CHARLOTTE & PETER FIELL

CONTEMPORARY GRAPHIC DESIGN

Grafikdesign der Gegenwart
Le graphisme contemporain

TASCHEN

CONTENTS
INHALT
SOMMAIRE

SURROUNDING US EVERY MINUTE OF EVERY DAY…

Surrounding us every minute of every day – from packaging, print and signage to television identities and web pages – graphic design is an omnipresent aspect of modern life. Complex and ever changing in form, it synthesizes and transmits information to the public while, at the same time, reflecting society's cultural aspirations and moral values.

The seven years since we published *Graphic Design for the 21st Century* (TASCHEN, 2003) have witnessed many developments in the practice of graphic design, and significant shifts of emphasis in both style and content. For example, the ever-growing interactivity of computers has transformed graphic design from an essentially static medium to one that increasingly involves movement. The greater sophistication of software solutions has also refined image manipulation, and graphic designers worldwide have creatively exploited the blurring of fiction and reality that this facilitates. Even that most respected of newsgathering agencies, Reuters, has been hoodwinked by images doctored to maximize their impact.

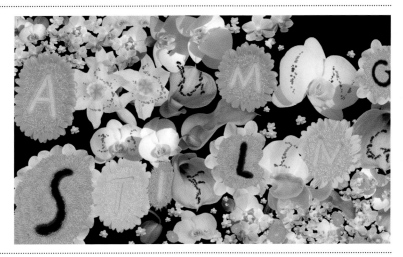

Stefan Sagmeister
Project: *Annual report
for DDD Gallery in Osaka
and GGG Gallery in Tokyo,*

*2005 (photo: Matthias
Ernstberger)*
Client: *Dai Nippon
Printing Company*

Many designers – and, of course, film makers – have exploited these potentialities to the full, generating hyper-real artificial environments in which even the laws of physics can be broken at will. This has given media of all kinds a rather surreal air, promoting greater skepticism among audiences who are no longer prepared to trust the evidence of their eyes. Indeed, the more polished the message and its delivery have become, the more distrust they seem to breed. Unsurprisingly, this trend has inspired many graphic designers to reconnect their work with the 'authentic' and hand-drawn – employing scratched, shaky or blotched visuals to suggest a trustworthy simplicity. Taken to extremes, this approach has spawned a variety of campaigns clearly constructed on the principle that, "if the ad is crap, the product must be good." The almost cult success of the *Cillit Bang* campaign featuring the over-enthusiastic "Barry" and his cleaning products, revisited in endless spoofs and remixes on the web, succeeds precisely because of its garish 'naffness'. Similarly, the huge impact of *Dove's Real Women* campaign owes much to its parodying of 'glamour' advertisements and the rigidly idealized portrayal of female beauty that they display.

To the same extent popular web sites such as *YouTube*, a video-sharing portal which allows easy-to-access self-broadcasting, have fundamentally changed the nature of user participation by offering media exposure on the audience's own terms. In some ways this digital ascendancy has eroded the professional graphic designer's status – now everyone with access to a personal computer thinks he or she is a design maestro, regardless of talent. This do-it-yourself ability has also eroded the line between homage and plagiarism, with the result that designers in professional practice really have to be on the creative ball to stay ahead of the digital game. At the same time, however, this digital revolution has also led to a greater freedom within graphic design – the sophisticated software at designers' fingertips allows them to play freely with ideas that would otherwise have taken hours if not days to work up. John L. Walters, the editor of *Eye* magazine, recently summarized the current situation as follows, "Today, any engagement with process usually touches on the digital."

After all, many of the younger generation of graphic designers working today grew up with computers and have a detailed understanding of programming. Fundamentally, they are technophiles rather than technophobes. Rather than being intimidated by technology, they are prepared to experiment with

and subvert it. Indeed, designers have frequently cracked commercial software codes so as to adapt it to their own requirements. For example, the *Scriptographer* plugin (designed in 2001 by Jürg Lehni) is a wayward child of the ubiquitous *Adobe Illustrator™*, and uses *JavaScript* to extend the original software's functionality allowing, according to its web site, "the creation of mouse controlled drawing-tools, effects that modify existing graphics and scripts that create new ones". Many of *Scriptographer's* tools are designed to generate visual complexity – *Tree* script sprouts seemingly random branches; *Fiddlehead* script grows fern-like tendrils; *Tile Tool* script has an engaging block-like quality; *Faust* script has a topographical 3D quality; and (our personal favourite) *Stroke-Raster* script translates the pixel value of an image into diagonal lines of varying thickness.

This type of advanced software has led to a strong re-emergence of ornamental complexity within graphic design, and a post-modern delight in 'more' rather than 'less'. In the past, hard-line Modernists believed ornament itself was linked to immorality. In his 1908 design manifesto *Ornament and Crime*, Adolf Loos famously asserted that, "the evolution of culture marches with the elimination of ornament." This current renaissance of the decorative rejects such strictures for an exuberant and playful naivety. In part, this can be seen as an attempt to humanize communications, and to re-connect the audience with the message in an increasingly atomized and coldly corporate world.

The digital revolution has also led to the dissolving of many creative boundaries, allowing an ever-greater melding of graphic design with fine art, illustration, music and fashion – in fact many of the graphic designers featured in the coming pages are also artists, fashion designers, musicians, animators and filmmakers. Today it is not unusual for graphic designers to go on to have 'post-graphic-design' careers as art directors and production designers. The leap from 2D to 3D design has been facilitated by the introduction of software such as *Maya*, *Previs* and *Studio Tools*, and their honed skills of composition can, therefore, be readily adapted to other media.

Understanding the technology used by designers does not, however, explain their motives for designing. For many, if not most, of the designers included in this publication, graphic design is not simply a job but a way of life and a source of identity. A significant number weave intellectual ambitions and agendas into

Bruce Willen/Post Typography   Client: *Heeb Magazine*
Project: *"The Chosen"*
illustration for Jewish
cultural magazine, 2007

Jonathan Barnbrook
Project: *"You Can't Bomb an*
Idea" political message, 2003
Client: *Self*

their work, most commonly reflected in a left-leaning political outlook and a desire to highlight ethical and environmental concerns. In this regard, graphic designers are alert to the powerful tools of persuasion at their disposal. The same skills that can market fizzy drinks and soap powder can also be employed to change public attitudes on a whole raft of issues, be it sweatshop labour, environmental destruction, unfair trade practices, gender-discrimination or the war-fueling greed for oil. One of the most high profile graphic-designers-with-principles, Jonathan Barnbrook, declares his motivation to be, "an inner anger which is a response to all the unfairness that is in this world". His highly politicized work has conscientiously sought to challenge capitalist structures, and is as thought provoking as it is visually stimulating.

Similarly, in the last few years, the AIGA (American Institute of Graphic Arts) has begun to see its mission as promoting socially responsible design, rather than the reputations of individual designers. In a recent statement the Institute acknowledged that, "In today's world, complex problems are usually those defined by a complex context. And increasingly, as noted in the Kyoto protocols, the Johannesburg conference on sustainable development, the global tensions surrounding cultural terrorism or revulsion, and a stumbling of economic growth, the context involves economic, environmental and cultural dimensions." Consistent with these sentiments, the AIGA has begun sponsoring a number of ethically-driven initiatives, such as *The Urban Forest Project* in New York's Times Square (October 2007). Importantly, the web now allows for a greater dissemination of this type of work among communities of like-minded people, and graphic designers increasingly understand their role as providing a vital interface between high politics and public consciousness.

There can, however, be a sharp division between those who see themselves as socially-aware, anti-capitalist protesters, and the creative 'marketeers' who are proud of their commercial clout and their ability to raise brand awareness for their paying clientele. Of course, the economic realities of running a studio dictate that designers often have a foot in both camps, and face the seemingly intractable dichotomy of having ties to both the anti-globalization movement and big business. This balancing act often leads designers to intersperse straightforwardly commercial work with more culturally, if less financially rewarding projects for art galleries, museums and educational institutions.

Craig Holden Feinberg
Project: "Eating cigarettes"
graphic artwork – award-
winning entry for "Nagoya

Design Do!" competition, 2004
(photo: Namiko Kitaura)
Client: International Design
Center of Nagoya

Sweden Graphics
Project: "Territory" still from
animated short film, 2002
Clients: onedotzero/Channel 4

The lingering perception of graphic designers as the hired hands of big business – as well as the new mass availability of computerized design tools – perhaps also explains their eagerness to present themselves as members of a highly trained, professional design community. More than any other sub-group of the design profession, graphic designers use prizes, awards and membership of chartered organizations to establish and police the boundaries of their professional territory. A large percentage of graphic designers also combine lecturing responsibilities with their other activities. The resulting cross-fertilization between practice and academia does much to underpin the internal coherence and professional status of graphic design.

Political and commercial developments, and the extraordinary power of the web, have also recast the geographical and cultural configuration of graphic design. The integration of former Eastern Bloc countries and China into global cultural and business networks has been highly influential. This survey features designers from Russia, Slovenia, Hong Kong and Turkey, alongside work from countries more traditionally associated with avant-garde graphic design practice, namely Britain, Germany, Switzerland, Holland and France. Many of the designers included emphasize their national cultural roots and draw on them in their work; others are more interested in universal solutions that transcend national and cultural boundaries, and that reflect globalism rather than globalization. Either way, they are all trying to connect people to the ideas and opinions transmitted by their work in the most engaging way possible.

One of the most startling characteristics of the designers featured here is their youth – with the vast majority belonging to Generation X (born between 1965 and 1980), with its post-baby-boom cynicism and love of irony. It is not surprising that this generation – weaned on MTV, grunge and skateboarding – has a very different approach to media production than its predecessors. Much of their work references youth culture and is used by companies to inject their products with the essential hip credibility. Interestingly, their thoughts, as revealed here, are noticeably self-reflective, referring back to their adolescent experiences – it is as though the teen in them has never really grown up. A recent phenomenon has also been the appearance of 'viral marketing' as a way of tapping into the idealistic, optimistic, and flexible mindset of the still younger Generation Y (born between 1980 and 2000), or as it is sometimes known GenY. Even more resilient

to traditional marketing techniques than its older brother, this grouping shows how the Internet has created a swing away from television and print advertising towards web-based community platforms (which are already being infiltrated using viral marketing techniques). To get their message across, today's graphic designers have to be evermore aware of the fast-moving currents of youth culture, which like its demographic, are characterized by short attention spans and a natural empathy for technology.

In an attempt to engage the ever-shortening attention span of today's media-savvy-yet-weary audience, many media producers are increasingly using sexual imagery to sell all kinds of products. The problem is that like the games junkie who becomes anaesthetized to violence, the audience of potential consumers becomes so jaded with titillation that images have to become more and more raunchy in order to create an impact. What would have been seen as explicit even ten years ago is now deemed mainstream in many western cultures – it is no wonder that a scary backlash of religious fundamentalism (both Islamic and Christian) has emerged. Rejecting this type of overt porno-graphic-design, our selection prioritizes those designers, like Francesca Granato, who use sexualized imagery from a very different feminized and subversive standpoint. Regrettably while many of the graphic designers featured here have conscientiously laboured to critique the iniquities of contemporary industrial society, much of today's media appears to be working just as energetically to extend its moral bankruptcy, sensationalism and celebrity worship.

If graphic design is to remain a vital force within the contemporary cultural landscape, its practitioners must take on board not only the plethora of new media platforms, but also the fact that it is indeed possible to be a successful graphic designer without selling your soul – and many of the designers selected for this survey are shining examples of this belief. They are prepared to respond to their new global responsibilities with work that is aesthetically and conceptually fresh. The contributors to this publication have also very kindly written in their own words about their approaches to the design process, and the underlying motivations behind their work. We hope, therefore, that *Contemporary Graphic Design* will not only offer a visually engaging snapshot of contemporary graphic design, but will also generate ideas and values that will provide an ethical compass for its professional practice today.

ES UMGIBT UNS IN JEDER MINUTE JEDEN TAGES …

Jede Minute jedes Tages sind wir von Grafikdesign umgeben – auf Verpackungen, in Druckerzeugnissen, auf Schildern, im Fernsehen und auf Internetseiten. Grafikdesign ist ein allgegenwärtiger Bestandteil des modernen Lebens. Komplex und in stets wechselnder Form reiht es Informationen aneinander und übermittelt sie der Öffentlichkeit, während es zugleich gesellschaftliche, kulturelle und ethische Werte darstellt.

In den sieben Jahren seit Erscheinen von *Graphic Design for the 21st Century* (TASCHEN, 2003) hat es in der Praxis des Grafikdesigns zahlreiche neue Entwicklungen und – was Stil und Inhalt angeht – erhebliche Schwerpunktverlagerungen gegeben. Zum Beispiel hat die wachsende Interaktivität von Computern das Grafikdesign von einem im Wesentlichen statischen in ein zunehmend dynamisch bewegtes Medium verwandelt. Auch haben in den letzten Jahren weitaus komplexere Software-Programme die Bildbearbeitung so verfeinert, dass Grafiker in aller Welt heute auf kreative Weise die Grenzen zwischen Fiktion und Realität verwischen können.

Slavimir Stojanovic   Client: *Futro*
Project: *"Futro Fanzine 012 –*
Educative and Therapeutic"
fanzine, 2004

Vladimir Dubko
Project: *"Dandi" T-shirt image*
and logo, 2006
Client: *3nity*

Selbst die renommierteste aller Nachrichtenagenturen – Reuters – ist Bildern „auf den Leim gegangen", die der größeren Wirkung wegen „frisiert" worden waren.

Viele Designer – und natürlich auch Filmemacher – haben schon jetzt diese neuen Potenziale voll ausgeschöpft und damit hyper-reale künstliche Lebenswelten geschaffen, in denen sich die Gesetze der Physik beliebig biegen und brechen lassen. Dadurch haftet Medien aller Art etwas Surreales an, was größere Skepsis bei den Menschen hervorruft, die nicht länger bereit sind, ihren Augen zu trauen. Tatsächlich, so scheint es, weckt eine Botschaft und ihre Darstellung um so mehr Misstrauen, je makelloser sie gestylt wurde. Es überrascht daher nicht, dass dieser Trend viele Grafikdesigner dazu veranlasst hat, in ihrer Arbeit zum „Authentischen" und zur Handzeichnung zurückzukehren, wobei sie Bilder mit Kratzspuren, zittrigen Linien oder Flecken schaffen, um vertrauenswürdige Einfachheit zu suggerieren. Im Extremfall hat dieser Ansatz zu verschiedenen Werbekampagnen geführt, die ganz deutlich dem Motto folgten: „Wenn die Anzeige Mist ist, muss das Produkt gut sein." Der fast schon Kult gewordene Erfolg der *Cillit-Bang*-Werbung mit dem übereifrigen Barry und seinen Reinigungsmitteln – unzählige Male parodistisch verarbeitet und im Internet neu gemischt – beruht gerade darauf, dass sie so schrillbunt und „ordinär" ist. Ganz ähnlich die *Dove*-Werbung *Real Women*: Sie ist deshalb so erfolgreich, weil sie die Glamour-Anzeigen anderer Firmen und deren unnatürliche, strikt idealisierten weiblichen Schönheiten parodiert.

In gleichem Maße haben beliebte Internetseiten wie *YouTube* (ein Videoportal, über das man leicht zugängliche Videos senden und von anderen Nutzern empfangen kann) die Art der Internet-Nutzerbeteiligung von Grund auf verändert, indem sie mediale Auftritte von Zuschauern für Zuschauer zu deren eigenen Bedingungen verbreiten. In gewisser Weise hat dieser digitale Aufstieg des Durchschnittsnutzers den professionellen Status des Grafikdesigners herabgewürdigt: Heute denken alle, die Zugang zu einem PC haben, sie seien Meister des Designs – ob sie nun Talent haben oder nicht. Diese „Selbst-ist-der-Mann/die-Frau"-Haltung hat auch die Trennungslinie zwischen Hommage und Plagiat verwischt mit dem Ergebnis, dass professionelle Designer stets sozusagen ganz nah am Ball bleiben müssen, um im digitalen Kreativspiel zu gewinnen. Gleichzeitig hat die digitale Revolution innerhalb des Grafikdesigns aber auch zu einer größeren Freiheit geführt, denn die jederzeit mit einem Klick zugänglichen, aus-

geklügelten Computerprogramme erlauben es den Designern, schnell einmal spielerisch verschiedene Bildideen zu entwickeln, deren Ausarbeitung früher Stunden, wenn nicht gar Tage, in Anspruch genommen hätte. John L. Walters, Chefredakteur der Zeitschrift *Eye*, hat die derzeitige Situation vor Kurzem so beschrieben: „Heute hat man es bei der Beschäftigung mit Prozessen für gewöhnlich auch mit digitalen Prozessen zu tun."

Schließlich sind ja die meisten jungen Grafikdesigner schon mit Computern aufgewachsen und verfügen über gründliche Softwarekenntnisse. Grundsätzlich sind sie technophil und nicht technophob. Statt sich von Technologie einschüchtern zu lassen, sind sie bereit und in der Lage, damit zu experimentieren und sie zu manipulieren. Tatsächlich haben viele Designer die Codes handelsüblicher Software „geknackt", um diese nach eigenen Bedürfnissen umzumodeln. Die 2001 von Jürg Lehni entwickelte *Scriptographer*-Programm zum Beispiel ist ein aus der Art geschlagener Sprössling des allgegenwärtigen *Adobe Illustrator*™ und nutzt *JavaScript*, um die Funktionen der ursprünglichen Software zu erweitern und dadurch (so die Internetseite) „die Anwendung Maus-kontrollierter Zeichenwerkzeuge" zu ermöglichen und Effekte zu erzeugen, „die bereits vorhandene Grafiken und Skripts modifizieren, so dass man damit neue erzeugen kann". Viele Werkzeuge von *Scriptographer* wurden entwickelt, um komplexe Bilder zu entwerfen: das Anwendungsprogramm *Tree* lässt scheinbar zufällig weitere Zweige sprießen; *Fiddlehead* wächst sich ähnlich wie Farn zu zarten Wedeln aus; *Tile Tool* ist von ansprechend kompakter, blockähnlicher Art und *Faust* von topografischer 3D-Qualität, während *Stroke-Raster* (unser persönliches Lieblingsskript) die Pixelwerte eines Bildes in verschieden dicke Diagonallinien übersetzt.

Diese Art hoch entwickelte Programme haben im Grafikdesign zu einem Wiedererstarken ornamentaler Komplexität und zur postmodernen Freude am „mehr" statt am „weniger" geführt. Früher war das Ornament für den harten Kern der Modernisten geradezu etwas Unmoralisches. In seinem berühmten Manifest „Ornament und Verbrechen" von 1908 behauptet Adolf Loos sogar: „evolution der kultur ist gleichbedeutend mit dem entfernen des ornamentes aus dem gebrauchsgegenstande." Die gegenwärtige Renaissance des Dekorativen lehnt derartige Einschränkungen ab und bevorzugt statt dessen überschäumende, spielerische Naivität. Teilweise lässt sich das als Versuch interpretieren, das Kommunikationswesen menschlicher zu gestalten und das Publikum in einer zunehmend

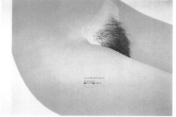

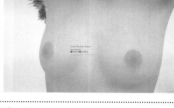

Christina Föllmer
Project: "Road Safety"
poster campaign proposal
for the World Health

Organization, 2005 (developed
at Fabrica with Eric Ravelo –
photo: Rebekka Ehlers)
Client: Fabrica

Makoto Saito
Project: "Love Mother Earth"
advertising print campaign, 2001

Clients: Green Homes Co.
Ltd./Toppan Printing Co. Ltd

kalten, in kleinste Einheiten gespaltenen Unternehmenswelt wieder emotional an die (Werbe)Botschaft zu binden.

Die digitale Revolution hat außerdem zahlreiche Grenzen der Kreativität aufgehoben und die zunehmende Verschmelzung von Grafikdesign, bildender Kunst, Illustration, Musik und Mode ermöglicht. Tatsächlich sind viele auf den folgenden Seiten vorgestellten Grafikdesigner außerdem Künstler, Modedesigner, Musiker, Animateuren und Filmemacher. Es ist nichts Ungewöhnliches mehr, dass ein Grafiker als Art Director und Produktionsdesigner beim Film „post-graphische" Karriere macht. Der Sprung vom zwei- zum dreidimensionalen Entwurf wurde durch die Einführung entsprechender Software wie *Maya*, *Previs* und *Studio Tools* gefördert, deren ausgeklügelte Kompositionstechniken sich auf andere Medien übertragen lassen.

Die Kenntnis der verwendeten Designtechniken und -technologien erklärt aber noch lange nicht die Motivation des jeweiligen Anwenders. Für viele, wenn nicht gar die meisten in diesem Buch vorgestellten Protagonisten ist Grafikdesign nicht nur ein Job, sondern ihr Leben und die Quelle ihres Selbstverständnisses. Nicht wenige verarbeiten geistige Ambitionen und Zielsetzungen in ihren Werken, die sich in den meisten Fällen in links-politischen Auffassungen und dem Wunsch spiegeln, bevorzugt ethische Fragen und Umweltthemen darzustellen. Deshalb wissen sie auch ganz genau, welche mächtigen Mittel der Überzeugungs- und Überredungskunst ihnen zur Verfügung stehen. Mit der Befähigung und dem Geschick zur Vermarktung von Sprudelgetränken und Waschpulver kann man ebenso gut die öffentliche Meinung zu einer ganzen Reihe verschiedenster Themen beeinflussen, von Kinderarbeit und Umweltzerstörung bis hin zu unfairen Handelspraktiken, Geschlechterdiskriminierung oder der kriegstreiberischen Gier nach Erdöl. Einer der angesehensten Grafikdesigner mit Prinzipien, Jonathan Barnbrook, erklärt, ihn treibe „ein tiefsitzender Zorn über all die Ungerechtigkeit in dieser Welt" an. Mit seinen hoch politischen, visuell stimulierenden und zum Nachdenken anregenden Arbeiten stellt er stets gewissenhaft kapitalistische Strukturen in Frage.

In ähnlicher Weise hat das AIGA (American Institute of Grafic Arts) in den letzten Jahren begonnen, seine Aufgabe eher in der Förderung von sozial verantwortlichem Werbedesign zu sehen, statt in der Förderung einzelner Grafiker. In einer kürzlich veröffentlichten Erklärung des Instituts heißt es: „In der

Welt von heute erwachsen vielschichtige Probleme für gewöhnlich aus vielschichtigen Situationen. Wie in den Protokollen von Kyoto vermerkt, findet die Konferenz über nachhaltige Entwicklung in Johannesburg, und finden die internationalen Auseinandersetzungen über Kulturterrorismus oder über den Hass auf bestimmte Kulturen und nachlassendes Wirtschaftswachstum stets in vielschichtigen Situationen mit ökonomischen, ökologischen und kulturellen Dimensionen statt." Übereinstimmung mit dieser Einschätzung hat das AIGA begonnen, eine Reihe ethisch motivierter Initiativen zu sponsern, unter anderem das für Oktober 2007 auf dem New Yorker Times Square geplante *Urban Forest Project* (Stadtwald-Projekt). Das Internet ermöglicht heute eine größere Verbreitung dieser Art Projekte unter Gleichgesinnten in aller Welt, und Grafikdesigner sehen ihre Aufgabe zunehmend darin, wichtige „Schnittstellen" zwischen der Politik und dem öffentlichen Bewusstsein zu liefern.

Es kann jedoch zu einer scharfen Trennung kommen zwischen den antikapitalistischen Aktivisten, die sich selbst gesellschaftliches Bewusstsein attestieren, und den kreativen „Vermarktern", die stolz sind auf ihre kommerzielle Schlagkraft und ihre Fähigkeit, für gut zahlende Auftraggeber das Markenbewusstsein der Käufer zu steigern. Natürlich sind selbstständige Grafiker mit eigenen Büros aus ökonomischen Gründen oft gezwungen, mit je einem Fuß in beiden Lagern zu stehen, und sehen sich vor der unlösbaren Dichotomie, Geschäftsbeziehungen sowohl mit der Anti-Globalisierungs-Bewegung als auch mit internationalen Großkonzernen zu pflegen. Dieser Balanceakt veranlasst viele Designer dazu, neben Werbung für Wirtschaftsunternehmen immer wieder auch kulturell wertvollere – obschon weniger lukrative – Aufträge für Kunstgalerien, Museen und Bildungseinrichtungen anzunehmen.

Die immer noch verbreitete Auffassung vom Grafiker als Handlanger des Großkapitals – ebenso wie die neue massenhafte Verfügbarkeit computerisierter Entwurfswerkzeuge – erklärt vielleicht auch, warum Grafiker sich selbst so gerne als Angehörige einer bestens ausgebildeten, hoch professionellen Designergemeinschaft präsentieren. In stärkerem Maße als jede andere Gruppe von Designern nutzen Grafiker Preise, Auszeichnungen und Unternehmensteilhaberschaften, um ihr berufliches Territorium abzustecken und zu schützen. Ein großer Prozentsatz von Grafikern verbindet mit der eigentlichen Designarbeit auch Lehrtätigkeiten. Die sich daraus ergebende wechselseitige Befruchtung von

Jay Prynne/Esterson Associates
Project: *"Eye: Issue 60" maga-*
zine cover, 2006 *(image manipu-*
lated using Jürg Lehni's "Stroke-

Raster" script)
Client: *Eye magazine*

Walter Schönauer
Project: *"Chicks on Speed"*
book (spread), 2003
Client: *Booth-Clibborn Editions*

Praxis und Lehre trägt in nicht geringem Maße dazu bei, den inneren Zusammenhalt und Status des Berufsstands zu fördern und zu untermauern.

Politische und wirtschaftliche Entwicklungen sowie der enorme Einfluss des Internets haben auch die geografischen und kulturellen Konfigurationen des Grafikdesigns verändert. Die Integration der früheren Ostblockstaaten und Chinas in globale kulturelle und wirtschaftliche Netzwerke hat dabei eine große Rolle gespielt. Das vorliegende Buch gibt einen Überblick und stellt Grafiker aus Russland, Slowenien, Hong Kong und der Türkei ebenso vor wie Designer aus den traditionell mit modernem Grafikdesign in Verbindung gebrachten Ländern Großbritannien, Deutschland, Frankreich, der Schweiz und den Niederlanden. Nicht wenige, die auf den folgenden Seiten zu Wort (und Bild) kommen, betonen ihre nationalen kulturellen Wurzeln und schöpfen aus ihnen; andere interessieren sich stärker für universelle Lösungen über nationale und kulturelle Grenzen hinweg und vertreten damit zwar Internationalität, aber nicht Globalisierung. So oder so versuchen sie alle, mit ihren Arbeiten den Menschen auf möglichst ansprechende und überzeugende Art Ideen und Meinungen zu vermitteln.

Eines der auffallendsten Merkmale der hier vorgestellten Grafikdesigner ist ihr jugendliches Alter: die allermeisten gehören zur Generation X (zwischen 1965 und 1980 geboren) mit ihrem Post-Babyboom-Zynismus und der Vorliebe für Ironie. Es überrascht nicht, dass diese Generation, die mit MTV, Grunge und Skateboard-Fahren aufgewachsen ist, ganz anders an die Gestaltung von Medien herangeht als ihre Vorgänger. Viele ihrer Arbeiten beziehen sich auf die Jugendkultur, was von Firmen verlangt wird, die ihren Produkten essenzielle Hip-Kredibilität geben wollen. Interessanterweise verweisen die in diesem Buch geäußerten Ideen deutlich auf eigene Erlebnisse aus der Jugendzeit der Designer, so als ob der Teenager in ihnen nie erwachsen geworden wäre. Ein ganz neues Phänomen ist das „virale Marketing" als Möglichkeit, das idealistische, optimistische und flexible Denken der jüngsten Generation Y – auch Gen Y genannt und zwischen 1980 und 2000 geboren – anzuzapfen. Diese Jüngsten unserer Gesellschaft sind gegen die herkömmlichen Marketingtechniken resistenter als die etwas Älteren, was beweist, dass das Internet eine Abkehr von der Werbung im Fernsehen und in den Printmedien hin zu Internetportalen bewirkt hat (die bereits von viralen Marketingtechniken infiltriert werden). Um ihre Botschaft „rüberzubringen", müssen Grafikdesigner heutzutage unbedingt auf dem Laufenden sein, was die schnell-

lebigen Trends der Jugendkultur angeht, die der Tatsache Rechnung tragen, dass Jugendliche heute generell eine geringe Konzentrationsfähigkeit und eine natürliche Empathie für alles Technische besitzen.

Im Bemühen, die „Kurzzeit-Konzentration" ihres heutigen, medial überfütterten und medienmüden Publikums auszunutzen, verlassen sich viele Produzenten der verschiedenen Medien zunehmend auf erotische Bildassoziationen, um ihre Produkte abzusetzen. Das Problem besteht darin, dass deren potenzielle Konsumenten ebenso wie der Spielsüchtige, der gegenüber Gewaltszenen völlig abstumpft, für sexuelle Stimulanzien derart unempfänglich werden, dass die Bilder immer schlüpfriger sein müssen, um überhaupt noch zu wirken. Was noch vor zehn Jahren allzu eindeutig war, gilt heute in vielen westlichen Ländern als üblich und reizlos.

Kein Wunder, dass man als Reaktion darauf die Zunahme eines beängstigenden religiösen (islamischen wie christlichen) Fundamentalismus' beobachtet. Auch wir lehnen eine derart offenkundig „porno-grafisches" Design ab und haben für dieses Buch Designer wie Francesca Granato ausgewählt, die zwar auch erotische Bilder und Symbole verwenden, aber aus einem ganz anderen, weiblicheren und subversiven Blickwinkel. Während viele der hier vorgestellten Grafiker sich gewissenhaft bemühen, die Verderbtheit der modernen Industriegesellschaft anzuprangern, scheinen viele Medien heute leider deren moralisch-ethischen Bankrott, Sensationslüsternheit und Starkult ebenso energisch zu fördern.

Wenn das Grafikdesign in der zeitgenössischen Kultur eine wichtige treibende Kraft bleiben will, müssen Grafiker nicht nur die ganze Palette neuer Medienplattformen nutzen, sondern auch die Tatsache akzeptieren, dass es möglich ist, als Grafikdesigner erfolgreich zu sein, ohne seine Seele zu verkaufen – und viele der für dieses Buch ausgewählten Designer sind leuchtende Beispiele hierfür. Sie sind bereit, ihre neue globale Verantwortung auf sich zu nehmen und Designs zu entwickeln, die ästhetisch wie konzeptionell frisch und lebendig sind. Auf den folgenden Seiten erklären sie selbst, wie sie an das Entwerfen herangehen und welche Motive ihrer Arbeit zugrunde liegen. Wir hoffen daher, dass *Contemporary Graphic Design* nicht nur optisch ansprechende Momentaufnahmen des zeitgenössischen Grafikdesigns bieten, sondern auch Ideen und Werte fördern wird, die den auf diesem Gebiet Tätigen einen ethischen Kompass für ihren beruflichen Weg an die Hand geben.

IL EST DANS NOTRE CHAMP DE VISION À CHAQUE MINUTE DU JOUR ...

Il est dans notre champ de vision à chaque minute du jour, sur les emballages, les imprimés et les panneaux de signalisation, à la télévision et sur les pages Internet : le graphisme est omniprésent dans la vie moderne. Complexe et en perpétuelle métamorphose, il synthétise l'information et la transmet au public tout en reflétant les aspirations culturelles et les valeurs morales de la société.

Les sept années qui se sont écoulées depuis que nous avons publié *Graphic Design for the 21st Century* (TASCHEN, 2003) ont vu intervenir de nombreuses évolutions dans la pratique du graphisme ainsi que des changements significatifs de perspective tant sur le fond que sur la forme. L'interactivité toujours croissante que permettent les ordinateurs, par exemple, a transformé la création graphique, au départ un média essentiellement statique, en une discipline qui intègre de plus en plus le mouvement. La plus grande sophistication des logiciels a aussi perfectionné la manipulation des images et les graphistes du monde entier ont exploité avec une grande créativité l'ambiguïté qu'ils autorisent entre fiction et réalité.

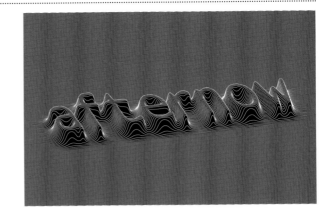

Jürg Lehni
Project: *"Object Rotation
Raster"/"Stroke Rotation
Raster"/"Stroke Raster"/*

"Object Raster" scripts, 2006
Client: *Self*
(www.scriptographer.com)

Jürg Lehni
Project: *"Afternow" poster
designed for and in collaboration with the Swiss artist*

*Philippe Decrauzat using
"Faust" 3D script, 2006*
Client: *Philippe Decrauzat*

Même la très respectée agence de presse Reuters s'est laissée tromper par des images retouchées par ordinateur.

Un grand nombre de créatifs, et bien sûr de réalisateurs de films, ont exploité ce potentiel pour donner naissance à des environnements artificiels hyperréalistes dans lesquels même les lois élémentaires de la physique peuvent être enfreintes à volonté. Ces possibilités nouvelles ont donné aux médias de tous poils une allure plutôt surréaliste et ont par ailleurs rendu plus sceptique encore un public qui n'était déjà plus disposé à prendre ce qu'il voyait pour argent comptant. De fait, plus le message et la manière dont il est délivré ont été lissés, plus il semble provoquer la défiance. Cette tendance encourage bien sûr les graphistes à revenir à un travail plus «authentique», en employant des supports visuels esquissés, tremblés ou tachés pour donner une impression de spontanéité «à main levée». Poussée à l'extrême, cette approche a engendré toute une série de campagnes clairement élaborées sur le principe que: «si la pub est pourrie, le produit doit être bon». Le succès presque légendaire de la campagne pour *Cillit Bang* où l'extatique «Barry» vante les mérites de ses produits ménagers, objet de dizaines de parodies et de variantes sur le Web, s'explique précisément par sa ringardise criarde. De la même manière, l'immense impact de la campagne «Real Women» de *Dove* doit beaucoup à son appropriation parodique de l'idéal de beauté féminine véhiculé par les publicités «glamour».

Des sites Internet très populaires comme *YouTube*, un portail de partage de vidéos amateur très facile à utiliser, ont eux aussi radicalement changé la nature des relations entre commerciaux et usagers en permettant aux uns et aux autres d'être exposés médiatiquement selon les termes fixés par le public. D'une certaine manière, cet ascendant du numérique a émoussé le statut du graphiste professionnel – aujourd'hui, quiconque a accès à un ordinateur se prend pour un maître du graphisme, quel que soit son talent. Cette aptitude autodidacte a également brouillé les frontières entre hommage et plagiat, ce qui oblige les graphistes professionnels à se maintenir au meilleur niveau créatif pour conserver les rênes du jeu. Et pourtant, dans le même temps, cette révolution numérique a donné davantage de liberté à cet art — les logiciels sophistiqués auxquels ont aujourd'hui accès les graphistes leur permettent de jouer librement avec les idées d'une manière qui aurait demandé des heures sinon des jours de travail il y a quelques années encore. John L. Walters, l'éditeur du magazine *Eye*, résumait récemment la situa-

tion actuelle en ces termes: «Aujourd'hui, tout processus créatif long implique un recours au numérique».

Après tout, nombre de graphistes de la dernière génération ont grandi avec les ordinateurs et ont des connaissances précises en matière de programmation. Ils sont fondamentalement plus technophiles que technophobes. Loin d'être intimidés par la technologie, ils sont aptes à la contourner et à la corrompre. De fait, les graphistes ont souvent déchiffré et détourné les codes de logiciels commerciaux afin de les adapter à leurs propres exigences. Le plug-in *Scriptographer* (créé par Jürg Lehni en 2001), par exemple, est un enfant rebelle de l'omniprésent *Adobe Illustrator*™, et utilise *JavaScript* pour étendre la fonctionnalité du logiciel original et permettre, à ce qu'affirme son site Internet, «la création d'outils de dessin contrôlés par la souris, d'effets qui modifient des graphismes existants et de scriptes qui en créent de nouveaux». Un grand nombre des outils de *Scriptographer* sont destinés à générer de la complexité visuelle – le script *Tree* semble faire pousser des branches au hasard; le *Fiddlehead*, lui, déverse des vrilles de fougères; le *Tile Tool* est d'une robustesse charmante; le *Faust* est intéressant pour la topographie en 3D; et enfin (notre préféré) le script *Stroke-Raster* traduit la valeur en pixels d'une image en lignes diagonales d'épaisseurs variées.

L'avènement de ce type de logiciels de haute qualité a provoqué une forte résurgence de la complexité ornementale dans le graphisme, et un goût post-moderne assumé pour le 'plus' davantage que pour le 'moins'. Dans le passé, les Modernistes intransigeants considéraient l'ornement comme intrinsèquement immoral. Dans son manifeste de 1908, *Ornement et Crime*, Adolf Loos a cette affirmation restée célèbre: «L'évolution de la culture va dans le sens de l'expulsion de l'ornement hors de l'objet d'usage.» L'actuelle renaissance du décoratif rejette ces restrictions au profit d'une naïveté exubérante et espiègle, en partie pour tenter d'humaniser les outils de communication et renouer le lien entre le public et le message dans un monde de plus en plus atomisé et froid.

La révolution numérique a aussi conduit à la disparition d'un grand nombre de limites à la création en autorisant tous les mélanges entre le graphisme et les beaux-arts, l'illustration, la musique et la mode: une bonne partie des graphistes dont le travail est présenté dans ce livre sont d'ailleurs aussi artistes, créateurs de mode, musiciens, animateurs ou réalisateurs. Il n'est pas inhabituel aujourd'hui que des graphistes se lancent dans une seconde carrière en tant que

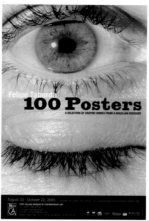

Felipe Taborda
Project: "Cinema Polonês
Hoje" exhibition poster, 2005

Client: *Espaço Unibanco Belas
Artes*

Felipe Taborda
Project: "100 Posters by Felipe
Taborda" exhibition poster,
2004/05 (event held at the

*8th International Poster
Biennial in Mexico)*
Client: *8th International
Poster Biennial, Mexico*

directeurs artistiques ou créatifs de publicité. Le passage du graphisme de la 2D à la 3D a été facilité par l'arrivée de logiciels comme *Maya*, *Previs* et *Studio Tools*, et leur dextérité en matière de composition peut dès lors être aisément adaptée à d'autres médias.

Comprendre quelle technologie les graphistes utilisent n'explique pas pour autant les raisons pour lesquelles ils font ce métier. Pour une bonne partie des créateurs présentés dans ce volume, si ce n'est pour la majorité d'entre eux, le graphisme n'est pas un métier mais un style de vie, où ils puisent leur identité. Beaucoup nourrissent leur travail de convictions ou d'ambitions intellectuelles, généralement exprimées dans une perspective politique axée à gauche et un désir de mettre en avant des préoccupations éthiques et environnementales. De ce point de vue, les graphistes sont très au fait des outils de persuasion qu'ils ont à leur disposition. Les compétences auxquelles on a recours pour vendre une boisson gazeuse ou de la lessive en poudre peuvent aussi bien être employées pour faire évoluer l'opinion publique sur tout un éventail de sujets, du travail au noir à la destruction de l'environnement en passant par les pratiques commerciales inéquitables, la discrimination sexuelle ou la demande globale de pétrole, source de conflits. Jonathan Barnbrook, graphiste-avec-des-principes parmi les plus réputés, déclare que sa motivation est « une colère intérieure qui vient répondre à toute l'injustice de ce monde ». Son travail, extrêmement politisé, cherche volontairement à défier les structures capitalistes et suscite la réflexion autant qu'il stimule le regard.

De la même façon, au cours des dernières années, l'AIGA (American Institute of Graphic Arts) a commencé à considérer que sa mission devait être de promouvoir une création socialement responsable plutôt que la réputation de créateurs particuliers. L'Institut a récemment reconnu que « dans le monde actuel, les problèmes complexes se définissent généralement par un contexte complexe. Et de plus en plus, comme le montrent le protocole de Kyoto, la conférence de Johannesburg sur le développement durable, les tensions internationales autour du terrorisme culturel ou du gaspillage, et les ratés de la croissance économique, le contexte a des dimensions économiques, environnementales et culturelles. »

Fidèle à ses convictions, l'AIGA s'est mis à parrainer un grand nombre d'initiatives éthiques, comme *l'Urban Forest Project* prévu pour Times Square, à New York (octobre 2007). L'Internet favorise d'ailleurs une meilleure dissémination de ce type de travail parmi des communautés de même sensibilité idéologique, et les graphistes ont de plus en plus tendance à penser que leur rôle est de servir d'interface entre politique internationale et conscience populaire.

Il peut toutefois exister un net clivage entre ceux qui se considèrent comme des militants anti-capitalistes engagés et les créatifs 'vendus à l'économie de marché' qui sont fiers de leur valeur commerciale et de leur talent, bien rémunéré, à faire connaître une marque. Les contingences économiques liées à la gestion d'un studio de création obligent bien sûr bon nombre de graphistes à avoir un pied dans chaque camp. Cette dichotomie apparemment insoluble, qui fait qu'ils ont des liens à la fois avec le mouvement alter-mondialiste et avec le monde des affaires, conduit souvent les graphistes à alterner leur travail ouvertement commercial avec des projets culturellement, si ce n'est financièrement, plus enrichissants pour le compte de galeries d'art, de musées ou d'instituts de formation.

L'idée reçue, persistante, selon laquelle les graphistes sont les émissaires des multinationales – qui rejoint celle de l'accessibilité des outils de graphisme par ordinateur – contribue à expliquer qu'ils tiennent tant à se présenter comme les membres formés et expérimentés d'une communauté de professionnels du design. Plus qu'aucun des autres sous-groupes qui forment cette dernière, les graphistes utilisent les prix, les récompenses et leur implication dans le monde de l'entreprise pour établir les frontières de leur territoire professionnel. Nombre de graphistes enseignent aussi en marge de leurs activités de création. La fertilisation croisée entre pratique et monde universitaire qui en résulte étaye grandement la cohérence interne et le statut professionnel de la création graphique.

L'actualité politique et commerciale, associée à l'extraordinaire pouvoir de l'Internet, ont également remanié la configuration géographique et culturelle de la profession. L'arrivée des pays de l'Est et de la Chine dans les réseaux commerciaux et culturels internationaux a eu une influence tout aussi décisive. Notre ouvrage présente des créateurs de Russie, de Slovénie, de Hong Kong et de Turquie au même rang que d'autres, originaires de pays plus traditionnellement associés à l'avant-garde en matière de graphisme, c'est-à-dire la Grande-Bretagne, l'Allemagne, la Suisse, la Hollande et la France. Un grand nombre d'entre eux insistent sur leurs racines culturelles nationales et montrent leur influence dans

Leslie Chan
Project: *"The Urban Impres-*
sions of Taipei 3" poster, 2005

Client: *China Productivity*
Center, Taipei

Rafael Esquer/Alfalfa
Project: *"Forever Now"*
banner for "The Urban Forest
Project", Times Square,

New York, 2006
Clients: *Times Square Alliance,*
AIGA New York Chapter and
Worldstudio Foundation

leur travail ; d'autres s'intéressent davantage à des solutions universelles qui transcendent les frontières nationales et culturelles pour refléter le mondialisme plutôt que la mondialisation. Dans un cas comme dans l'autre, ils tentent de rallier les gens aux idées et aux opinions transmises par leur travail de la façon la plus captivante possible.

Une des caractéristiques les plus frappantes des graphistes réunis ici est leur jeune âge : la grande majorité d'entre eux appartiennent à la Génération X (nés entre 1965 et 1980), caractérisée par son cynisme post-baby-boom et son goût pour l'ironie. Il n'est pas étonnant que cette génération, élevée avec MTV, le grunge et le skateboard, aborde la production médiatique très différemment de ses prédécesseurs. Les entreprises utilisent leur travail, nourri de références à la culture jeune, pour conférer à leurs produits une crédibilité 'branchée' essentielle. Comme le montrent leurs textes de présentation de façon très intéressante, ils s'inspirent beaucoup de leur histoire personnelle et de leurs expériences adolescentes – c'est comme si l'ado en eux n'avait jamais vraiment grandi. Autre phénomène récent : l'apparition du « marketing viral » qui permet d'accéder à la toute jeune Génération Y (née entre 1980 et 2000), parfois surnommée GenY, plus idéaliste, optimiste et flexible. Encore plus résistants aux techniques traditionnelles de marketing que leurs aînés, ces GenYs vont pousser la publicité à délaisser la télévision ou la presse écrite au profit de l'Internet et des plateformes communautaires qu'il héberge (et qui commencent déjà à être infiltrés grâce aux techniques du marketing viral). Pour faire passer leur message, les graphistes d'aujourd'hui doivent rester plus connectés que jamais aux tendances éphémères de la culture jeune, qui se caractérise, comme ceux qui la véhiculent, par une grande versatilité et une empathie naturelle avec la technologie. Afin de retenir l'attention versatile de ce public rusé mais blasé, un grand nombre de publicitaires utilisent de plus en plus l'imagerie sexuelle pour vendre toutes sortes de produits. Le problème, c'est que, tout comme le drogué de jeux vidéos devient insensible à la violence, la perception des consommateurs potentiels est aujourd'hui tellement saturée de stimulations que les images doivent devenir de plus en plus torrides pour créer un impact. Ce qui aurait semblé explicite il y a seulement dix ans est aujourd'hui jugé conventionnel dans la plupart des cultures occidentales – pas étonnant que le fondamentalisme religieux (islamique ou chrétien) fasse un retour si brutal et effrayant. Notre sélection exclut ce

style de porno-graphisme et privilégie les créateurs comme Francesca Granato, qui utilise l'iconographie sexuelle dans une perspective féminine et subversive bien différente. Malheureusement, alors que la plupart des graphistes présentés ici ont consciencieusement œuvré à une critique des iniquités de la société industrielle contemporaine, les médias actuels semblent sacrifier avec tout autant d'ardeur qu'autrefois à la faillite morale, au sensationnalisme et au culte de la célébrité.

Si le graphisme doit demeurer une force vive dans le paysage culturel contemporain, ses praticiens doivent prendre en compte non seulement la pléthore de nouveaux supports médiatiques mais aussi le fait qu'il est réellement possible d'être un graphiste reconnu sans vendre son âme – et bien des créateurs sélectionnés pour ce volume sont de brillants exemples de cette conviction. Ils sont prêts à assumer leurs nouvelles responsabilités grâce à la fraîcheur esthétique et conceptuelle de leur travail. Ces jeunes graphistes ont aussi très généreusement accepté de décrire eux-mêmes leur conception du processus créatif et les motivations qui sous-tendent leur travail. Nous espérons donc que *Contemporary Graphic Design* offrira un panorama visuellement séduisant du graphisme contemporain, mais générera en outre des idées et des valeurs qui serviront de boussole éthique à cette pratique professionnelle aujourd'hui.

3KG

*"Progress means simplifying,
not complicating." (Bruno Munari)*

3KG
3F Iwasa Building
N3E5 Chuo-ku
Sapporo, Hokkaido 060-0033
Japan
T +81 11 219 330 9
hello@kgkgkg.com
www.kgkgkg.com

Design group history
2002 Co-founded by Hiroaki Shirai and Shin Sasaki in Sapporo, Japan
2003 Tomoko Takano joined creative studio

Founders' biographies
Hiroaki Shirai
1976 Born in Sapporo, Japan

1994–1997 Studied graphic design, Hokkaido College of Art and Design, Sapporo
1998–2000 Worked as graphic designer at Suda Printing, Sapporo
2000–2002 Worked as freelance graphic designer
Shin Sasaki
1974 Born in Sapporo, Japan
1992–1996 Studied English

language and western culture, Hokkai-Gakuen University, Sapporo
1997–2000 Worked as graphic designer at Shimooka Office, Sapporo
2000–2002 Worked as graphic designer at Extra Design, Sapporo

Recent exhibitions
2002 "Vector Lounge", Singapore
2003/04 "Source of Wonder", London/Tokyo

Recent awards
2001 Hiroshi Yonemura Prize and Bronze Award, Sapporo Art Directors Club
2002 Gold Award (x2),

Sapporo Art Directors Club
2004 Members Selection, Sapporo Art Directors Club

Clients
Allrightsreserved; Cartoon Network; Hokkaido International Airlines; IdN; onedotzero

［デス］
des
des special-edition: Macromedia
for Web Designers & Developers

design experimental square

Webデザインとマクロメディアの特集号です
U.S.のWebデザイン　ケータイやブログにおけるFlash
中村勇吾／遠崎寿義／福井信蔵／長谷川踏太 ほか

Dreamweaver　Flash　ColdFusion　Director　Contribute　FlashPaper

Webを触発する
マクロメディアを、
1冊にまとめました。

SE des［デス］マクロメディア特集号
SHOEISHA　定価●本体1,895円＋税

The Reverse Side of
Creative Expression

INT

Name:
Tota Hasegawa

Company:
Tomato

SHINZO
&
KEN KITAMU

What is RIA?

FLASH Lite
The possibility of Flash on
cellular phone interface

Web Design Guide in U.S.
San Francisco + Silicon Valley
&
MAX 2004 in New Orleans

Special
Part
01

FLASH BLOG

macromedia
FLASH MX
2004

SEO for FLASH
Accessibility of FLASH

FLASH / MX200

A Guide to COLDFUSION

CSS of DREAMWEAVER
macromedia
DREAMWEAVER
2004

PLEASE LABEL YOUR BAGGAGE

macromedia
CONTRIBUTE 3

CMS

VARIOUS USES OF
FLASH
There is no only right usage of FLASH
Dissection of the hot Flash website / How to show the
photograph on Flash / The contents related to Flash
from various viewpoints
Special Part-02

MAX IN JAPAN
2004 Retrospective and 2005 Perspective

BAGGAGE IDENTIFICATION TAG

SYMPOSIUM:
The Origin Of Creative Drive

RUSH URGENT

macromedia

FLASH & XML

31-12-23

"We listen to what our clients say and communicate what we think. We like working closely with our clients as a small creative studio. Also we believe that graphic design can add extra value to anything from printed matter, websites, daily necessities, television screens – in fact whatever surrounds you."

»Wir hören uns an, was unsere Auftraggeber von uns wollen, und teilen ihnen dann mit, was wir darüber denken. Als kleines Kreativbüro arbeiten wir gerne eng mit unseren Auftraggebern zusammen. Wir glauben, dass Grafikdesign den Wert aller möglichen Produkte steigern kann, von Druckerzeugnissen und Internetseiten, Artikeln des täglichen Bedarfs bis zu Fernsehgestaltung – einfach für alles, was einen täglich umgibt.«

«Nous écoutons ce que nos clients disent et nous communiquons ce que nous pensons. Nous aimons travailler en étroite collaboration avec nos clients, comme un petit studio de création. Nous pensons aussi que le graphisme peut apporter une valeur ajoutée à la presse, aux sites Internet, aux produits de consommation courante, aux publicités télévisées – en fait à tout ce qui vous entoure. »

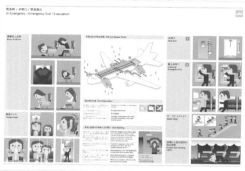

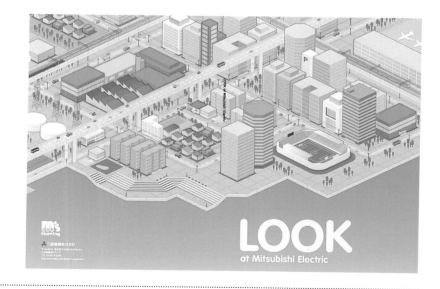

Page 19:
Project: "des (design experimental square)" magazine cover, 2004
Client: Shoeisha

Previous page:
Project: "Museselection 4"
book/CD packaging, 2004
Client: Museselection

Top:
Project: "Safety Instructions"
(unpublished), 2004
Client: AIR DO

Above:
Project: "LOOK at Mitsubishi
Electric" book, 2005
Client: Mitsubishi Electric

ADAPTER

"Sonic collage"

Adapter
5F Sasaki Building
1-1-13 Taishido Setagaya-ku
Tokyo 154 0004
Japan
T +81 03 577 973 74
info@adapter.jp
www.adapter.jp

Design group history
2003 Founded by Kenjiro
Harigai in Tokyo, Japan

Founder's biography
Kenjiro Harigai
1977 Born in Japan

Recent exhibitions
2004 "Beams T", Rocket
Gallery, Tokyo
2005 "More than Human",
Surface to Air, Paris
2006 "Memai", Nanzuka
Underground, Tokyo

Clients
And A.; Beams; Brutus; Com-
posite; Dazed and Confused;
Levi's; Medicomtoy; Nike;
Parco; Relax; Studiovoice

"We design like we draw a picture. We mix the elements of illustration, photography and typography and try not to limit our expression by having no particular style."

»Wir entwerfen so, wie wir ein Bild zeichnen. Wir mischen die Elemente Illustration, Fotografie und Typografie und versuchen, unsere Ausdrucksmöglichkeiten nicht durch einen festgelegten Stil zu beschränken.«

« Nous créons nos visuels comme si nous dessinions un tableau. Nous mêlons les éléments d'illustration, de photographie et de typographie et tentons de ne pas enfermer notre expression dans un style particulier. »

Previous page:
Project: *"I Hate You for US Army" T-shirt image, 2006*
Client: *Adamite*

Above:
Project: *"P.I.C.S." company overview brochure, 2005*
Client: *PICS Co. Ltd*

Following page:
Project: *"P.I.C.S." DVD cover, 2005*
Client: *PICS Co. Ltd*

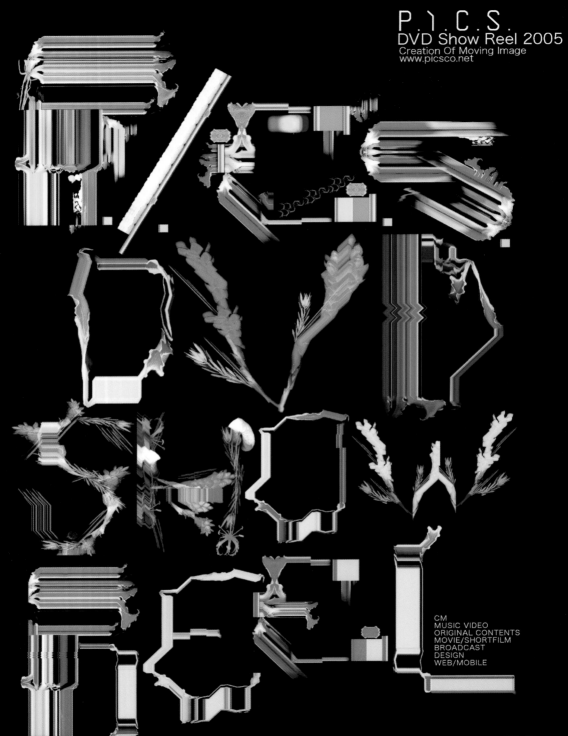

P . I . C . S .
DVD Show Reel 2005
Creation Of Moving Image
www.picsco.net

CM
MUSIC VIDEO
ORIGINAL CONTENTS
MOVIE/SHORTFILM
BROADCAST
DESIGN
WEB/MOBILE

Top:
Project: *"Chisako Mikami: Here"* CD cover, 2005
Client: *Creage, Yamaha Corp.*

Above left:
Project: *"More than Human 01"* poster, 2005
Client: *Self*

Above right:
Project: *"More than Human 02"* poster, 2005
Client: *Self*

Following page:
Project: *"Tao"* T-shirt image, 2005
Client: *Beams T*

PETER ANDERSON

"Graphics has a unique position of interaction and therefore influence with the everyday world. I believe it is our responsibility to act on this."

Peter Anderson Studio Ltd
8 Flitcroft Street
London WC2H 8DL
UK
T +44 207 836 338 0
peter@
peterandersonstudio.co.uk
www.
peterandersonstudio.co.uk

Biography
1969 Born in Belfast, Northern Ireland
1989–1992 Studied graphic design, Central Saint Martins College of Art & Design, London
1992–1994 Advanced postgraduate, Fine Art Printmaking and Photomedia, Central Saint Martins College of Art & Design, London

Professional experience
1994–1997 Gravitaz collaborative project with photographer Platon
1994–1997 Established Resonator Buzz Publications
1997–2006 Founded Interfield Design Ltd, London
2006 Founded Peter Anderson Studio Ltd, London

Recent exhibitions
1999–2001 "Ultravision", British Council Millennium world touring exhibition
2001 "British Experiment", Westside Gallery, New York; "Innovation Stories", British Design Council world touring exhibition
2005 "Local Stories", town centre typographic installation, Castleford, West Yorkshire

2006 "Chelsea Art Fair", London; "Spoken with Eyes", Davis Design Museum, University of California, Sacramento

Recent awards
2005 Shortlisted, "X Man of the Year", Arena magazine, London

Clients
Alive and Well; Altnagelvin Hospital; BBC; British Council; Central Saint Martins College of Art & Design; Channel 4; Paul Rankin Group; Red Cell HHCL

"Graphic language is growing to become a new art, cheap publishing and Internet access are becoming the new galleries. We are in a wonderful time where we can access innovation much more easily and increased choice makes this more relevant than ever before. This coupled with commercial collaboration and the brilliance of great functionality sets the stage for an ever-inspiring and challenging arena. I hope to continue to experiment and function, explore and invent with young and experienced eyes."

»Grafikdesign entwickelt sich allmählich zu einer neuen Kunstform, als deren Galerien preiswerte Druckerzeugnisse und Internetportale fungieren. Wir leben in einer wunderbaren Zeit, in der wir viel leichter Zugang zu Innovationen haben, was aufgrund des riesigen Angebots wichtiger denn je ist. In Verbindung mit geschäftlicher Professionalität und hervorragender Funktionalität ergibt das die Voraussetzungen für eine stets inspirierende und anspruchsvolle Arena des Grafikdesigns. Ich hoffe, auch weiterhin mit sowohl jungen als auch erfahrenen Augen zu experimentieren und zu arbeiten, zu forschen und zu erfinden.«

« Le langage graphique est en train de devenir une nouvelle discipline artistique dont l'édition bon marché et l'accès à Internet sont les nouvelles galeries. Nous vivons une merveilleuse époque où l'innovation est bien plus accessible, ce qui est d'autant plus intéressant que le choix est plus vaste que jamais. Conjuguée à la commercialisation et une fonctionnalité exceptionelle, cette évolution a contribué à l'émergence d'un terrain d'action à la fois inspirant et plein de défis. J'espère continuer à fonctionner, expérimenter, explorer et inventer avec un regard jeune et expérimenté. »

ANTOINE+ MANUEL

"It's time for graphic designers to come to power."

Antoine+Manuel
8, rue Charlot
75003 Paris
France
T +33 1 44 61 99 00
c@antoineetmanuel.com
www.antoineetmanuel.com

Design group history
1993 Co-founded by Antoine Audiau and Manuel Warosz in Paris, France

Founders' biographies
Antoine Audiau
Studied fashion design, l'Atelier Letellier, Paris

Manuel Warosz
Studied industrial design, École Nationale Supérieure des Arts Décoratifs, Paris

Recent exhibitions
2006 "Papier peint: la peau intérieure", Galerie Blanche, Unité d'habitation Le Cor- busier, Briey; "Domestic Wall Stickers: Troy, Possession, Waterfall", Galerie Colette, Paris; "100 affiches contempo- raines françaises", École Supérieure d'Art de Grenoble 2007 "Domestic Vases", Espace Modem, Paris

Clients
Cartier; CCNT; Centre Georges Pompidou; Christian Lacroix; CNDC; Collection Lambert en Avignon; Domes- tic; École Nationale Supérieure des Beaux-Arts; Galeries Lafayette; Habitat; La Comédie de Clermont-Ferrand; Larousse; Manufacture nationale de Sèvres; Musée d'art moderne de la ville de Paris; Musée des Arts Décora- tifs, Paris; Tarkett; Théâtre national Dijon Bourgogne; Yves Saint Laurent; Yvon Lambert

"For each project we begin the design process by inventing an entire system of forms, with its own vocabulary and rules. In this phase of conceptualizing, we focus on shape and on the story we want to tell. We always keep in mind that the objects we create are aimed at an audience, and we want to provoke emotions. Since we are our first audience, this emotion has to work on us."

»Bei jedem neuen Projekt beginnt bei uns der Designprozess damit, dass wir ein ganz neues Formensystem mit eigenem Vokabular und eigenen Regeln erfinden. In dieser Konzeptionsphase konzentrieren wir uns auf die Form und die Gestalt sowie auf die Geschichte, die wir erzählen wollen. Wir denken dabei immer daran, dass die von uns geschaffenen Arbeiten für ein Publikum bestimmt sind und dass wir Emotionen auslösen wollen. Da wir selbst unser erstes Publikum sind, muss die Emotion auch uns ergreifen.«

« Pour chaque projet, notre processus créatif commence par l'invention d'un système complet de formes, avec son vocabulaire et sa grammaire propres. Durant cette phase de conceptualisation, nous nous concentrons sur la forme et sur l'histoire que nous voulons raconter. Nous gardons toujours à l'esprit que les objets que nous créons sont destinés à un public et nous voulons provoquer des émotions. Parce que nous sommes notre premier public, cette émotion doit d'abord nous affecter. »

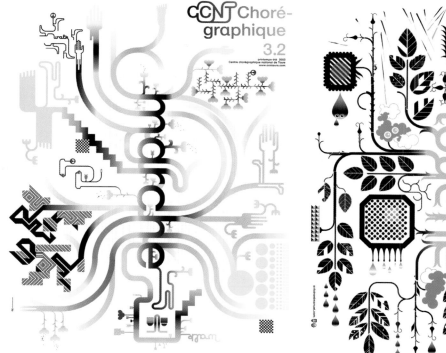

Previous page:
Project: *"À Fripon Fripon et Demi" poster, 2004*
Client: *Collection Lambert en Avignon*

Above left:
Project: *"3.2, marche"*
poster, 2003
Client: *CCNT (Centre Chorégraphique National de Tours)*

Above right:
Project: *"3.3, touche"*
poster, 2003
Client: *CCNT (Centre Chorégraphique National de Tours)*

Following page:
Project: *"1.3, Automne"*
poster, 2003
Client: *CCNT (Centre Chorégraphique National de Tours)*

cCNT Choré-
graphique
1.3

Centre chorégraphique national de Tours
Direction Daniel Larrieu

PHILIPPE APELOIG

"I attempt to preserve the elements of type and their meanings that have a tendency to become forgotten."

Studio Philippe Apeloig
41, rue La Fayette
75009 Paris
France
T +33 1 435 534 29
apeloig.philippe@wanadoo.fr
www.apeloig.com

Biography
1962 Born in Paris, France
1981–1985 Studied art and applied arts, École Nationale Supérieure des Arts Appliqués/École Nationale Supérieure des Arts Décoratifs, Paris
1984 Diplôme of the École Nationale Supérieure des Arts Appliqués; BTS Visual Arts (Brevet de Technicien Supérieur), Paris

Professional experience
1983 & 1985 Internships, Total Design, Amsterdam
1985–1987 Graphic designer, Musée d'Orsay, Paris
1988 Internship, April Greiman's studio, Los Angeles
1989 Founded Philippe Apeloig Design, Paris
1992–1998 Lecturer in Typography, École Nationale Supérieure des Arts Décoratifs, Paris
1993 Art Director, Le Jardin des Modes, Paris
1993/94 Grant from the French Ministry of Culture to spend one year researching typography at the French Academy of Art, Rome
1997+ Design consultant and subsequently Art Director,

Musée du Louvre, Paris
1999–2002 Professor of Graphic Design, Cooper Union School of Art, New York
2000–2003 Curator, Herb Lubalin Study Center of Design and Typography, Cooper Union School of Art, New York

Recent exhibitions
2003 "Affiches", Mediatine, Brussels
2004 "Affiches", touring exhibition, Galerija Avla NLB, Ljubljana/Grafist, Istanbul/ Dawson College of Design, Montreal

2005 "Typo/Typé", Carré Sainte-Anne, Montpellier, in collaboration with Galerie Anatome; "Typo/Typé", Russian Art Museum, Kiev, in collaboration with the French Institute of Ukraine
2006 "Play Type", Rosenwald-Wolf Gallery, University of the Arts, Philadelphia

Recent awards
2004 Premier Award, International Typographic Awards, International Society of Typographic Designers; Golden Bee Award, Moscow International Biennale of Graphic Design

2006 Five Star Award, International Invitational Poster Biennale, Osaka University of Arts

Clients
Achim Moeller Fine Art; Châtelet; Cité du Livre, Aix-en-Provence; Cultures France; Éditions Odile Jacob; Éditions Robert Laffont; French Institute, New York; Institut National d'Histoire de l'Art; Musée d'Art et d'Histoire du Judaïsme; Musée du Louvre; Réunion des Musées Nationaux

APELOIG

AFFICHES

PHILIPPE APELOIG / TYPO / TYPÉ

8 AVRIL – 22 MAI 2005

CARRÉ SAINTE ANNE. MONTPELLIER. 2 RUE PHILIPPY

13H – 18H DU MARDI AU DIMANCHE

"I like messages to be strictly minimalist in expression: they should be functional. Sometimes, however, I move into more experimental and emotional design by adding 'non-functional' elements. Early in my career, I explored increasingly complex grids and typography in compositions. Yet, the core of typography remains the interaction of letters and meanings, which tends to be overlooked. Recently, graphic designers have become dissatisfied with merely obediently delivering the client's message. Sidestepping the designer's traditional neutrality, many are adding self-conscious critiques, humour, irony, irreverence and self-deprecating concepts that speak to the reader on a number of levels. In my view, the strongest part of my design work is its fragility, which may demand a less commercial and more intellectual understanding. I try in my work to speak to and touch the audience by exploiting the form and function of my messages. Through working with clients and helping them to communicate their messages, the graphic design community anticipates the future of culture."

»Ich mag streng minimalistische Ausdrucksformen, die auch funktional sein sollten. Manchmal bin ich aber auch experimenteller oder emotionaler in meinen Designs. Schon am Anfang meiner Berufstätigkeit habe ich in meinen Kompositionen zunehmend komplexe Raster und Typografien verwendet. Im Kern bleibt jedoch die Typografie eine Interaktion von Buchstaben und Bedeutungen, was gerne übersehen wird. Seit kurzem geben sich Grafiker generell nicht mehr damit zufrieden, gehorsam die Botschaft des Auftraggebers abzuliefern. Viele umgehen die traditionelle Neutralität des Werbegrafikers und lassen eigene Kritik, Humor, Frechheit, Ironie und Selbstironie in ihre Entwürfe einfließen, die den Betrachter auf mehreren Ebenen ansprechen. Meiner Ansicht nach liegt die Stärke meiner Arbeiten in ihren Brüchen, die ein weniger kommerziell orientiertes und dafür stärker intellektuelles Verständnis erfordern. Ich versuche das Publikum anzusprechen und innerlich zu berühren, indem ich die Form und Funktion meiner Grafiken kreativ ausschöpfe. Durch die Zusammenarbeit mit den Auftraggebern, denen man hilft ihre Aussagen zu kommunizieren, nimmt jeder Grafiker die Kultur der Zukunft vorweg.«

« J'aime que les messages soient strictement minimalistes dans leur expression: ils doivent être fonctionnels. Parfois, pourtant, je m'aventure sur des terrains plus expérimentaux et émotionnels en ajoutant à mon graphisme des éléments 'non fonctionnels'. Au début de ma carrière, j'ai exploré des grilles et des typographies extrêmement complexes dans mes compositions. Mais l'essence de la typographie demeure l'interaction entre lettres et sens, qui est trop souvent négligée. Depuis peu, les graphistes ne se contentent plus de sagement délivrer le message du client. Prenant leurs distances avec la traditionnelle neutralité du graphiste, un grand nombre d'entre eux ajoutent éléments d'autocritique, humour, ironie et irrévérence à leurs concepts pour s'adresser au public sur plusieurs niveaux. De mon point de vue, le trait le plus important de mon travail graphique est sa fragilité, qui peut exiger une appréhension moins commerciale et plus intellectuelle. Dans mon travail, j'essaie de parler au public et de le toucher à travers la forme et la fonction de mes messages. En travaillant avec les clients et en les aidant à communiquer leurs messages, la communauté du graphisme annonce la culture de l'avenir. »

Previous page:
Project: *"Typo / Typé"*
exhibition poster, 2005
Client: *Carré Sainte-Anne,*
Montpellier

Above left:
Project: *"ŌÉ, I am once again*
a man" festival poster, 2006
Client: *Cité du livre, Aix-en-*
Provence

Above right:
Project: *"Demain la bibliothè-*
que" (Tomorrow, the Library)
poster for annual convention,
2006

Client: *Association des biblio-*
thécaires français

Following page:
Project: *"9ᵉ Semaine de la*
langue française" poster, 2004
Client: *Ministère de la Culture*

JONATHAN BARNBROOK

"Design is both a political and cultural force for change, although most designers choose not to think about the power it has."

Barnbrook Design
Studio 12
10–11 Archer Street
London W1D 7AZ
UK
T +44 207 287 384 8
us@barnbrook.net
www.barnbrook.net
www.virusfonts.com

Biography
1966 Born in Luton, England
1988 BA (Hons) Graphic Design, Central Saint Martins College of Art & Design, London
1989 MA Graphic Design, Royal College of Art, London

Professional experience
1990 Founded Barnbrook Design and Virusfonts, London

Recent exhibitions
2003 "Graf Exhibition: My Room, Somehow", Osaka/Taipei; "Buy Me/Bomb Me", Rocket Gallery, Tokyo
2004 "Tomorrow's Truth: The Graphic Agitation of Jonathan Barnbrook", Seoul Arts Centre; "Friendly Fire: The Work of Barnbrook Design", GGG Gallery, Tokyo/ DDD Gallery, Osaka

Clients
Adbusters; Barbican Gallery, London; David Bowie; Émigré; Damien Hirst; Mori Art Museum, Tokyo; Museum of Contemporary Art, Los Angeles; Roppongi Hills, Tokyo; Saatchi Gallery, London; White Cube Gallery, London

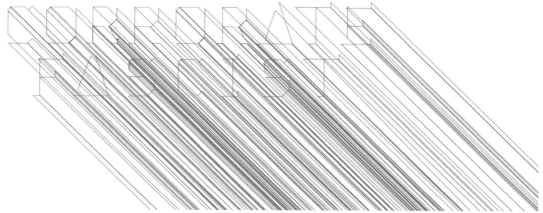

"Any kind of information does not change people immediately. For instance, if you see a commercial for a car, you don't say: 'That's a great car!' and then go and buy that car. It works over time and it filters through into your consciousness, as does work with a political message. If you look through history, you'll see that nothing has ever been directly changed by one poster or one campaign. The work I do adds to the political ideological landscape of a society. You put things on the agenda and I know it is successful, because globalization is on the agenda now and it wasn't just 10 years ago. This is through the pressure of protest from ordinary citizens. You can't ignore what companies are doing in relation to various political situations in the world and you can't ignore the role of graphic design within that. There is a political, social and psychological impact of what you do as a designer. People shouldn't pretend that they are not responsible, because they are. We all are."

»Menschen werden durch irgendwelche neuen Informationen nicht augenblicklich veranlasst, anders zu denken oder zu handeln. Wenn man zum Beispiel eine Werbung für ein Auto sieht, sagt man nicht gleich: ›Das ist ja ein tolles Auto!‹ und geht hin und kauft es. Die Werbung wirkt und infiltriert das Bewusstsein peu à peu; genauso funktioniert das bei politischer Propaganda. Wenn man sich geschichtliche Entwicklungen anschaut, erkennt man, dass sich nichts jemals durch ein einziges Plakat oder eine einzige Kampagne geändert hat. Meine Arbeit trägt zur politisch-ideologischen Situation in einer Gesellschaft bei. Man setzt bestimmte Themen auf die Tagesordnung. Ich weiß, der Erfolg ist gewiss, denn Globalisierung steht heute auf der Tagesordnung (was vor zehn Jahren einfach nicht der Fall war), und zwar auf Druck von Bürgerprotesten. Man kann nicht ignorieren, welche Auswirkungen unternehmerisches Handeln international auf verschiedene politische Konstellationen hat und man kann auch den Anteil der Werbegrafik an diesen Auswirkungen nicht ignorieren. Was man als Werbegrafiker macht, hat politische, soziale und psychologische Folgen. Die Leute sollten nicht so tun, als ob sie nicht dafür verantwortlich wären, denn sie sind es. Wir sind es alle.«

« Une information, quelle qu'elle soit, ne change pas les gens instantanément. Par exemple, si vous voyez une publicité pour une voiture, vous ne vous dites pas tout de suite : 'Ça, c'est une voiture géniale !' avant de courir l'acheter. Cela prend du temps et cela s'infiltre dans votre conscience, tout comme le font les slogans politiques. L'histoire a démontré que rien n'a jamais été directement changé par une affiche ou même une campagne. Le travail que je fais agrémente le paysage politique et idéologique d'une société. Il met en avant certaines choses dont je sais qu'elles auront du succès, parce que la mondialisation est à l'ordre du jour et que ce n'était pas le cas il y a seulement dix ans. Et tout cela se fait sous la pression de citoyens ordinaires mécontents. Vous ne pouvez plus ignorer ce que les entreprises font dans telle ou telle situation de politique internationale et vous ne pouvez pas ignorer le rôle que joue le graphisme dans tout cela. Ce que nous faisons en tant que graphistes a des conséquences politiques, sociales et psychologiques. Les gens ne devraient pas faire comme s'ils n'étaient pas responsables, parce qu'ils le sont. Nous le sommes tous. »

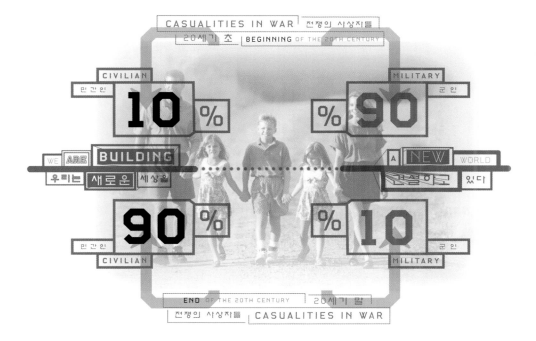

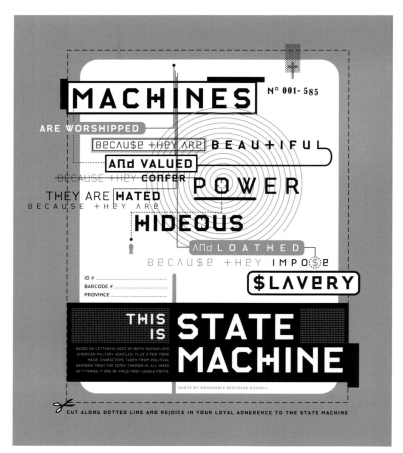

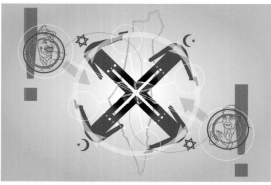

Page 41:
Project: *"Tomorrow's Truth: Globanalization – Corporate Fascist"*
political message, 2001
Client: *Self*

Previous page:
Project: *"Tomorrow's Truth: Collateral Damage – We are Building a New World"*
political message, 2004
Client: *Self*

Above:
Project: *"Tomorrow's Truth: Collateral Damage – Violence is a Cycle" political message, 2004*
Client: *Self*

Top:
Project: *"State Machine" illustration showing font, 2004*
Client: *Virusfonts*

Top left:
Project: *"Tomorrow's Truth:*
Gulf War II – America"
political message, 2003
Client: *Self*

Top right:
Project: *"Tomorrow's Truth:*
Globanalization – Rosama

McLaden" political message,
2003
Client: *Self*

Above left:
Project: *"Tomorrow's Truth: Col-*
lateral Damage – U. N.Ilateral"
political message, 2004
Client: *Self*

Following page top left:
Project: *"Tomorrow's Truth:*
Gulf War II – What Should Bush

Above right:
Project: *"Tomorrow's Truth:*
Collateral Damage – U. S.Rael"
political message, 2002
Client: *Self*

Following page top right:
Project: *"Tomorrow's Truth:*
Gulf War II – What Should Kim
Jong II Really Be Saying?"
political message, 2003

Really Be Saying?"
political message, 2003
Client: *Self*

Following page bottom left:
Project: *"Tomorrow's Truth:*
Gulf War II – B-liar"
political message, 2003
Client: *Self*

Client: *Self*

Following page bottom right:
Project: *"Tomorrow's Truth:*
Gulf War II – What Should
Annan Really Be Saying?"
political message, 2003
Client: *Self*

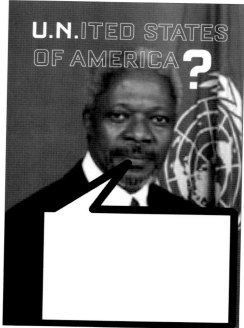

NICHOLAS BLECHMAN

"Designers are also citizens, and we have a responsibility to use our images in ways that benefit society."

Knickerbocker Design
416 West 13th Street, #309
New York, NY 10014
USA
T + 1 212 229 283 1
nb@
knickerbockerdesign.com
www.
knickerbockerdesign.com

Biography
1967 Born in New York City, USA
1990 BA Art History and Studio Arts, Oberlin College, Ohio

Professional experience
1996–2000 Art Director, op-ed and editorial pages, The New York Times
2000+ Freelance illustrator,

published in Dwell, GQ, Maxim, New York, The New York Times, Newsweek, Wired
2001 Founder and principal of Knickerbocker Design
2004+ Art Director, "Week in Review" section, The New York Times

Recent exhibitions
2006 "National Design Triennial", Cooper Hewitt National Design Museum, New York

Recent awards
1996 Award of Excellence, Society of News Design, Rhode Island; Communication Graphics Award, AIGA, New York

1998 Gold Medal, Society of Publication Designers, New York
2004 "50 Books/50 Covers", American Institute of Graphic Arts, New York
2005 "50 Books/50 Covers", American Institute of Graphic Arts, New York; Award of Excellence, Society of Publication Designers, New York
2006 Award of Excellence,

Society of Publication Designers, New York

Clients
Glimmerglass Opera; Grand Street; Greenpeace; Harper Collins; Housing Works; Little; Brown and Co.; Penguin; Simon & Schuster; United Nations

"1. Design is a means, not an end, and is most effective when articulating an idea; 2. Design is not an individual pursuit but a public one, and I rely on the collaborative back and forth between clients and colleagues to help stimulate and open up projects; 3. Illustration features prominently in my work, and I often integrate drawing into my design; 4. Politics plays an integral role in my creative thinking. I believe design can encourage social change."

»1. Design ist das Mittel zum Zweck, nicht das Ziel, und am effektivsten, wenn es eine Idee formuliert. 2. Design ist kein Privatvergnügen, sondern von öffentlichem Interesse. Daher brauche ich das ständige Feedback von Auftraggebern und Kollegen, um das Beste aus einem Projekt zu machen. 3. Illustrationen sind ein wichtiger Teil meiner Arbeiten, in die ich häufig Zeichnungen integriere. 4. Politik spielt in meinen schöpferischen Denkprozessen eine große Rolle. Ich bin davon überzeugt, dass Grafikdesign gesellschaftliche Veränderungen fördern kann.«

«1. Le graphisme n'est pas une fin en soi mais un moyen, et le plus efficace lorsqu'il articule une idée. 2. Le graphisme n'est pas une quête individuelle mais publique, et je me repose sur une collaboration constante entre mes collègues et nos clients pour dynamiser et élargir les projets. 3. L'illustration a une place dominante dans mon travail et j'intègre souvent du dessin à mes créations. 4. La politique fait partie intégrante de ma réflexion. Je pense que le design peut faire changer la société. »

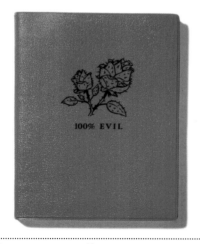

Previous page:
Project: *"Nozone IX – Empire"*
magazine cover, 2004
Client: *Princeton Architectural Press*

Above:
Project: *"100% Evil" book cover and spread, 2005*
(illustrators: Nicholas Blechman and Christoph Niemann)
Client: *Princeton Architectural Press*

Following page top:
Project: *"Nozone – States of the Union" magazine illustration, 2004*
(illustrator: Christoph Niemann)
Client: *Princeton Architectural Press*

Following page bottom:
Project: *"Nozone IX – Empire" table of contents and "Condoleezza Rice" magazine spreads, 2004 (illustrator: Paul Sahre)*
Client: *Princeton Architectural Press*

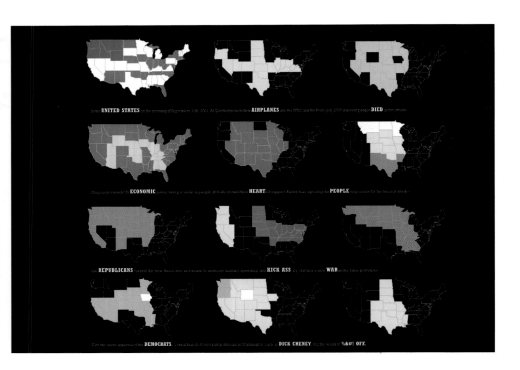

In the **UNITED STATES** on the morning of September 11th, 2001 Al Qaeda terrorists flew **AIRPLANES** into the WTC and the Pentagon; 2700 innocent people **DIED** in the attacks.

Meanwhile, towards the **ECONOMIC** power, were put under especially gleefully stressed their **HEART**-felt support. Rather than capturing the **PEOPLE** responsible for the terrorist attacks,

the **REPUBLICANS** turned the new threat into an excuse to increase military spending and **KICK ASS** by starting a new **WAR** under false pretenses.

With the tacent approval of the **DEMOCRATS**, a small bunch of arrogant politicians in Washington made a **DICK CHENEY** tell the world to %&#! OFF.

CONTENTS

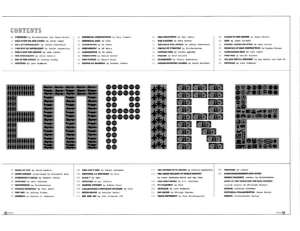

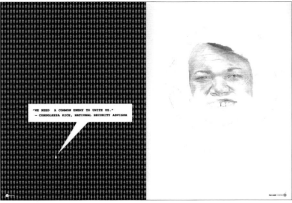

"WE NEED A COMMON ENEMY TO UNITE US."
— CONDOLEEZA RICE, NATIONAL SECURITY ADVISOR

IRMA BOOM

"Every book is a different story."

Irma Boom Office
Koninginneweg 174
1075 EH Amsterdam
The Netherlands
T +31 20 627 189 5
office@irmaboom.nl
www.irmaboom.nl

Biography
1960 Born in Lochem,
The Netherlands
1979–1985 Studied at the
School for Fine Art, Enschede

Professional experience
1985–1990 Senior designer,
Government Publishing,
Printing Office, The Hague
1991+ Founded own studio,
Irma Boom Office,
Amsterdam
1992+ Lecturer, Yale University,
New Haven
1998–2000 Tutor, Jan van Eyck
Academie, Maastricht

Exhibitions
2003 "BOOM!", solo exhibition, Bigli University, Istanbul
2003–2005 "The European
Design Show", touring exhibition, Design Museum, London
2005 "Ontwerper &
Opdrachtgever", Universiteits-
bibliotheek Amsterdam
2005/06 "Foreign Affairs",
touring exhibition
2006 "Books from: M. C.
Escher, Jan Bons, Otto Treuch-
mann, Willem Sandberg, Irma
Boom", Archive Stichting de
Roos 1945–2005, Museum
Meermanno, The Hague
2006/07 "Best Designed

Books", Stedelijk Museum
Amsterdam; "Schönste Bücher
aus aller Welt", Leipzig

Recent awards
1998 Overall Winner, Lutki &
Smit Annual Report Competition, Culemborg
1999 Award (x4), Collectieve
Propaganda van het Neder-
landse Boek (CPNB)
2000 Gold Medal, Schönste
Bücher Aller Welt, Leipzig
2001 Award (x3), Collectieve
Propaganda van het Neder-
landse Boek (CPNB); The
Gutenberg Prize, Institut für
Buchkunst, funded by the

Cultural Administration of
Leipzig
2002 Silver Medal, Schönste
Bücher aus aller Welt, Leipzig

Clients
Architectural Association,
London; AVL/Joep van
Lieshout; Berlin Biennale;
Birkhäuser Verlag; Camper;
Centraal Museum Utrecht;
Ferrari; Forum for African
Arts (Cornell University);
Stichting De Appel; Het
Financieele Dagblad; Inside
Outside; Koninklijke
Tichelaar; KPN/Royal PTT
Nederlands; Mondrian Foun-

dation; Museum Boijmans
Van Beuningen; NAi publish-
ers; Oeuvre AKZO Coatings;
Oktagon Verlag; OMA/Rem
Koolhaas; Paul Fentener van
Vlissingen; Paul Kasmin
Gallery; Prince Claus Fund;
Prins Bernhard Foundation;
Royal Ahrend NV; Royal
Library; Rijksmuseum; SHV
Holdings NV; Slewe Galerie;
Stedelijk Museum; Stichting
CPNB; Stichting De Roos;
Stroom hcbk; Thoth publish-
ers; United Nations; Vitra
International; World Wide
Video Festival; Zumtobel
GmbH

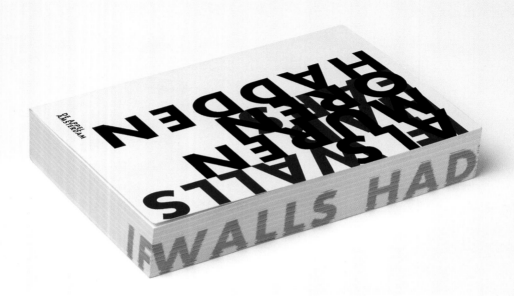

"Happily through books, the past, present and future can take on profoundly contemporary results and become part of our everyday. My role in making books is to give another life to a story. Working with different worlds, exchanging thoughts and ideas is one of the most valuable ingredients in my practice. What has always been important to me is the complete trust of my commissioner. I immediately drop my 'pen' if there is no collaboration, and if I feel we're not on the same track, there's no use in continuing. But if it works, then the object that we've collectively created hopefully pushes the boundaries of the definition of a book."

»Glücklicherweise können Vergangenheit, Gegenwart und Zukunft durch Bücher Teil unseres Lebens werden. Meine Aufgabe als Buchgestalterin ist es, Geschichten lebendig werden zu lassen. Die Arbeit in verschiedenen Welten, der Austausch von Gedanken und Ideen gehört zu den wertvollsten Aspekten meiner Tätigkeit. Es ist sehr wichtig für mich, dass ein Auftraggeber mir vollkommen vertraut. Wenn keine echte Zusammenarbeit zustande kommt, lasse ich sofort den ›Griffel‹ fallen. Wenn ich spüre, dass wir nicht auf der gleichen Wellenlänge liegen, hat es keinen Sinn weiterzumachen. Wenn aber die Wellenlänge stimmt, wird das, was wir gemeinsam schaffen, hoffentlich die Grenzen dessen sprengen, was man ein Buch nennt.«

«Grâce aux livres, le passé, le présent et l'avenir se colorent d'aspects radicalement contemporains et font partie de notre quotidien. Mon rôle dans la fabrication d'un livre est d'offrir une nouvelle vie à une histoire. Dans la pratique, il est très précieux de travailler avec des mondes différents, d'échanger pensées et idées. Ce qui a toujours beaucoup compté pour moi, c'est la confiance totale de mon client. Je laisse immédiatement tomber mon crayon s'il n'y a pas de collaboration entre nous, et si je sens que nous ne sommes pas sur la même longueur d'onde, ce n'est pas la peine de continuer. Mais si ça fonctionne, avec un peu de chance, l'objet que nous avons créé collectivement repousse les limites de ce qu'est un livre».

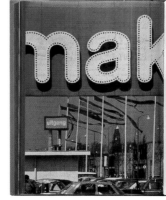

Previous page:
Project: "If Walls Had Ears" book, 2005
Client: Stichting De Appel

Above:
Project: "Frits" visual biography/ book (cover and spread), 2004
Client: Marthe Foch

Following page:
Project: "Rotterdams Kookboek" cook book, 2004
Client: Stichting Madame Jeanet

52   Irma Boom

BÜRO
WEISS

"Design is more than a façade."

Büro Weiss
Gabriel-Max-Str. 4
10 245 Berlin
Germany
T +49 30 780 837 80
post@bueroweiss.de
www.bueroweiss.de

Design group history
2003 Co-founded by
Christoph Bebermeier,
Marc Bürger, David Krause
and Jan Pauls in Berlin, Germany
2005 Christoph Bebermeier
appointed manager of Büro
Weiss

Founders' biographies
Christoph Bebermeier
1970 Born in Duderstadt,
Germany
2002 Diploma in Visual Communications, University of
Applied Sciences, Dortmund

David Krause
1971 Born in Düsseldorf,
Germany
2002 Diploma in Visual
Communications, University of Applied Sciences,
Dortmund
Marc Bürger
1971 Born in Düsseldorf,
Germany
2005 Diploma in Visual
Communications, University of Applied Sciences,
Dortmund
Jan Pauls
1973 Born in Neuwied,
Germany

2000 Diploma in Visual Arts,
Academy of Visual Arts, Leipzig

Recent exhibitions
2002 "Die 100 besten Plakate",
Berlin; "Type Directors Show",
New York
2005 "Die 100 besten Plakate",
Berlin
2006 "International Poster
Exhibition Japan", Tokushima;
"Festival d'Affiches de Chaumont"; "Freispiel", Forum
Junges Design, Munich; "Type
Directors Show", New York;
"Die 100 besten Plakate",
Berlin

Recent awards
2001 Best of the Best, Red Dot
Award
2002 Junior Award, Art Directors Club, Berlin; Joseph
Binder Award
2003 Joseph Binder Award;
Red Dot Award; Sappi–Ideas
that Matter; Art Directors
Club Award, Berlin
2004 Sappi–Ideas that Matter
2005 Best of the Best, Red Dot
Award; Plakat- und Media
Grand-Prix, Fachverband
Außenwerbung; "Die 100
besten Plakate", 100 Beste
Plakate e. V.

2006 Excellence Award, New
York Type Directors Club;
"Die 100 besten Plakate", 100
Beste Plakate e. V.; iF Gold
Award; iF Communication
Design Award; Joseph Binder
Award

Clients
Adolf Grimme Institut; Dummy Magazine; Festspielhaus
Hellerau; FIRMA; Fritz Bauer
Institut; Maiami; Reporter
ohne Grenzen; Shoa.de; Stiftung Brandenburgische Gedenkstätten; Stiftung Warentest; Zefa Visual Media

Gestaltung: BÜRO WEISS

"Design is more than a façade. Design catches the eye. Design is beautiful, exciting and intelligent. It tells stories and gives you food for thought. Design is different. It is not entirely customer oriented. It may, for instance, be hard to read. If design permanently caters to the consumer's taste, it creates weak, undefined brands with no clear direction."

»Gestaltung ist mehr als Fassade. Gestaltung ist auffällig, schön, spannend und intelligent. Sie erzählt Geschichten, lädt zum Mitdenken ein, gibt Impulse. Gestaltung ist anders. Sie ist nicht ausschließlich kundenorientiert. Sie kann auch mal schlecht lesbar sein. Die ewige Orientierung am Geschmack des Verbrauchers macht Marken schwach, unscharf und unklar.«

« Le graphisme est bien plus qu'une façade. Le graphisme attire le regard. Le graphisme est beau, stimulant et intelligent. Il raconte des histoires et nourrit votre réflexion. Le graphisme est différent. Il ne s'intéresse pas qu'au client. Il peut par exemple être difficile à lire. Si le graphisme se contente de docilement satisfaire le goût des consommateurs, il ne crée que des marques faibles et floues, sans direction claire. »

Previous page:
Project: "Dummy Revolution" magazine cover, 2005
Client: Dummy Magazine

Top and above:
Project: "Dummy Revolution" magazine spreads, 2005
Client: Dummy Magazine

Following page:
Project: "The Time After" poster, 2000 (in collaboration with Thomas Armborst)
Client: FH Dortmund

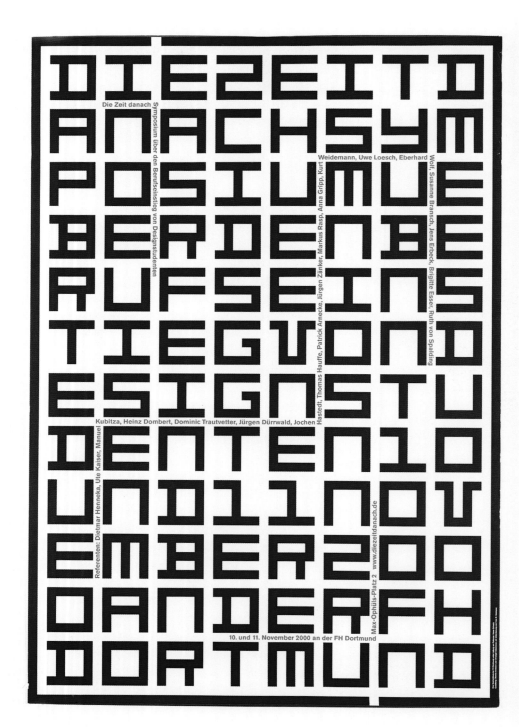

DIEZEITD ANACHSYM POSIUMUE BERDENBE RUFSEIND TIEGVOND ESIGNSTU DENTEN10 UND11NOV EMBER200 0ANDERFH DORTMUND

Die Zeit danach

Symposium über den Berufseinstieg von Designstudenten

Weidemann, Uwe Loesch, Eberhard Wolf, Susanne Bransch, Jens Erbeck, Brigitte Esser, Ruth von Spalding

Hastedt, Thomas Hauffe, Patrick Arnecke, Jürgen Zänker, Markus Rasp, Anna Gripp, Kurt

Kubitza, Heinz Dombert, Dominic Trautvetter, Jürgen Dürrwald, Jochen

Referenten: Dietmar Henneka, Ute Kaiser, Manuel

Max-Ophüls-Platz 2   www.diezeitdanach.de

10. und 11. November 2000 an der FH Dortmund

LESLIE CHAN

*"A splendid design can't come
out of others' minds."*

Leslie Chan Design Co Ltd
*4th Floor, 115 Nanjing East
Road / Section 4
Taipei 105
Taiwan*
*T +886 2 254 554 35
leslie@lcdesign.com.tw*

Biography
1963 Born in Hong Kong
1982–1984 Studied at the
Caritas Bianchi College of
Career, Art & Design Dept.,
Hong Kong
1987–1991 Art Director and
later Associate Creative
Director, Leo Burnett
Advertising Co., Taiwan
1991 Established own design
office in Taiwan
1994 Affiliate Member of
Hong Kong Designers
Association
1995 Communication
Design Lecturer of China
Productivity Center; Pack-
aging Design & Graphic
Design Lecturer of China
External Trade Development
Council

2006/07 Executive Supervisor
of Taiwan Graphic Design
Association; President of
Taiwan Poster Design Association

Recent exhibitions
2000 "Tokyo Type Directors
Club Annual Exhibition",
GGG Gallery, Japan; "TDC 46
the Type Directors Club
Annual Exhibition", Aronson
Gallery, New York
2001 "Hong Kong Interna-
tional Poster Triennial",
Hong Kong Heritage
Museum; "13th Lahti Poster
Biennial", Lahti Art Museum
2002 "The Colorado Interna-
tional Invitation Poster
Exhibition", Colorado State
University, Hatton and

Curfman Galleries; "Hong
Kong Design Show of Asia
Region", Hong Kong
Connection and Exhibition
Center
2003 "7th International Poster
Triennial Toyoma", The Muse-
um of Modern Art Toyama;
"14th Lahti Poster Biennial",
Lahti Art Museum
2004 "Hong Kong Interna-
tional Poster Triennial", Hong
Kong Heritage Museum
2006 "8th International Poster
Triennial Toyoma", The Muse-
um of Modern Art Toyama;
"17th International Poster
and Graphic Arts Festival of
Chaumont", Silos/Maison du
Livre et de l'Affiche

Recent awards
2000 Grand Prize & Gold
Award (x3), International
Exhibition of Visual Design,
Taiwan; Certificate of Typo-
graphic Excellence, The Type
Directors Club Awards, New
York
2002 The Mayor of the City
of Brno Award, 20th Interna-
tional Biennale of Graphic
Design Brno
2003 Grand Prize, 5th Seoul
Triennial Exhibition of Asia
Graphic Poster
2004 Selected for the 8th
Tehran International Poster
Biennial
2005 Selected by the Tokyo
Type Director Club; Bronze
and Excellence Award (x2),
Hong Kong Design Awards

2006 Selection in the 17th
International Poster and
Graphic Arts Festival (x3),
Chaumont; Silver and Bronze
Awards, 2nd Taiwan Interna-
tional Poster Design; Gold
Award, Taiwan Design Award;
Best of the Best, Red Dot
Award, Germany

Clients
British American Tobacco;
Christian Dior; Coca-Cola; Far
Eastone Telecommunications;
GSK; Master Kong Foods;
President Group; SC Johnson;
Sony; Taiwan External Trade
Development Council;
Unilever

"The main motivation behind my work is to strengthen the contacts between the graphic design community in Taiwan and other nations (such as Iran), while assisting the commercial development, the cultivation of creative design ability and the advancement of international competitiveness of my country. I also strive for my design work to be simple, uncomplicated and original, while retaining a specific rhythm of design that emphasizes visual tension in order to increase the layout's appeal."

«Die Hauptmotivation in meiner Tätigkeit liegt darin, die Kontakte zwischen den Grafikern in Taiwan und denen anderer Länder (zum Beispiel im Iran) zu stärken und dabei gleichzeitig meinen Beitrag zur wirtschaftlichen Entwicklung unseres Landes, zur Förderung kreativer Gestalter und zur internationalen Wettbewerbsfähigkeit Taiwans zu leisten. Ich versuche meine Entwürfe einfach, unkompliziert und originell zu gestalten. Gleichzeitig versuche ich einen spezifischen Designstil aufrechtzuerhalten, der visuelle Spannungen betont und die Attraktivität meiner Arbeiten zusätzlich steigert.«

«Ce qui me motive principalement dans mon travail, c'est de renforcer les liens entre les graphistes de Taiwan et ceux des autres nations (comme l'Iran), tout en participant au développement du commerce, d'une culture du graphisme et de la compétitivité internationale de mon pays. Je fais aussi tout mon possible pour que mon graphisme soit simple, sans complications et original, tout en restant fidèle à un rythme créatif particulier, qui insiste sur la tension visuelle afin de renforcer l'attrait de la composition.»

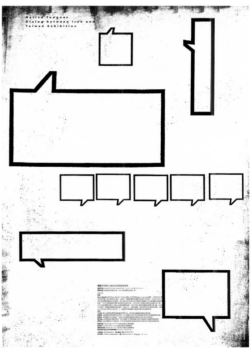

Previous page:
Project: "Chinese Character – Apprehensible" poster, 2004
Client: Taiwan Poster Design Association

Above:
Project: "Native Tongues Dialog Between Iran and Taiwan Exhibition" posters, 2006
Client: China Productivity Center

Following page top:
Project: "Green & Life" poster, 2004
Client: Taiwan Poster Design Association

Following page bottom:
Project: "The Urban Impressions of Taipei" posters, 2005
Client: China Productivity Center

green & Life

CYAN

"We attempt to meld text, images, paper into a unified entity, which is not intended to be easily consumed, either aesthetically or with regard to its content. A single glance is not sufficient to digest it."

Cyan
Strelizer Str. 61
10 115 Berlin
Germany
T +49 30 283 300 4
post@cyan.de
www.cyan.de

Design group history
1992 Founded by Daniela Haufe and Detlef Fiedler in Berlin, Germany
1996 Cyanpress founded for the design and publication of books
2000 Susanne Bax (b. 1973) joined Cyan
2000+ Haufe and Fiedler lecture at the Academy of Visual Arts, Leipzig

2001 Katja Schwalenberg (b. 1975) joined Cyan
2001+ Haufe and Fiedler became members of AGI
2004 Julia Fuchs (b. 1975) joined Cyan

Founders' biographies
Daniela Haufe
1966 Born in Berlin, Germany
Self-taught

Detlef Fiedler
1955 Born in Magdeburg, Germany
1977–1982 Studied architecture, Hochschule für Architektur und Bauwesen, Weimar

Recent exhibitions
2005 "Cyan–13 years in Berlin" DDD Gallery, Osaka
2006 "Cyan Berlin", GGG Gallery, Tokyo/Galerie Anatome, Paris

Recent awards
2002–2006 "Award (x4) 100 Best Posters–Germany, Austria, Switzerland"
2005 Silver Medal, 16th International Poster and Graphic Design Festival of Chaumont; Gold Cube, New York Art Directors Club

Clients
Academy of Fine Arts, Berlin; Bauhaus Dessau Foundation; Berlin National Gallery; The British Council; Institut für Auslandsbeziehungen; State Opera Berlin

CYAN

"We attempt to meld text, images, paper into a unified entity, which is not intended to be easily consumed, either aesthetically or with regard to its content. A single glance is not sufficient to digest it."

Cyan
Strelitzer Str. 61
10 115 Berlin
Germany
T +49 30 283 300 4
post@cyan.de
www.cyan.de

Design group history
1992 Founded by Daniela Haufe and Detlef Fiedler in Berlin, Germany
1996 Cyanpress founded for the design and publication of books
2000 Susanne Bax (b. 1973) joined Cyan
2000+ Haufe and Fiedler lecture at the Academy of Visual Arts, Leipzig
2001 Katja Schwalenberg (b. 1975) joined Cyan
2001+ Haufe and Fiedler became members of AGI
2004 Julia Fuchs (b. 1975) joined Cyan

Founders' biographies
Daniela Haufe
1966 Born in Berlin, Germany
Self-taught

Detlef Fiedler
1955 Born in Magdeburg, Germany
1977–1982 Studied architecture, Hochschule für Architektur und Bauwesen, Weimar

Recent exhibitions
2005 "Cyan–13 years in Berlin" DDD Gallery, Osaka
2006 "Cyan Berlin", GGG

Gallery, Tokyo/Galerie Anatome, Paris

Recent awards
2002–2006 "Award (x4) 100 Best Posters–Germany, Austria, Switzerland"
2005 Silver Medal, 16th International Poster and Graphic Design Festival of Chaumont; Gold Cube, New York Art Directors Club

Clients
Academy of Fine Arts, Berlin; Bauhaus Dessau Foundation; Berlin National Gallery; The British Council; Institut für Auslandsbeziehungen; State Opera Berlin

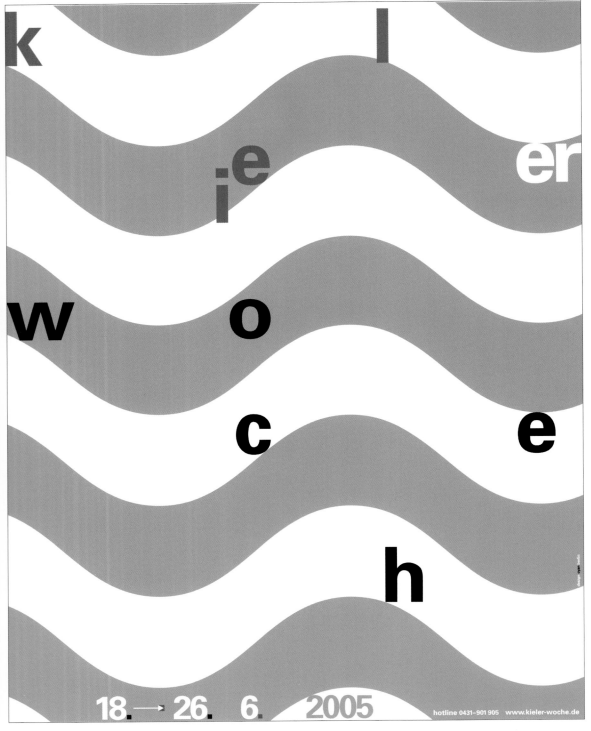

kiel er
woche
18. → 26. 6. 2005
hotline 0431–901 905   www.kieler-woche.de

"We are commissioned by cultural institutions and government initiatives. We can only achieve these low-to-no budget projects by saving costs on conventional lithography, photosetting and secretarial support. Generally, there is a clear choice between ever more colourful and costly products, and results that are sound in terms of aesthetics, ecology and economy. Maybe our work does not submit to conventional ideas of good typography. Certainly it is not supposed to address the question of 'good form'. In order to support quick and easy consumption, meaning and form have been reduced to a mundane banality. Opposing this position, our work aims to maintain the idea of reading as an occupation directed at the gaining of experience and based on visual sensitivity. Reading, we believe, needs engagement and awareness. This approach – directed against fast food communication and the mere consumption of sensationalism and entertainment – needs substantial, culturally innovative subjects."

»Unsere Auftraggeber sind Kulturinstitutionen und staatliche Einrichtungen. Wir können deren Projekte mit knappen oder gar keinen Budgets nur realisieren, wenn wir die Kosten für herkömmliche Lithografien, Fotosatz und Sekretariat sparen. Generell muss man sich zwischen immer bunteren teuren Produkten einerseits und ästhetisch, ökologisch und ökonomisch vernünftigen Lösungen andererseits entscheiden. Vielleicht entsprechen unsere Arbeiten nicht der gewohnten Vorstellung von guter Typografie. Auf jeden Fall sollen sie nicht mit den Maßstäben der sogenannt ›guten Form‹ gemessen werden. Um schnellen, mühelosen Verbrauch zu fördern, werden Inhalt und Form üblicherweise auf Alltäglichkeit und Binsenweisheit getrimmt. Im Gegensatz zu dieser Position hat unsere Tätigkeit zum Ziel, die Vorstellung vom Lesen als Beschäftigung zu bewahren, die auf Wissens- und Erfahrungszuwachs angelegt ist und auf visueller Sensibilität beruht. Lesen erfordert innere Beteiligung und bewusste Wahrnehmung. Dieser Ansatz richtet sich gegen Fastfood-Kommunikation, gegen das bloße Konsumieren von Sensationen und Unterhaltung und braucht substanzielle, kulturell innovative Themen.«

«Nous sommes engagés par des institutions culturelles et des organisations gouvernementales. Nous ne pouvons mener à bien ces projets à budget modéré ou nul qu'en économisant sur la lithographie conventionnelle, la photocomposition et le secrétariat. Il faut généralement faire un choix tranché entre des produits plus pittoresques et coûteux et des résultats esthétiquement, écologiquement et économiquement sains. Peut-être notre travail ne se soumet-il pas aux conventions définissant ce qu'est la bonne typographie. Il n'a en tous cas pas pour objectif de répondre à une question de 'belle forme'. Afin de faciliter une consommation rapide et irréfléchie, le sens et la forme sont souvent réduits à une totale banalité. À l'opposé de cette conception, nous voulons, par notre travail, affirmer l'idée que la lecture doit permettre d'acquérir une expérience et se fonde sur la sensibilité visuelle. Nous pensons que la lecture mobilise engagement et conscience. Cette approche – qui s'oppose à la communication 'fast food' et à la simple consommation de divertissement et de sensationnalisme – exige des sujets solides et culturellement novateurs. »

Previous page:
Project: "Kieler Woche 2005" poster, 2005
Client: City of Kiel

Above:
Project: "Olafur Eliasson: The Blind Pavillion"
(50th Venice Biennale), catalogue cover and spread, 2003
Client: Danish Contemporary Art Foundation

Following page:
Project: "Friedrich Christian Flick Collection" catalogue cover and spreads, 2004
Client: Hamburger Bahnhof – Museum für Gegenwartskunst, Berlin

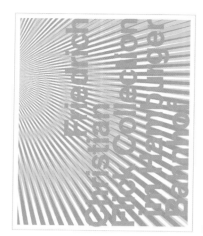

Friedrich
Christian
Flick
Collection
Rawwohlinger

Marcel **Broodthaers**

Larry Clark

Stan Douglas

Duane Hanson

Martin **Kippenberger**

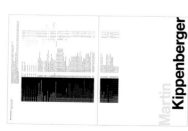

Above:
Project: *"Singuhr 2004 – Benoît
Maubrey/Brandon LaBelle"*
posters, 2004
Client: *Singuhr*

Following page:
Project: *"Singuhr 2005 –
Bernhard Leitner" poster, 2005*
Client: *Singuhr*

DED
ASSOCIATES

"Design happy!"

DED Associates
Workstation
15, Paternoster Row
Sheffield S1 2BX
UK
T +44 114 249393 9
info@dedass.com
www.dedass.com

Design group history
1991 Founded by Jon and Nik Daughtry in Sheffield, England
2004 Rob Barber joined the studio

Founders' biographies
Jon Daughtry
1970 Born in Sheffield, England

1988–1990 Studied graphic design, Lincoln College of Art & Design
1990–1992 Studied graphic design, Central Saint Martins College of Art & Design, London
Nik Daughtry
1970 Born in Sheffield, England
1988–1990 Studied

communication graphics, Sheffield College
1990–1992 Studied graphic design, Central Saint Martins College of Art & Design, London

Recent exhibitions
2005 "Pictoplasma–Characters at War", Berlin; "Qee Expo",

Toy2r and Playlounge, London; "Rockpile exhibition–Gigantic Brand", New York
2006 "Zarjaz–Puma, 2000AD", Playlounge, London
2006 University of California Design Museum

Clients
180 Amsterdam; Cohn & Wolfe; Don't Panic; ESPN; FX Channel; London Zoo; Lucozade; Mustoes; Ogilvy; Puma; Science Museum; Universal Music; Weber Shandwick

"Treating our clients' imagery and words as raw materials, we create active and often anarchic visual environments that beg exploration."

»Wir behandeln die Bilder und Texte, die uns unsere Auftraggeber liefern, als Rohmaterial und machen daraus aktiv-dynamische, oft anarchisch visuelle Welten, die erforscht werden wollen.«

« Avec l'univers visuel et verbal de nos clients comme matière première, nous créons des environnements visuels actifs et souvent anarchiques demandent à être explorés. »

Previous page:
Project: *"Peer Pressure"*
poster, 2006
Client: *Don't Panic Media*

Above:
Project: *"The End"*
book illustration, 2006
Client: *Ogilvy*

Following page:
Project: *"Judge Fire"*
T-shirt design, 2006
Clients: *Playlounge/Puma/*
2000AD

70   **DED Associates**

Judge Fire

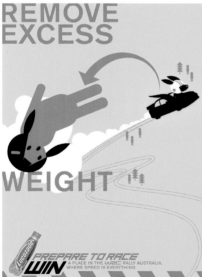

Top left:
Project: *"The Greatest Shows on Earth" poster, 2006*
Client: *FX/Fox*

Top right:
Project: *"Geisha" experimental project, 2006*
Client: *Self*

Above left:
Project: *"Remove Excess" poster, 2005*
Client: *Ogilvy/Lucozade*

Above right:
Project: *"No Loo" poster, 2005*
Client: *Ogilvy/Lucozade*

Following page:
Project: *"Sex and Violence" exhibition poster, 2006*
Client: *Davis Design Museum, University of California*

DELAWARE

"We are not artists,
we are ARTOONists."

Delaware
2C Tokiwamatsu
1-20-6 Higashi Shibuya-ku
Tokyo 150-0011
Japan
T +81 3 340 949 44
mail@delaware.gr.jp
www.delaware.gr.jp

Design group history
1993 Founded by Masato
Samata in Tokyo, Japan

Founder's biography
Masato Samata
1959 Born in Gumma, Japan
Self-taught

Recent exhibitions
2004 Solo exhibition,
RAS Gallery, Barcelona
2005 "D-Day, Design Today",
Centre Pompidou, Paris
2006 "From Mars", Moravian
Gallery, 22nd International
Biennale of Graphic Design,

Brno; "Too Slow To Live", 7th
album and 5th exhibition,
online

Clients
Actar; AG Ideas; DoCoMo;
Espai Pupu; Pitti Uomo

"Designin' In The Rain
* i am designin' in the rain
% just graphic designin' in the rain
$ red yellow green blue black & white
stripe check bitmap free freehand
brightness & contrast color balance
like a james brown, like a haiku
* (repeat)
% (repeat)
air beat shit deep yeah enough jean
ouch eye jar hey hell amp end
oh peep cool ah essay tea woo
beer dub tax wine zzzziiiiiiiiiiiiiiiit
$ (repeat)
% (repeat)"

»Entwerfen im Regen
* Ich entwerfe im Regen,
% einfach grafisch designe im Regen
$ rot gelb grün blau schwarz & weiß
Streifen Karo Bitmap mit freier Hand
Helligkeit & Kontrast farbliche Ausgewogenheit
wie ein James Brown wie ein Haiku
* (da capo)
% (da capo)
Luft Beat Scheiß Tief Jawoll Genug Jean
Autsch Auge Krug Hallo Hölle AMP Ende
oh piep cool ah Essay Tee wuh
Bier Dub-Musik Steuern Wein zzzziiiiiiiiiiiiiiit
$ (da capo)
% (da capo). «

« Je dessine sous la pluie
* je dessine sous la pluie
% je dessine simplement sous la pluie
$ rouge jaune vert bleu noir & blanc
rayure carreau image matricielle libre à main levée
clarté & contraste équilibrage des couleurs
comme un james brown, comme un haïku
* (répéter)
% (répéter)
air rythme merde profond yeah assez jean
aïe œil bol hey enfer ampli fin
oh peep cool ah essai thé wou
bière dub taxe vin zzzziiiiiiiiiiiiiiiit
$ (répéter)
% (répéter) »

Previous page:
Project: *"We Are Alone"*
experimental project for

"Buzz Club" exposition, 2001
Client: *P. S. 1 MoMA*

Above:
Project: *"Stairway To Heaven"*
installation for men's fashion

trade fair, 2003
Client: *Pitti Uomo*

Above:
Project: *"Take A Walk"*
experimental project for

"Customize Me" exhibition, 2005
Client: *Espai Pupu/Vans*

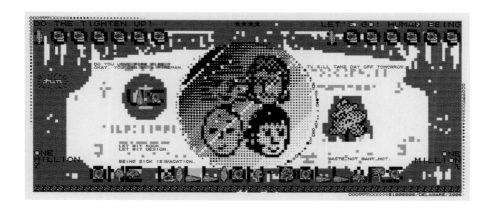

Top:
Project: *"Designin' In The Rain"*
book cover/spread, 2004
Client: *Actar*

Above:
Project: *Background picture for*
"$1 000 000", display for
"CTIA Wireless", 2006
Client: *NTT DoCoMo*

Following page:
Project: *Background picture for*
"Waterfall" display for
"3GSM World Congress", 2006
Client: *NTT DoCoMo*

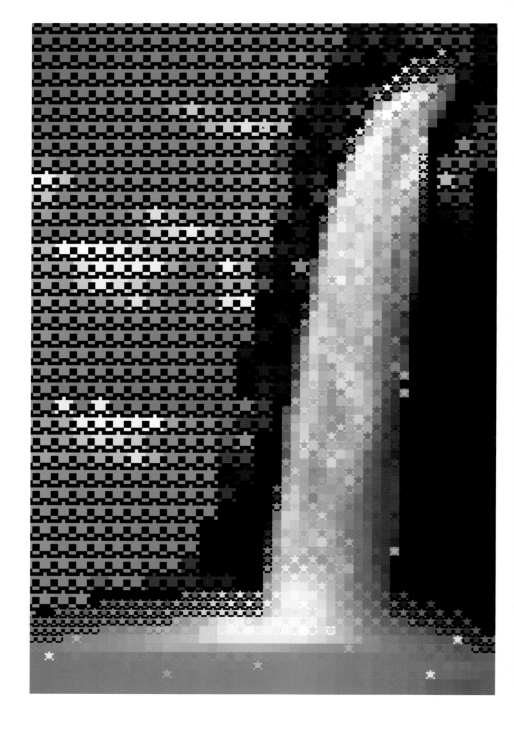

DEXTRO

"My opinion about abstract images seems to be opposed to the common view."

Dextro
dextro@dextro.org
www.dextro.org

Biography
1978 Born in Austria
Self-taught freelance designer
in Vienna, Tokyo and Berlin

Recent exhibitions
2003 "Abstraction Now",
Künstlerhaus, Vienna; "Lovebytes", Public Art Space,
Sheffield; "6th Biennale Graz",
Kunsthaus Graz
2004 "International Symposium of Interactive Media
Design", Yeditepe University,

Istanbul; "Muesli", Salle
d'Escrime, Montpellier;
"aadg.at", Museo Tamayo,
Mexico City; "Sound x Vision",
Graf Media GM, Osaka
2004/05 "Cimatics",
Mediaruimte, Brussels

2005 "International Symposium of Interactive Media
Design", Yeditepe University,
Istanbul; "Soundtoys", Water-
shed Media Centre, Bristol;
"Hexa Project", Shanghai Duol-
un Museum of Modern Art

2006 "International Sympo-
sium of Interactive Media
Design", Yeditepe University,
Istanbul; "Mixed Media",
Hangar Bicocca, Milan

"I think abstract images and animations can, through their shapes and relations between objects, mirror universal thought patterns and thereby provoke a reaction in the viewer on a level so deep that it is the same in all people. Therefore abstract images, in my view, leave no room for interpretation. Only if we try to see real objects in them do they become ambiguous."

»Ich denke, dass abstrakte Bilder und Animationen mit ihren Formen und Objektbezügen universelle Denkmuster reflektieren und deshalb auf einer ganz tiefen geistigen und emotionalen Ebene beim Betrachter ankommen, die überall in allen Menschen angelegt ist. Deshalb lassen abstrakte Bilder meiner Meinung nach keinen Interpretationsspielraum. Sie werden nur mehrdeutig, wenn man versucht, irgendwelche realen Dinge in ihnen zu sehen.«

« Je pense que les images abstraites et les animations peuvent, à travers leurs formes et les relations qu'elles tissent entre les objets, refléter des systèmes de pensée universels et ainsi provoquer chez le spectateur une réaction si profonde qu'elle est partagée par tous. Voilà pourquoi les images abstraites ne laissent de mon point de vue aucune place à l'interprétation. Ce n'est que si nous tentons d'y voir des objets réels qu'elles deviennent ambiguës. »

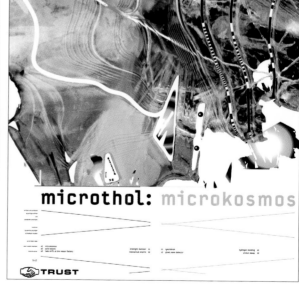

Previous page:
Project: *"K413_P2"*
algorithmic image, 2006
Client: *Self*

Above left:
Project: *"Just/Krawall"*
record sleeve, 2006
Client: *Pomelo Records*

Above right:
Project: *"Microthol"*
record sleeve, 2006
Client: *Trust Records*

Top left:
Project: *"Epy"*
music CD labels, 2005
Client: *Trust Records*

Bottom left:
Project: *"Microthol"*
music CD labels, 2006
Client: *Trust Records*

Right:
Project: *"11 idea_02.002"*
3D image, 2003
Client: *Idea Magazine*

DRESS CODE

"Never Sleep We."

dress code
68 Richardson St., #504
Brooklyn, NY 11211
USA
T +1 425 417 849 0
casual@dresscodeny.com
www.dresscodeny.com

Design group history
2002 Founded by Andre Andreev and G. Dan Covert in San Francisco, California, USA
2004 Studio relocated to Manhattan, New York
2005 Hired their first employee
2005+ Began teaching Typography and Graphic Design, Pratt Institute, New York
2006 Studio relocated to Brooklyn, New York

Founders' biographies
G. Dan Covert
1981 Born in Cincinnati, Ohio
2001–2004 Studied graphic design, California College of the Arts, San Francisco
2004–2006 Senior Designer, On-Air design department, MTV
Andre Andreev
1984 Born in Pernik, Bulgaria
2001–2004 Studied graphic design, California College of the Arts, San Francisco
2004–2006 Senior Designer, On-Air Design department, MTV

Recent exhibitions
2003 "Audiographic", Old Federal Reserve Bank Building, San Francisco; "Within 4 Walls", Dogpatch Studios, San Francisco
2004 "Adobe Design Achievement Awards", Yerba Buena Center for the Arts, San Francisco; "The Art Directors Club", Art Directors Club Gallery, New York
2005 "The Design of Dissent", School of Visual Arts, New York; "The Type Directors Club", Cooper Union Gallery, New York
2006 "Spoken With Eyes", Davis Design Museum, University of California, Sacramento; "Agit Prop", The Center for the Study of Political Graphics, Los Angeles; "ADC Young Guns", Art Directors Club Gallery, New York
2007 "Design Politics", Museum of Contemporary Art, Santiago; "Luxury to Performance", Fila Flagship Store, New York; "100 Years of CCA", San Francisco Museum of Modern Art

Recent awards
2004 First Place, Adobe Design Achievement Awards–Print Category

Clients
Adobe; Amazing; Bathtub Records; California College of the Arts; Cincinnati Council on Child Abuse; CMT; Compo Digital; DDB; Definitive Jux Records; Destroy Clothing; Empire State Clothing; Exhibition Prints; Fila; Good-Human Magazine; MTV; New York Arts Collective; Nike; Pratt Institute; Revelation Records; Southern Exposure; Threadless; Tribal DDB; West of January Records; Westminister Social Club; Xlarge

"We try to:
Talk to our Moms often.
Not be too cocky.
Teach us teaching.
Get our girlfriends milk at night.
Look big and stay small.
Do work that makes us happy.
Water the plant.
Travel places where we point to get stuff.
Look up at the clouds.
Hire people more talented than us.
Help others be happy.
Listen to music not too loud.
Make an OK living.
Work with big ideas.
Think wrong.
Win awards and polish them.
Never go to work.
Let our friends know we care (Jimm too).
Think of funny games involving a paper ball.
Take photos of naked people.
Steal ideas only when we plan on returning them.
Say 'contrived' daily.
Design everything.
Smile."

»Wir versuchen:
oft mit unseren Muttis zu reden,
nicht großspurig zu sein,
uns selbst das Unterrichten beizubringen,
unseren Freundinnen in der Nacht Milch zu besorgen,
groß auszusehen und klein zu bleiben,
Aufträge zu bearbeiten, die uns glücklich machen,
die Topfpflanze zu gießen,
an exotische Orte zu reisen,
hoch in die Wolken zu schauen,
Leute einzustellen, die talentierter sind als wir selbst,
anderen zu helfen, glücklich zu sein,
nicht zu laut Musik zu hören,
unser Auskommen zu finden,
mit großen Ideen zu arbeiten,
auch mal verkehrt zu denken,
Medaillen zu gewinnen und sie blank zu polieren,
nie zur Arbeit zu gehen,
uns um unsere Freunde zu kümmern (auch um Jimm),
uns lustige Spiele mit einem Papierball auszudenken,
Fotos von nackten Leuten zu schießen,
Ideen nur dann zu klauen, wenn wir vorhaben, sie zurückzugeben,
täglich ›gekünstelt‹ zu sagen,
alles zu designen,
zu lächeln.«

« Nous essayons de :
Parler souvent à nos mamans.
Ne pas être trop impudents.
Apprendre à enseigner.
Apporter du lait à nos copines la nuit.
Paraître grands et rester petits.
Faire un travail qui nous rend heureux.
Arroser la plante.
Voyager dans des endroits pour en rapporter des trucs.
Lever les yeux vers les nuages.
Embaucher des gens plus doués que nous.
Aider les autres à être heureux.
Écouter de la musique pas trop fort.
Bien gagner notre vie.
Travailler avec de grandes idées.
Nous tromper.
Remporter des prix et les astiquer.
Ne jamais aller au bureau.
Dire à nos amis que nous les aimons (Jimm aussi).
Inventer des jeux rigolos avec une boule de papier.
Prendre des photos de gens nus.
Ne voler des idées que lorsqu'on a l'intention de les rendre.
Dire ‹ forcé › quotidiennement.
Tout créer.
Sourire. »

Top left:
Project: *"Balloons"*
T-shirt, 2006
Client: *Definitive Jux Records*

Top right:
Project: *"Ski Mask Tee"*
T-shirt, 2006
Client: *Empire State Clothing
and The Beard*

Centre left:
Project: *"Direct Effect"*
*logo for an MTV hip-hop show,
2006*
Client: *MTV On-Air Design*

Above:
Project: *"Lonely for Stereo"*
*illustration for CD packaging,
2005*
Client: *Alison Rose Bailey*

DANIEL EATOCK

"My objective is to go beyond the surface, presenting dematerialised concepts and ideas within the context of art and graphic design."

Eatock Ltd
7 Minerva Street
London E2 9EH
UK
T +44 207 739 017 4
daniel@eatock.com
www.eatock.com

Biography
1975 Born in Boulton, England
1996–1999 Studied graphic design, Royal College of Art, London
1998–1999 Graphic design intern at the Walker Art Center, Minneapolis
1999 Co-founded Foundation 33 in London with the architect Sam Solhaug, a multi-disciplinary practice that later merged with creative agency boymeetsgirl
2000–2004 Senior Lecturer, Graphic Design, University of Brighton
2005 Founded Eatock Ltd

Exhibitions
2001 "Design Now", Design Museum, London; "Multi-Ply Furniture", Pentagram Gallery, London
2006 "The Urban Forest Project", Times Square, New York

Awards
1998 Graphic Design Award, Creative Futures, Creative Review, London
2000 Annual Design Review Award; 40 under 30 Award, I.D. Magazine

Clients
ADC-LTSN; Alex Poots Artistic Events; Channel 4; Design Museum, London; Eatock Family; Maguffin; Mazorca Projects; Opus Magnum; Walker Art Center, Minneapolis

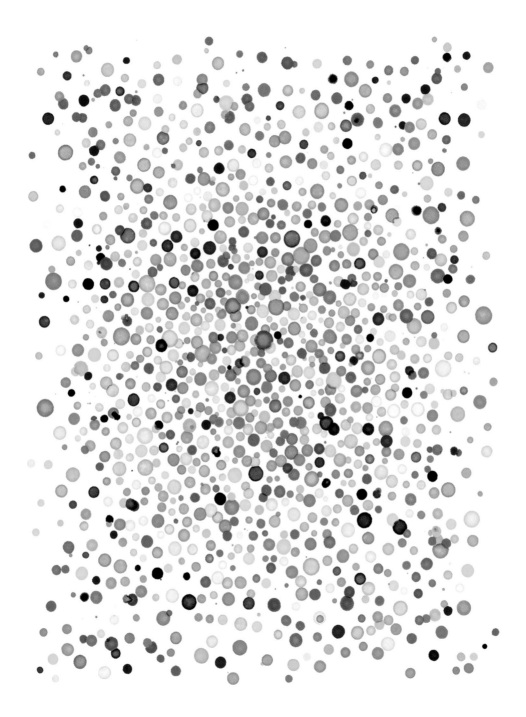

"Manifesto: Begins with ideas – Merges graphic design and art – Knows banal ideas cannot be rescued by beautiful execution – Eliminates superfluous elements – Subverts the expectation – Believes complex ideas can produce simple objects – Trusts the process – Allows material/research/concept to determine form – Reduces material and production to their essence – Sustains the integrity of an idea – Proposes honesty as a solution – Removes subjectivity.
Ethos: I would never use a female body in an objectified way to sell products – I would not make work for a tobacco company, online casino or anybody who is irresponsible – I would love to be commissioned to think of ways that encourage people to not drop litter or quit smoking – I would enjoy promoting healthy food or well-made sustainable products – I enjoy being involved with art, museums, education, entertainment and culture."

»Manifest: Beginnt mit Ideen – mischt Werbegrafik und Kunst – weiß, dass banale Ideen nicht durch wunderbare Ausführungen zu retten sind – lässt überflüssige Elemente weg – unterminiert Erwartungen – glaubt, dass aus komplexen Gedankengängen einfache Objekte entstehen können – vertraut dem Arbeitsprozess – erlaubt es dem Material/den Forschungsergebnissen/dem Konzept, die Form zu bestimmen – reduziert Material und Produktion auf das Wesentliche – hält ohne Abstriche an einer richtigen Idee fest – schlägt Ehrlichkeit als Lösung vor – strebt nach Objektivität. Arbeitsethos: Ich würde niemals einen weiblichen Körper als Objekt einsetzen, um ein Produkt zu verkaufen. – Ich würde nicht für einen Tabakwarenhersteller, ein Online-Kasino oder irgendeinen anderen verantwortungslosen Auftraggeber arbeiten. – Ich würde liebend gerne den Auftrag erhalten, über Dinge nachzudenken, die Menschen dazu auffordern, mit dem Rauchen aufzuhören und ihren Müll nicht auf die Straße zu werfen. – Es würde mir Spaß machen, für gesunde Ernährung oder solide verarbeitete, langlebige Produkte zu werben. – Ich arbeite gern in den Bereichen Kunst, Museen, Bildung, Unterhaltung und Kultur.«

«Manifeste: Commence par des idées – Unifie graphisme et art – Sait que les idées banales ne peuvent être sauvées par un exécution brillante – Élimine les éléments superflus – Bouleverse les attentes – Croit que les idées complexes peuvent produire des objets simples – Se fie au développement – Permet au matériau/à la recherche/au concept de déterminer la forme – Réduit matériel et production à leur essence – Soutient l'intégrité d'une idée – Propose comme solution la franchise – Écarte toute subjectivité. Éthique: Je n'utiliserais jamais un corps féminin comme objet pour vendre un produit – Je ne travaillerais pas pour l'industrie du tabac, un casino en ligne ou qui que ce soit d'irresponsable – J'adorerais qu'on me demande de réfléchir à des moyens d'encourager les gens à arrêter de polluer ou de fumer – Je prendrais plaisir à faire la promotion d'une alimentation saine ou de produits durables et bien pensés – J'aime travailler dans l'art, les musées, l'éducation, le divertissement et la culture.»

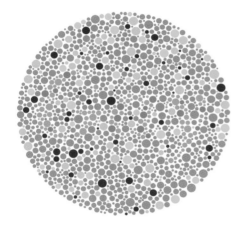

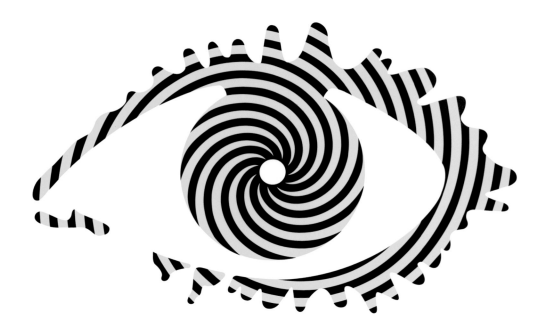

Above:
Project: *"This postcard is temporarily out of stock"/"Junk Mail"/"Email" and "Envelope" postcards, 2004*
Client: *Self*

Top:
Project: *"Big Brother 7" logo/television programme identity, 2006*
Client: *Channel 4*

RAFAEL ESQUER

"Make the idea clear and simple,
but the design surprising and beautiful."

Alfalfa Studio
255 Centre Street, 7th Floor,
New York, NY 10013
USA
T +1 212 629 955 0
raf@rafaelesquer.com
www.rafaelesquer.com

Biography
1966 Born in Alamos, Sonora,
Mexico
1986 Moved to Mexico City
and studied at Coyoacan
School of Photography
1987 Studied communication
design at Universidad
Autónoma Metropolitana in
Mexico City
1988 Moved to Los Angeles
1991 Studied sculpture and
painting at Hollywood Art
Center School under the
direction of Mona Lovins

1991–1993 Director, Enfoque
magazine, Los Angeles
1995–1996 Apprenticeship in
graphic design under Rebeca
Méndez in Los Angeles
1996 BFA with Distinction in
Graphic Design, Art Center
College of Design, Pasadena
1996 Moved to New York
1997–2004 Art Director (and
later Creative Director) for
@radicalmedia design group
in New York and also served
a term on the board of the
New York Chapter of the

American Institute of Graphic
Arts
2004 Established Alfalfa
Studio in New York

Recent exhibitions
2006 "The Urban Forest
Project", Times Square, New
York; "365: AIGA Year in
Design 27", AIGA National
Design Center, New York;
"TDC 52: The 52nd Annual
Type Directors Club Exhibi-
tion", New York (worldwide
touring exhibition); "Mohawk

Show 7" (touring exhibition
shown in over 50 venues in the
USA)

Recent awards
2003 Merit Award, New York
Art Directors Club; Gold (x2)
and Bronze Industrial Design
Excellence Awards (IDEA)
2004 National Design Award,
Cooper-Hewitt National
Design Museum
2005 Winner, STEP Design 100
Competition
2006 Selected, 365: AIGA

Annual Design Competitions
27; Typographic Excellence
Award, TDC 52; Winner, STEP
Design 100 Competition

Clients
AIGA; Björk; Elle Magazine;
IBM; MTV; Nike; Scholastic;
Target; Tommy Boy Records;
The New York Times Maga-
zine; The Robin Hood Foun-
dation

"In my experience, integrity should be one of the highest values in graphic design, as in the world in general. A designer with integrity is original and designs with responsibility. I seek to bring integrity to my work by approaching every project as if it were my first and last. I do not follow formulas or rules but search instead for a unique solution to the design problem at hand. I begin with a white canvas, so to speak, as if the project were a painting. But my canvas is always stretched by my personal journeys through many worlds: language, love, literature, film, fine art, pop culture, music, science, politics, travel, and dreams. What keeps me excited about going to work every day is the challenge of adding another drop of integrity to the world through simplicity, surprise and beauty."

»Meiner Erfahrung nach sollte Integrität auch im Grafikdesign – wie überhaupt in der Welt – einer der höchsten Werte sein. Ein integerer Designer ist originell und entwirft im Bewusstsein seiner Verantwortung für die Wirkung seiner Arbeiten. Ich versuche, Integrität in meine Tätigkeit einzuführen, indem ich jedes Projekt so in Angriff nehme, als sei es mein erstes und letztes. Ich folge weder Formeln noch Regeln, sondern suche nach der einzigartigen Lösung für die jeweilige Aufgabe. Jedes Mal beginne ich sozusagen mit einer weißen Leinwand, wie beim Malen eines Ölgemäldes. Aber meine Leinwand dehnt sich durch meine persönlichen Streifzüge in verschiedenen Welten aus: Sprache, Liebe, Literatur, Film, bildende Kunst, Popkultur, Musik, Naturwissenschaften, Politik, Reisen und Träume. Ich finde es immer noch spannend, zur Arbeit zu gehen, weil jeder Tag die Herausforderung bringt, durch Einfachheit, Überraschungseffekte und Schönheit der Welt einen weiteren kleinen Tropfen Integrität einzuflößen.«

« D'après mon expérience, l'intégrité devrait être une des valeurs maîtresses du graphisme en particulier et du monde en général. Un graphiste intègre est original et crée de façon responsable. Je cherche à apporter de l'intégrité à mon travail en abordant chaque projet comme s'il était le premier et le dernier. Je ne suis ni formules ni règles : je cherche au contraire une solution unique au problème créatif posé. Je commence par une toile blanche, pour ainsi dire, comme si le projet était un tableau. Mais ma toile se tend toujours sur un cadre composé de mes pérégrinations dans divers mondes : langage, amour, littérature, cinéma, beaux-arts, culture pop, musique, science, politique, voyages et rêves. Ce qui fait que je vais travailler avec enthousiasme chaque matin, c'est le défi d'ajouter une autre touche d'intégrité au monde grâce à la simplicité, à la surprise et à la beauté. »

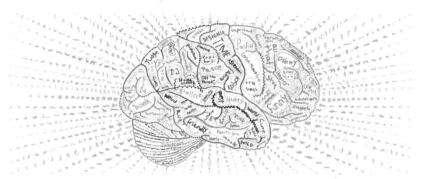

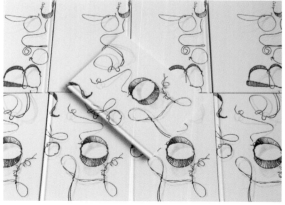

Previous page:
Project: "AIGA membership campaign" stickers, 2006
Client: AIGA

Top:
Title: "The L!brary Initiative Mural" mural, 2007
Client: The Robin Hood Foundation

Above:
Project: "Bonds of Love" book, 2005
Client: John Connelly Presents

Following page top:
Project: "AIGA membership campaign" postcard, 2006
Client: AIGA

Following page bottom:
Project: "AIGA membership campaign" poster, 2006
Client: AIGA

94 *Rafael Esquer*

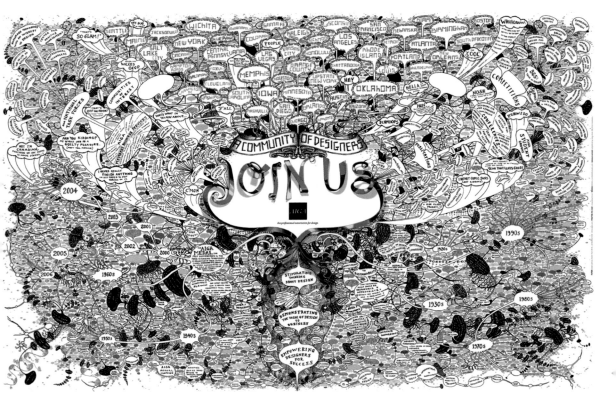

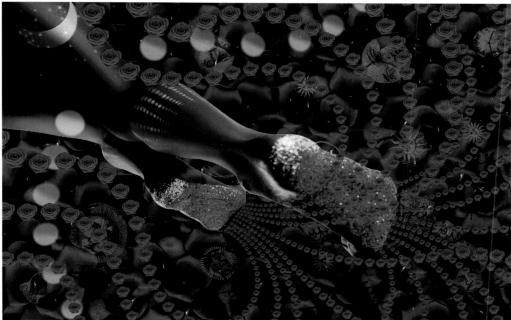

Above (both images):
Project: *"Legs"*
editorial spreads, 2006
Client: *Elle*

Following page top:
Project: *"Vote" poster, 2004*
Client: *AIGA*

Following page bottom left:
Project: *"Below the Belt"*
poster, 2006
Client: *Amphibian Stage*
Productions

Following page bottom centre:
Project: *"Fully Committed"*
poster, 2006
Client: *Amphibian Stage*
Productions

Following page bottom right:
Project: *"The Credeaux Canvas"*
poster, 2006
Client: *Amphibian Stage*
Productions

Good design makes choices clear.

EXPERI-MENTAL JETSET

"We have an almost anachronistic interest in the idea of 'thing-ness': the designed object as an artefact, as a materialised idea, as a container that carries its own meaning."

Experimental Jetset
Jan Hanzenstraat 37/1
1053 SK Amsterdam
The Netherlands
T +31 20 468 603 6
experimental@jetset.nl
www.experimentaljetset.nl

Founders' biographies
Erwin Brinkers
1973 Born in Rotterdam, The Netherlands
1993–1998 Studied graphic design at the Gerrit Rietveld Academy, Amsterdam
Marieke Stolk
1967 Born in Amsterdam, The Netherlands
1993–1997 Studied graphic design at the Gerrit Rietveld Academy, Amsterdam
2000+ Teaches at the Gerrit

Design group history
1997 Co-founded by Erwin Brinkers, Marieke Stolk and Danny van den Dungen in Amsterdam, The Netherlands

Rietveld Academy, Amsterdam
Danny van den Dungen
1971 Born in Rotterdam, The Netherlands
1992–1997 Studied graphic design at the Gerrit Rietveld Academy, Amsterdam
2000+ Teaches at the Gerrit Rietveld Academy, Amsterdam

Recent exhibitions
2002 "Commitment", Las Palmas, Rotterdam
2003 "Reality Machines", NAi (Netherlands Architecture Institute), Rotterdam; "Gnome Sweet Gnome (White Dots)", Keukenhof, Lisse; "Jungle

LP Show (The Dark Side of Bauhaus)", Rocket Gallery, Tokyo; "Now: 90 Years Pastoe", Centraal Museum, Utrecht; "Somewhere Totally Else", Design Museum, London
2004 "Public Address System", Henry Peacock Gallery, London; "The Free Library", The Riviera, Brooklyn; "Club Canyon", Harmony Gallery, Hollywood; "Terminal Five", JFK Airport, New York; "Under a Tenner", Design Museum, London
2005 "The Free Library 2", Space 1026, Philadelphia; "Poster Plakate Affiche", Swinburne University, Melbourne; "The Free Library

3", M+R Gallery, London; "Hide & Seek", Nakayoku Project, Hong Kong; "Now & Again", Dutch Design Centre, Utrecht; "The Future is Bright", Vivid, Rotterdam; "Music For The Artists (Love Aktion Machine)", De Veemvloer, Amsterdam
2006 "Going Underground", Mornington Hotel, Stockholm; "Did You Mention Design?", MUDAC, Lausanne; "Ten Years of Posters", Kemistry Gallery, London

Clients
Artimo A-Z; Boijmans Van Beuningen Museum; Casco Projects; Centre Georges

Pompidou; Colette; Stichting De Appel; De Theatercompagnie; Droog Design; Dutch Post Group/TPG; Emigre Magazine; Gingham Inc.; IDEA Magazine; Johannes Schwartz (photographer); Netherlands Architecture Institute; Paradiso; Purple Institute; So by Alexander van Slobbe; Stedelijk Museum Amsterdam; W139; Witte De With

Experimental Jetset   04 /04 /06
Ten years of posters   30 /05 /06

10 years of licorice
10 years of popmusic
10 years of reading papers
10 years of staying up all night
10 years of feeling guilty
10 years of excuses
10 years of Fed-Ex
10 years of sunshine
10 years of posters
10 years of aspirin

Kemistry Gallery

"As graphic designers, we fully embrace the 'problem/solution' model, whilst at the same time accepting the inherent sadness of this model: the fact that there is no such thing as a perfect solution, as every solution inevitably leads to more problems. For us, it is exactly this sad side that gives the 'problem/solution' model its tragic beauty."

»Als Grafiker fühlen wir uns ganz dem Modell ›Problem/Lösung‹ verpflichtet. Gleichzeitig wissen wir, dass dieses Modell auch etwas Trauriges beinhaltet: Es gibt nämlich keine perfekte Lösung, da jede Lösung unweigerlich neue Fragen aufwirft. Für uns macht gerade diese Seite die tragische Schönheit des ›Problem/Lösung‹-Modells aus.«

«En tant que graphistes, nous avons pleinement conscience du modèle 'problème/solution' mais en même temps nous acceptons la tristesse intrinsèque de ce modèle: il n'existe pas de solution parfaite, chaque solution apportant inévitablement son lot de nouveaux problèmes. Pour nous, c'est exactement cela qui confère sa beauté tragique au modèle 'problème/solution'.»

Previous page:
Project: *"Ten Years of Posters"* invitation for solo exhibition, 2006
Client: *Kemistry Gallery, London*

Above:
Project: *"Time and Again"* title wall for exhibition, 2004
Client: *Stedelijk Museum CS, Amsterdam*

Stedelijk Museum CS

16.05 31.12
Tussenstand:
een keuze uit de
collectie
Intermission:
a choice from the
collection

16.05 03.10
20/20 Vision
Yesim Akdeniz Graf,
Francis Alÿs, Marc
Bijl, Germaine Kruip,
De Rijke/De Rooij,
Mathias Poledna,
Steve McQueen,
Torbjørn Rødland

16.05 29.08
Kramer vs. Rietveld
/Contrasten in
de meubelcollectie
Kramer vs. Rietveld
/Contrasts in the
furniture collection

www.stedelijk.nl

Top left:
Project: "Stedelijk Museum CS"
programme poster, 2004
Client: Stedelijk Museum CS,
Amsterdam

Top right:
Project: Button badges for
SMCS (selection), 2004
Client: Stedelijk Museum CS,
Amsterdam

Above (all images):
Project: "Four SMCS acrostics"
staircase installation, 2004
Client: Stedelijk Museum CS,
Amsterdam

FARROW

"Make things look better."

Farrow
23–24 Great James Street
Bloomsbury
London WC1N 3ES
UK
T +44 207 404 422 5
studio@farrowdesign.com
www.farrowdesign.com

Design group history
1995 Founded by Mark Farrow in London, England

Founder's biography
Mark Farrow
1960 Born in Manchester, England
Self-taught
1986–1990 Founded design studio 3A, London
1990+ Founded design studio Farrow, London

Recent exhibitions
2002 "Rewind: 40 Years of Design and Advertising from the D&AD Awards", Victoria & Albert Museum, London
2004 "Communicate: Independent Graphic Design since the Sixties", Barbican Art Gallery, London

Recent awards
2004 D&AD Silver Award; Nomination, Art Directors Club of Europe; "Most important graphic designer working today", Creative Review Peer Poll; AOP Zeitgeist Award
2005 AOP Zeitgeist Award

Clients
2CV Research; Atlantic Bar & Grill; Atlantic Records; BBC; Booth-Clibborn Editions; British Museum; Burt Bacharach; Channel 5; Cream; Cream Records; D&AD; David Gray; EMI Records; Epic Records; Gatecrasher; Harvey Nichols; Jasper Morrison; Jimmy Choo; Jonathan Glazer; KEF; Kylie Minogue; Levi Strauss Europe; London Records; Manic Street Preachers; Marc Newson; Mercury Records; Mash; MTV; Munkenbeck + Marshall Architects; Museum für Gegenwartskunst, Basel; Oliver Peyton; Palm Pictures; Parlophone Records; Pet Shop Boys; Rankin; Ross Lovegrove; Saatchi & Saatchi; Sadie Coles HQ; Sanctuary; Science Museum, London; SCP; Sony BMG; Spiritualized; Tate Modern; Terence Woodgate; Virgin Records; Vision on Publishing; WEA Records; Wilkinson Eyre Architects; William Ørbit

"It doesn't matter which we are working on, be it a 12-inch sleeve for Kylie Minogue, a gallery for the Science Museum or a global labelling system for Levi's, the aesthetic is the same and the approach identical."

»Egal, woran wir arbeiten – ein Plattencover für Kylie Minogue, ein Ausstellungsraum des Naturwissenschaftmuseums oder ein internationales Etikettiersystem für Levi's – die Ästhetik ist die gleiche, der Ansatz identisch.«

«Quel que soit le projet sur lequel nous sommes en train de travailler, qu'il s'agisse d'une pochette d'un disque 12 pouces de Kylie Minogue, d'une galerie pour le Musée de la Science ou d'un système d'étiquetage général pour Levi's, l'esthétique est la même et l'approche identique.»

Above:
Project: *"Peyton and Byrne"* Client: *Oliver Peyton*
retail identity and packaging,
2006

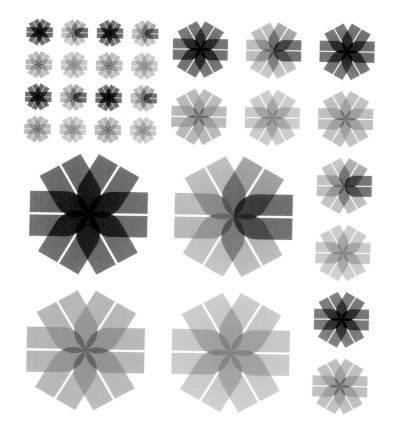

case

ject: *"Case logo and ele-*
ts" identity for furniture
pany, 2007

Client: *Case Furniture Ltd*

Above:
Project: *"Notime/Nightime/*
Finetime" clocks, 2003
Client: *SCP*

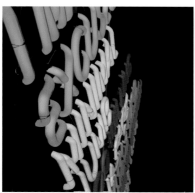

Top left:
Project: *"PSB T-Shirt" for*
"Fundamental-Pet Shop Boys"
music promotional campaign,
2006 (photo: John Ross)
Client: *PSB/Parlophone*

Centre right:
Project: *"PSB Minimal/*
Fundamenal-Pet Shop Boys"
music promotional campaign,
2006 (photo: John Ross)
Client: *PSB/Parlophone*

Bottom right:
Project: *"PSB Neon/Funda-*
mental-Pet Shop Boys" music
promotional campaign, 2006
(photo: John Ross)
Client: *PSB/Parlophone*

Following page top left:
Project: *"Amazing Grace –*
Spiritualized" CD cover, 2004
Client: *Spaceman*

Following page top right:
Project: *"Bailey/Rankin"*
photographic edition, 2005
Client: *Rankin*

Following page bottom:
Project: *"Pet Shop Boys: Mira-*
cles" 12-inch record album cover,
2004
Client: *PSB/Parlophone*

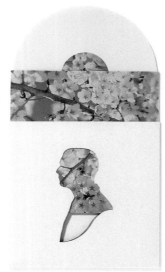

FELLOW DESIGNERS

"Simplify, surprise and enjoy!"

Fellow Designers AB
Högbergsgatan 28
116 20 Stockholm
Sweden
T +46 8 332 200
paul@fellowdesigners.com
eva@fellowdesigners.com
www.fellowdesigners.com

Design group history
1997 Co-founded by Paul Kühlhorn and Eva Liljefors in Stockholm, Sweden
2000 Fellow Designers joined Agent Form (Swedish design agency), Stockholm

Founders' biographies
Paul Kühlhorn
1971 Born in Stockholm, Sweden
1993–1997 Studied graphic design and illustration, Konstfack (University College of Arts, Crafts and Design), Stockholm
1998–2001 Lecturer, graphic design, Beckmans School of Design and Konstfack, Stockholm
Eva Liljefors
1969 Born in Uppsala, Sweden
1994–1997 Studied graphic design and advertising, Beckmans School of Design, Stockholm

1998–2001 Lecturer, Graphic Design, Beckmans School of Design and Konstfack, Stockholm

Recent exhibitions
2003 "Design Relay", Danish Design Centre, Copenhagen
2004 "Swedish Style in Tokyo", Gallery Speak For, Tokyo
2005 Istituto Europeo di Design, Madrid
2007 "Vad gör en Art Director", Malmö

Recent awards
2001 Silver Egg, The Golden Egg Awards
2002 Silver Egg, The Golden Egg Awards
2005 Silver (x3), Kolla! design competition

Clients
Acne; Adidas; Bang Magazine; Bon; Bonniers Förlag; BRIS; com hem; Dagens Nyheter; Grand Tone Music; Goran Kajfes; Kulturhuset; Linkim-age; Lindex; Liljevalchs Konsthall; Memfis Film; MNW; Respons; SF Film; Swedish Floorball Federation; Swedish State Railways; Sonet Film; Stockholm City Theatre; SVT; Swedish Society of Craft and Design; Ta4i; Telia; Vattenfall; Ylva Liljefors

Vårsalongen **Liljevalchs**
25 januari – 17 mars 2002 tisdag – söndag

"As we start working with a new assignment, we always stick to the first idea that pops up in our minds. We keep it as simple as possible and try to find a suitable graphic expression. This way we try to keep our work from getting unnecessarily influenced by other contemporary graphic design."

»Wenn wir an einem neuen Auftrag arbeiten, bleiben wir immer bei der ersten Idee, die uns in den Sinn gekommen ist. Wir vereinfachen sie so weit wie möglich und bemühen uns, den passenden grafischen Ausdruck dafür zu finden. Auf diese Weise versuchen wir uns nicht unnötig von anderen zeitgenössischen Grafikdesigns beeinflussen zu lassen.«

«Quand nous commençons à travailler sur une nouvelle commande, nous nous en tenons toujours à la première idée qui nous traverse l'esprit. Nous faisons tout pour qu'elle reste simple et tentons de trouver la meilleure manière de l'exprimer graphiquement. Nous cherchons ainsi à empêcher que notre travail ne soit inutilement influencé par le reste du graphisme contemporain. »

Previous page:
Project: *"Vårsalongen Lilje-valchs"* (Spring Salon), *art exhi-bition poster/catalogue, 2002*
Client: *Liljevalchs Konsthall*

Above left:
Project: *"Go to Hell"*
CD cover, *2004*
Client: *Grand Tone Music/ MNW*

Above right:
Project: *"Starring"*
logo designs, 2004
Client: *Starring*

Top left:
Project: *"Headspin"*
CD cover, 2004
Client: *Goran Kajfes*

Top right:
Project: *"Headspin"*
CD label, 2004
Client: *Goran Kajfes*

Above left:
Project: *"Fabrice Gygi – 1"*,
art exhibition poster, 2006
Client: *Magasin 3 Stockholm
Konsthall*

Above right:
Project: *"Fabrice Gygi – 2"*,
art exhibition poster, 2006
Client: *Magasin 3 Stockholm
Konsthall*

CHRISTINA FÖLLMER

"Nothing that we experience is ever lost."

Christina Föllmer
Marienstr. 64
63069 Offenbach
Germany
T +49 179 526 751 5
hallo@christinafoellmer.de
www.christinafoellmer.de

Biography
1977 Born in Aachen,
Germany
1998–2005 Studied visual
communication, Academy
of Art and Design,
Offenbach

Professional experience
2003/04 Scholarship
placement at Fabrica,
Catena di Villorba, Treviso
2004+ Freelance graphic
designer

Recent exhibitions
2000 "Digital World of
Images", Kreissparkasse
Recklinghausen
2003 "Time to take time",
Fabrica Features (Benetton),
Bologna

2006 "Time to …", American
Apparel, Frankfurt

Recent awards
2002 Nominated for the
backup.clipaward, Netzwerk
Filmfest e. V., Weimar

2006 Red Dot Award for
Communication Design

Clients
Fabrica; Sikora; Verein für
Kunstförderung Rhein-Main
e. V.

"What counts in life is the moment. Everyday moments are the source from which I draw the ideas and the inspiration for my work, which connects design with artistic expression. In this process, it is extremely important to me that the projects with which I am involved should carry meaning and artistic value, and should stand within a significant context. My approach is to apply aesthetic criteria to images constructed from what I have seen, experienced and remembered. In this way, and from this largely intuitive perspective, a clear concept seems to emerge almost naturally. I sense whether or not a solution is congruous and successful, and strive for every project to meet this standard. During the creative process it often seems to me that I am conducting a dialogue with my own intuition."

»Was im Leben zählt, ist der Augenblick. Alltägliche Momente sind die Quelle, aus der ich Ideen und Anregungen für meine Arbeit beziehe, in der ich Design mit künstlerischem Ausdruck verbinde. In diesem Prozess ist es für mich äußerst wichtig, dass die Projekte, an denen ich arbeite, sinnvoll und künstlerisch wertvoll sind und in einem bedeutungsvollen Kontext stehen. Mein Ansatz besteht darin, ästhetische Kriterien auf Bilder anzuwenden, die ich aus eigenen Erlebnissen und Erinnerungen zusammengestellt habe. Auf diese Weise, aus dieser weitgehend intuitiven Perspektive scheint sich ein klares Konzept fast wie von selbst zu ergeben. Ich spüre, ob eine Lösung stimmig und gelungen ist, und bemühe mich darum, dass jeder Entwurf diesem Standard entspricht. Beim schöpferischen Prozess scheint es mir oft so, als ob ich mit meiner eigenen Intuition einen Dialog führte.«

«Ce qui compte dans la vie c'est le moment. Les moments quotidiens sont à l'origine de mes idées et inspirent mon travail, qui fait le lien entre graphisme et expression artistique. Dans ce processus, il est très important pour moi que les projets auxquels je collabore soient porteurs d'un sens, d'une valeur artistique, et s'inscrivent dans un contexte significatif. Ma démarche est d'appliquer des critères esthétiques à des images construites à partir des choses que j'ai vues, expérimentées, dont je me suis souvenue. Si on se place dans cette perspective intuitive, un concept clair semble faire surface presque naturellement. Je sens si une solution est adaptée et gagnante et je me démène pour que chaque projet atteigne cet idéal. Au cours du processus créatif, j'ai souvent la sensation de dialoguer avec ma propre intuition.»

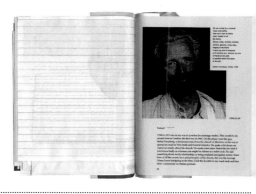

Previous page:
Project: "Time to take time" (quote from Sir John Lubbock), photograph for a calendar, 2003 (photo: Enrico Moro) Client: Fabrica

Top left, above left and right:
Project: "Festhalten" (Hold On), book, 2005 Client: Self

Top right:
Project: "Form ist äußere Identität aller Dinge" (Form is External Identity of All Things), image for book, 2004 Client: Self

Following page top:
Project: "Time to take time" (quote from an unknown source), photograph for a calendar, 2003 (photo: Enrico Moro) Client: Fabrica

Following page bottom left:
Project: "Time to take time" (quote from George Eliot), photograph for a calendar, 2003 (photo: Enrico Moro) Client: Fabrica

Following page bottom right:
Project: "Time to take time" (quote from Emily Dickinson), photograph for a calendar, 2003 (photo: Enrico Moro) Client: Fabrica

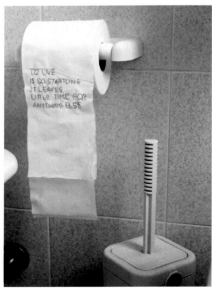

FORM

"We amplify our client's message."

Form
47 Tabernacle Street
London EC2A 4AA
UK
T +44 207 014 143 0
studio@form.uk.com
www.form.uk.com

Design group history
1991 Co-founded by Paul
West and Paula Benson in
London, England

Founders' biographies
Paul West
1965 Born in Weymouth,
England
1983/84 Art Foundation
course, Shelly Park School
of Foundation Studies,
Boscombet
1984–1987 Studied graphic
design, London College of
Printing
1987–1989 Designer, Peter
Saville Associates, London
1989 Freelance designer,
Vaughan Oliver/V23, London

1989/90 Designer, 3a (now
Farrow Design), London
1991 Co-founded Form,
London
1997 Co-founded UniForm
(clothing label), London
Paula Benson
1967 Born in Durham,
England
1984/85 Art Foundation
course, Gloucester College
of Arts & Technology,
Cheltenham
1985–1988 Studied graphic
design, Central Saint Martins
College of Art & Design,
London
1988/89 Designer, The Design
Solution, London
1989/90 Freelance designer

1991 Co-founded Form,
London
1997 Co-founded UniForm
(clothing label), London

Recent exhibitions
2002 "Design in Britain",
Tokyo
2004 "Swinging London",
Centre de Graphisme et de
la Communication visuelle
d'Échirolles, Grenoble
2005 "DesignUK", Creative
Forum, Bloomberg, Tokyo
2006 "Guadalajara–UK",
Auditorio Salón de Congresos
Tec de Monterrey, Guadalajara; "Designweek Monterrey",
Monterrey

Clients
Beck Greener; The Big Stretch;
British Embassy (Tokyo);
Caro Communications; CC
Girlz; dakini Books; Darkside
FX; Dazed and Confused;
Def Jam; Defected Records;
The Design Council; The
Discovery Channel; Dixon
Jones; Fabulous Films/Freman-
tle Media; Five; For Life
Records (Japan); Fuji TV;
Granite Colour; Hit It Now!
Records (LA); Imperial
Records (Japan); Indoor
Garden Design; Innocent
Records; International School
of Basel; Juice Vamoose; Knoll
International; Lifschutz
Davidson Sandilands;

Mathmos; Media Trust; Medi-
um Rare; Mercury Records;
Media Guardian Edinburgh
International Television
Festival; Ministry of Sound;
Mount Stuart Trust; The
Moving Picture Company;
MTV; Music On! TV (Japan);
Pilgrim Gallery; Polydor
Records; Prestige Manage-
ment; Ross + Bute by Anony-
mous; Graham Roxburgh;
RudaizkyRyan; Skint; Staver-
ton; St Lukes; Top Shop;
Translucis; Universal Island
Records; VH1; Vision On
Publishing; Warchild; Wild
Circle

"Our key area of expertise is in graphic design and branding for contemporary culture: music, design-led brands including architecture, furniture and fashion, for entertainment and media (including TV, film and DVD), and for the arts and events. We don't like to be pigeon-holed in our approach to design and branding, and our focus is on the value in the work we create, and that we remain respectful to the clients' wishes but also to surpass their expectations. We are driven by ideas and treat projects with enthusiasm and a love of our craft – no matter what the media. We are frequently invited to lecture on our work, and we contribute to magazines either as writers or with our opinions on graphic design."

»Unsere fachliche Kompetenz liegt im Grafik-design und in der Markenentwicklung für Kultur-produkte in den Bereichen Musik, Produktdesign (einschließlich Architektur), Möbel und Mode, Unterhaltung und Medien (Fernsehen, Film, DVD, etc.), bildende und darstellende Künste sowie Veranstaltungen. Wir lassen uns mit unserer Design- und Markenphilosophie nicht gern in eine Schublade stecken. Wir konzentrieren uns auf die Qualität unserer Arbeiten und darauf, dass wir die Wünsche unserer Auftraggeber berücksichtigen und ihre Erwartungen möglichst übertreffen. Wir werden von Ideen motiviert und bearbeiten die uns gestellten Aufgaben mit Begeisterung und Liebe zu unserem Beruf – egal in welchem Medium. Häufig werden wir gebeten, Vorträge über unsere Arbeit zu halten und liefern Beiträge für Zeitschriften, entweder als Autoren oder als Kritiker, zu Fragen des Grafikdesigns.«

« Nous sommes spécialisés dans le graphisme et la signature visuelle pour la culture contemporaine : musique, architecture, ameublement et mode, divertissement et médias (y compris la télévision, le cinéma et les DVD), arts et événements. Nous n'aimons pas être enfermés dans notre démarche créative ; nous nous concentrons sur la valeur du travail fourni en nous assurant non seulement qu'il respecte les souhaits du client mais aussi qu'il dépasse ses attentes. Nous sommes guidés par des idées et abordons les projets avec de l'enthousiasme et un amour profond pour notre métier – quel que soit le média. Nous sommes fréquemment invités à donner des conférences sur notre travail, et nous collaborons à des magazines en tant que rédacteurs ou graphistes. »

Previous page:
Project: *"Design UK"*
poster, 2005
Client: *British Embassy, Tokyo*

Above:
Project: *"Indoor Garden Design*
Re-brand" postcard set, 2001/02
Client: *Indoor Garden Design*

Following page top:
Project: *"Girls Aloud: Biology"*
CD *cover/music campaign, 2006*
Client: *Polydor*

Following page bottom:
Project: *"Sessions Compilation*
Series" CD covers/music
campaign, 2006
Client: *Ministry of Sound*

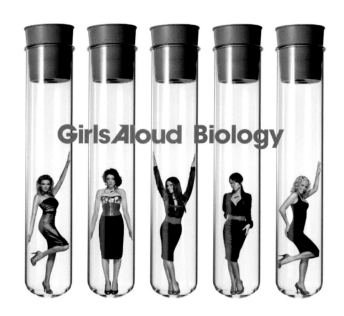

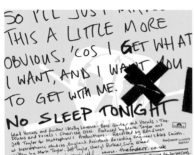

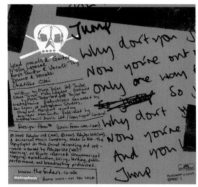

Above:
Project: "Faders Campaign"
CD promo covers / CD covers /
music campaign, 2005
Client: Polydor

Following page:
Project: "DSFX Branding"
branding / DVD / signage /
corporate identity, 2006
Client: Darkside FX

FUEL

"'What is the use of a book' thought Alice,
'without pictures or conversations?'"
(from Alice in Wonderland)

Murrey & Sorrell/FUEL
33 Fournier Street
Spitalfields
London E1 6QE
UK
T +44 207 377 269 7
fuel@fuel-design.com
www.fuel-design.com

Design group history
1991 Founded by Peter Miles,
Damon Murray and Stephen
Sorrell at the Royal College
of Art, London, England
1996 Published Pure Fuel
(Booth-Clibborn Editions)
2000 Published Fuel 3000
(Laurence King Publishing)
2004 Published Russian
Criminal Tattoo Encyclo-
paedia
2005 Published The Music
Library and Fleur

2006 Published Home-Made/
Contemporary Russian Folk
Artefacts and Russian Crimi-
nal Tattoo Encyclopaedia
Volume II

Founders' biographies
Peter Miles
1966 Born in Cuckfield,
Sussex, England
1990–1992 Studied graphic
design, Royal College of Art
Damon Murray
1967 Born in London, England

1990–1992 Studied graphic
design, Royal College of
Art
Stephen Sorrell
1968 Born in Maidstone,
England
1990–1992 Studied graphic
design, Royal College of Art

Exhibitions
1996 "Jam", Barbican Art
Gallery, London
1998 "Powerhouse: UK",
London

1999 "Lost & Found", British
Council touring exhibition
2000 "UK with NY", British
Design Council in New York
2004 "Communicate: Independent British Graphic Design
since the Sixties", Barbican Art
Gallery, London
2005 "European Design Show",
Design Museum, London

Awards
1995 Silver Nomination,
D&AD

1999 Honorary Mention,
Prix Ars Electronica
2005 Silver Award, D&AD

Clients
Autonomous Films; Jake
& Dinos Chapman; Tracey
Emin; Timothy Everest;
Thames & Hudson; The
Home Office; Modern Art
Oxford; Penguin; Phaidon;
White Cube Art Gallery

FUEL

London

------------------------   ------------------------

"In 1991 we were self-publishing our own magazines – often containing ambiguous and thought-provoking messages; these bold graphic statements served as a developing manifesto. *Pure Fuel* and *Fuel 3000* followed. Far from being monographs these books examined the accepted notions of graphic design illustrating our ideas and preoccupations to explore themes of authorship. In 2005 we formed FUEL Publishing. Producing books on a broad range of subjects that interest us, we deal with visual languages that uncover stories and open doors to other places."

»1991 haben wir unsere Zeitschriften – die häufig mehrdeutige und zum Nachdenken anregende Beiträge enthalten – im Eigenverlag herausgegeben. Diese kühnen grafischen Statements dienten als Manifeste unserer Entwicklung. Es folgten *Pure Fuel* und *Fuel 3000*. Weit davon entfernt, Monografien zu sein, analysieren diese Publikationen die üblichen Auffassungen von Grafikdesign; sie illustrieren unsere Vorstellungen und unsere Beschäftigung mit Fragen der Urheberschaft. 2005 gründeten wir den Verlag FUEL Publishing. Wir publizieren Bücher zu einer großen Bandbreite von Themen, die uns interessieren, und verwenden dafür Bildsprachen, die Hintergründe aufdecken und Türen zu anderen Welten aufstoßen.«

«En 1991, nous publiions nos propres magazines – qui contenaient souvent des messages ambigus qui stimulaient la réflexion; ces déclarations graphiques en caractères gras nous ont servi de manifeste de développement. *Pure Fuel* et *Fuel 3000* ont suivi. Loin d'être des monographies, ces livres se penchaient sur les notions de graphisme les plus communément admises qui illustraient nos idées et nos préoccupations en matière de paternité créative. En 2005, nous avons fondé la maison d'édition FUEL Publishing. Nous publions des livres sur un large éventail de sujets qui nous intéressent et, ce faisant, nous manipulons des langages visuels qui éclairent des histoires et ouvrent des portes vers d'autres univers. »

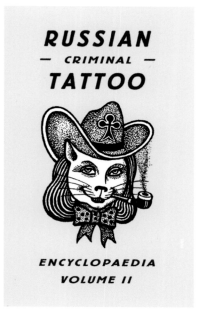

Previous page:
Project: *"FUEL"*
promotional poster, 2005
Client: *Self*

Above left:
Project: *"Russian Criminal Tattoo Encyclopaedia"*
book, 2003
Client: *Steidl/FUEL*

Above right:
Project: *"Russian Criminal Tattoo Encyclopaedia Volume II"*
book, 2006
Client: *FUEL Publishing*

Following page top:
Project: *"The Thrills: The Irish Keep Gate-crashing" poster, 2004*
Client: *Virgin Records*

Following page bottom right:
Project: *"The Thrills: Whatever Happened to Corey Haim?"*
record cover, 2004
Client: *Virgin Records*

Following page bottom left:
Project: *"The Thrills: Let's Bottle Bohemia"*
record cover, 2004
Client: *Virgin Records*

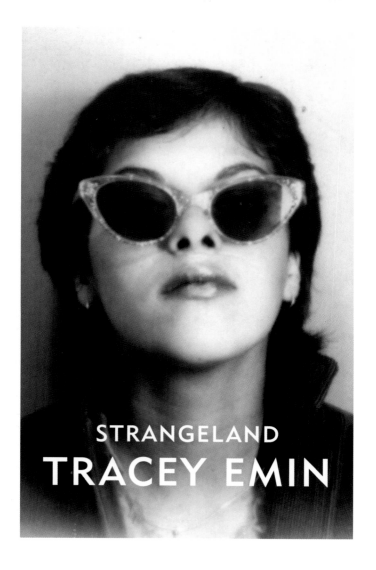

Executive Producers **Sara Giles, Michael Hamlyn**

The Proposition

Ray Winstone

Screenplay **Nick Cave**

GENEVIÈVE GAUCKLER

"I like creating an emotion while I'm working on an image. By creating a character or an atmosphere, I try to make something funny, sad, sweet, in a word emotional, because it creates a link between you, your creation and the viewer. It's magic."

Geneviève Gauckler
9, rue Saint Pierre
94 220 Charenton-le-Pont
France
T +33 1 497 793 27
genevieve@g2works.com
www.g2works.com

Biography
1967 Born in Lyon, France
1991 Graduated from the École Nationale Supérieure des Arts Décoratifs

Professional Experience
1991–1995 Graphic designer, F Communications, Paris

1996–1999 Worked with the directors Olivier Kuntzel and Florence Deygas, making promos for Dimitri from Paris, Pierre Henry, Sparks, commercials (Yves Saint Laurent's Live Jazz), titles (Arte) and short movies (Tigi, Velvet 99)

1999 Graphic designer/web designer, boo.com, creating online magazine, Boom magazine and website
2000 Graphic designer, Me Company, London
2001 Moved back to Paris

Recent exhibitions
2006 "Around The World", Someday Gallery, Melbourne

Clients
Beaux-Arts Magazine; Bourjois; Coca-Cola; Domestic; Flaunt; Fox Hotel; Galeries Lafayette; Hip; Isetan; Lane Crawford; Libération; Longchamp; Peugeot; Publicis; Renault; Virgin Records France

"I try to create some harmony in my images. I'm happy when it's energetic, not pretentious, simple, light. I'm not very interested in style, I'm just trying to build up a world like kids playing with toys, rather than trying to come up with a new style. I'm also very influenced by the tools I'm using (Illustrator, Photoshop, hand drawing). For example, when I'm using Illustrator to create a character; it's easier to get a simple and symmetrical character because the software is very rigid. I think also mixing is very important. By mixing bitmap and vector shapes, you get some very exciting images. Now, there's no more gap between photography and illustration, it's a very wide and rich field. I'm using illustration because it's straightforward... it has clear outlines. It's convenient to use it with typography. It's more related to childhood, while photography is more grown-up. Illustration and photography are like the yin and the yang of graphic design, both of them are necessary. I guess it's a way to mix the magic and the reality. It's a way to express the idea that magic stands in everyday life reality. It's only a question of the way you look at it."

»Ich versuche in meinen Bildern Harmonie zu erzeugen. Ich bin glücklich, wenn sie energiegeladen, unprätentiös, einfach und leicht sind. Stil interessiert mich relativ wenig. Ich versuche lediglich, eine Welt aufzubauen, so wie Kinder das mit ihrem Spielzeug tun. Die Medien, mit denen ich arbeite (Illustrator, Photoshop, freies Zeichnen), beeinflussen mich auch ziemlich stark. Wenn ich zum Beispiel mit Illustrator arbeite, um Schriftzeichen zu erzeugen, ist es leichter, einen schlichten, symmetrischen Buchstaben zu designen, weil die Software sehr starr ist. Die Mischung ist auch ganz wichtig. Wenn man Bitmap- und Vektorformen kombiniert, bekommt man manchmal spannende Bilder. Heute gibt es keine Kluft mehr zwischen Fotografie und Zeichnung – alles zusammen ist ein weites, vielfältiges Feld. Ich verwende gezeichnete Illustrationen, weil sie so klare Umrisse haben und sich gut mit typografischen Lösungen kombinieren lassen. Zeichnungen haben einen stärkeren Bezug zur Kindheit, Fotografie ist erwachsener. Zeichnungen und Fotos sind wie das Yin und Yang des Grafikdesigns; man braucht beide. Ich vermute, es ist eine Möglichkeit, Magie und Realität zu mischen. Man kann damit ausdrücken, dass auch in Alltäglichem ein Zauber liegt. Es kommt nur auf die Sichtweise an.«

« J'essaie de créer une harmonie dans mes images. Je suis satisfaite quand c'est énergique, sans prétention, simple, léger. Je ne m'intéresse pas beaucoup au style ; j'essaie de construire un univers, comme les enfants jouent avec des cubes, plutôt que d'inventer un nouveau style. Je suis aussi très influencée par les outils que j'utilise (Illustrator, Photoshop, dessin manuel). Par exemple, lorsque j'utilise Illustrator pour créer un caractère : il est plus facile d'obtenir un caractère simple et symétrique parce que le logiciel est très rigide. Je pense aussi que le mélange est très important. En mélangeant images matricielles et formes vectorielles on obtient des images très intéressantes. Aujourd'hui, il n'y a plus de fossé entre la photographie et l'illustration, c'est un champ d'exploration vaste et riche. J'utilise l'illustration parce qu'elle est franche... elle a des contours nets. C'est pratique de l'utiliser avec la typographie. Elle est davantage liée à l'enfance, alors que la photographie est plus adulte. L'illustration et la photographie sont comme le yin et le yang du graphisme, aussi nécessaires l'une que l'autre. J'imagine que c'est aussi un moyen de mélanger magie et réalité. C'est une manière d'exprimer l'idée que la magie est présente dans notre réalité quotidienne. Tout dépend de la façon dont on la regarde. »

Previous page:
Project: "Octobre"
editorial illustration, 2005
Client: Vue Sur La Ville

Left:
Project: "Hip Shampoo Collection" packaging design, 2005
Client: Hip

Right:
Project: "2040"
magazine cover, 2004
Client: Le Colette

Bottom:
Project: *"Love Peace Fun"*
painting for window display,
2005

Client: *Hankyu (Graffiti meets*
Windows project)

Top:
Project: *"Flaunt" magazine*
cover, 2005
Client: *Flaunt Magazine*

Geneviève Gauckler   133

JAMES GOGGIN

"Attempting to make simple, coherent compositions with layered meaning using words, pictures, shapes and colours."

Practise
Studio 2a
18–24 Shacklewell Lane
London E8 2EZ
UK
T +44 207 503 317 5
contact@practise.co.uk
www.practise.co.uk

Biography
1975 Born in Tamworth, Australia
1994–1997 Studied visual communication, Ravensbourne College of Design and Communication, London
1997–1999 Studied graphic design, Royal College of Art, London

Professional experience
1999 Established own studio, Practise, in London
1999–2006 Lectured and organised workshops in the UK, Belgium and Switzerland
2000 Started clothing label in collaboration with his wife, Shan, under the name Shan James
2001/02 Practise and Shan James moved to Auckland, New Zealand (for one year), continued working in UK, Europe and Japan
2002 Founded clothing label All Weather
2003 Practise studio returns to London
2003 Consulting Design Director at the Tate Britain and the Tate Modern
2006 Art Director of The Wire Magazine, London

Recent exhibitions
2001 "Inside Out", Kiasma Museum of Contemporary Art, Helsinki
2002 "GB: Graphic Britain", Magma, London
2003 "The Book Corner", British Council (touring exhibition); "Arts Foundation Awards", Pentagram, London
2004 "Communicate: Independent British Graphic Design since the Sixties", Barbican Art Gallery, London; "Interact1", London College of Communication, London; "The Free Library", Riviera, New York; "Public Address System", Henry Peacock Gallery, London
2005 "The Free Library", M+R Gallery, London; "TricoDesignLove!", Aram Gallery, London; "A Billion Pixels per Second", Lovebytes Digital Art Gallery, Sheffield; "The Free Library", Space 1026, Philadelphia; "You Are Here: The Design of Information", Design Museum, London
2006 "Felt-Tip", SEA Gallery, London; "Super Design Market", London Design Festival; "1 – An Exhibition in Mono", SEA Gallery, London; "From Mars", Moravian Gallery, Brno; "Graphic Design in the White Cube", Moravian Gallery, Brno

Clients
2K for Gingham; Analog Baroque; Artangel; Barbican Art Gallery, London; Book Works; British Council; Camden Arts Centre; Caruso St John Architects; Design Museum, London; Frieze Projects; Tate Britain; Tate Modern; Veenman Publishers; Victoria & Albert Museum; The Wire; White Cube Gallery

FRANCESCA GRANATO

"I believe graphic design can be approached in much the same way as fine art; I have inspirations and themes that are recurrent in my portfolio in the same way that an artist does."

Francesca Granato
88 Ridge Road
London N8 9NR
UK
T +44 785 442 452 3
francesca@dorasbox.com
www.dorasbox.com

Biography
1999–2000 Studied graphic design, University of Middlesex, London
2000–2003 Studied graphic design, University of Brighton

Professional experience
2004–2005 Graphic Design Department, Fabrica (Benetton Creative Centre), Catena di Villorba, Treviso
2005 Graphic Designer, Studio Myerscough, London
2005+ Graphic Designer, Unreal, London

Recent awards
2005 Awarded a NESTA Creative Pioneer 3-year sponsorship

Clients
Birth Rites; Electa Publishing; Fabrica; Greater London Authority; Hachette Livre; Amora–Academy of Sex & Relationships, London; Puffin Books; Scholastic; Time Warner Book Group

POPOLI IN CAMMINO

FESTAUNITA'
NAZIONALE GENOVA
FIERA OVEST
28 AGOSTO / 22 SETTEMBRE 2004

www.festaunita.it

Francesca Granato 139

"Much of my portfolio contains work about sex. It is this sexual theme that led me to art-direct the branding for the first museum of sex in the UK. I expect to continue working on projects concerned with sex and erotica; a truly under-designed area, I think. My thinking for a new brief is both instinctive and systematic. I would like to think that my work is always grounded in an idea. I find purely aesthetic design dull – the real substance in graphic design is in the concepts and how well they are communicated."

»In vielen meiner Arbeiten kommt Sex vor. Das hat dazu geführt, dass ich mit der künstlerischen Leitung der Markenentwicklung für das erste Sex-Museum in Großbritannien beauftragt worden bin. Ich gehe davon aus, dass ich auch weiterhin an Projekten arbeiten werde, die mit Sex und Erotika zu tun haben – einem, wie ich finde, echt unterdesignten Themenbereich. Ich gehe instinktiv, aber auch systematisch an jede neue Designaufgabe heran und wünsche mir, dass meine Arbeiten immer eine ideelle Grundlage haben. Ich finde rein ästhetisches Design öde. Die eigentliche Substanz des Grafikdesigns besteht nämlich aus den Konzepten und darin, wie gut sie vermittelt werden.«

« Mon portfolio contient beaucoup de travaux concernant le sexe. C'est cette thématique sexuelle qui m'a conduite à diriger la création de la plateforme graphique du premier musée britannique du sexe. J'espère continuer à travailler sur des projets touchant au sexe et à l'érotisme, un domaine largement déserté par le graphisme, à mon avis. À chaque nouveau projet, ma réflexion est à la fois instinctive et systématique. J'aimerais penser que mon travail se fonde toujours sur une idée. Je trouve le graphisme purement esthétique ennuyeux – la réelle substance du graphisme réside dans les concepts et dans la manière dont ils sont communiqués. »

Previous page:
Project: "Festaunitá"
(Festival of Unity) poster, 2004
Client: Democratici di Sinistra
(Left-Wing Democratic Party of
Italy)

Above:
Project: "Amora"
sex museum identity, 2005
Client: Amora – The Academy
of Sex & Relationships

Following page top:
Project: "Joy Frempong:
Because You are a Girl"
CD cover, 2004
Client: Fabrica

Following page bottom:
Project: "Alice in Wonderland" /
"Huckleberry Finn" /
"Treasure Island" / "Black Beauty"
children's book covers, 2005
Client: Puffin Books

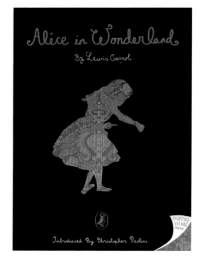

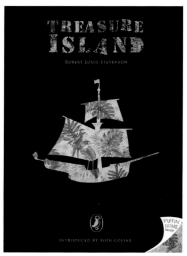

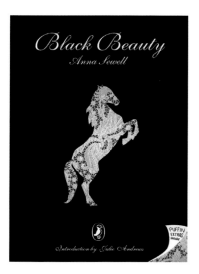

FERNANDO GUTIÉRREZ

"Good design speaks for itself."

**The Studio of
Fernando Gutiérrez**
28 Heath Street
London NW3 6TE
UK
T +44 207 431 005 0
info@fernandogutierrez.co.uk
www.fernandogutierrez.co.uk

Biography
1963 Born in London, England
1983–1986 Studied graphic
design, London College of
Printing

Professional experience
1986–1992 Graphic designer,
CDT Design, London
1990 Graphic designer,
Summa, Barcelona

1991 Associate, CDT Design,
London
1993–2000 Co-founding
partner of Grafica, Barcelona
1995+ Designer and Art
Director, Matador, Madrid
1997 Elected member of
Alliance Graphique
Internationale (AGI)
2000–2002 Creative Director,
Colors, Treviso

2000–2006 Partner, Pentagram,
London
2002+ Consultant Creative
Director, Prado Museum,
Madrid
2006 Founded own studio in
London

Recent exhibitions
2005 "Otros Quijotes",
touring exhibition, Spain

2006 "My London/My City",
International Society of
Typographic Design (ISTD)
& City Inn Westminster,
London; "The Present", Ithaca
Annual Poster Competition,
Ithaca/Athens; "Relics on
Spirit", Aiap Gallery, Milan

Clients
Asturias Television and Radio;
Banco Santander; Compañía
de Vinos Telmo Rodríguez;
CTA Transport; El País;
Hermès; Losada Publishing;
Phaidon Press; PhotoBolsillo;
Reina Sofía National Museum
of Contemporary Art; Telera-
ma; Vanidad

"encounter
understand
identify
visualise
refine
analyse
decide
implement
produce

These are the basic creative stages I follow but not necessarily in chronological order."

»begegnen
verstehen
identifizieren
visualisieren
verfeinern
analysieren
entscheiden
umsetzen
produzieren

Das sind die grundlegenden gestalterischen Stadien, die ich durchlaufe – allerdings nicht unbedingt immer in dieser Reihenfolge.«

« rencontrer
comprendre
identifier
visualiser
épurer
analyser
décider
exécuter
produire

Telles sont les étapes créatives fondamentales que je suis, mais pas nécessairement dans cet ordre. »

Previous page:
Project: *"My London My City"*
poster, 2006 (photo: John Ross)
Client: *Self*

Above left:
Project: *"Vanidad – Issue*
No. 108" magazine design, 2004
Client: *Vanidad*

Above right:
Project: *"Colors 57 – Slums"*
magazine design, 2003
Client: *Benetton*

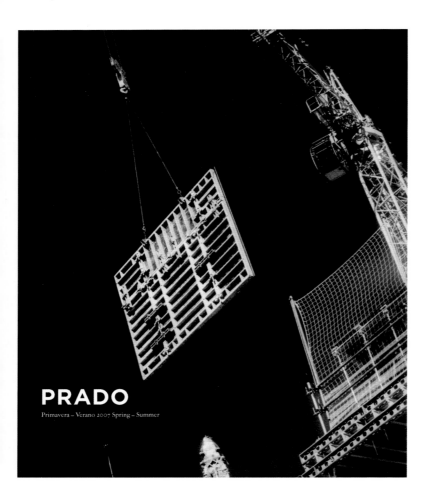

PRADO

Primavera – Verano 2007 Spring – Summer

Top:
Project: *"Prado"*
magazine design, 2007 (photo:
Phillip Sayer/Stefan Ruiz)
Client: *Museo Nacional del*
Prado

Above right:
Project: *"Duraton" identity*
for Spanish winery, 2006
Client: *Duraton*

Above far right:
Project: *"Viña 105, 2004"*
wine bottle label, 2005
Client: *Compañía de Vinos*
Telmo Rodríguez

HAMAN-SUTRA

"Using a simple system of just four basic elements – square, triangle, line and circle – it is possible to create a language to describe a multitude of other systems."

hamansutra
Buttermelcher Str. 21
80 469 Munich
Germany
T +49 89 212 686 88
info@hamansutra.com
www.hamansutra.com

Founder's biography
Haman Nimardani
1977 Born in Tehran, Iran
1999–2000 Studied design technology for the fashion industry, London College of Fashion
2000–2004 Studied fashion design and marketing, Central Saint Martins

College of Art & Design, London

Professional experience
1989–1998 Starts with graffiti through Munich's underground scene
1994–1998 Formed an artists' group funded by Munich City Council

1998–1999 Graphic designer, Jung von Matt advertising agency, Hamburg
2002 Assistant designer, Clothing Department of the German Military Forces, Munich
2002 Assistant designer, Kostas Murkudis, Munich
2003 Assistant designer,

Bavarian State Opera, Munich
2005+ Lecturer, Blocherer School of Design, Munich
2006 Lecturer, Miami Ad School, Hamburg
2006+ Lecturer, Academy of Fashion and Design (AMD), Munich

Clients
Amos; Booklet Magazine; Kickz Sportswear; Mey; Nike; Porsche Design; Saturn Hansa; Sonique; XBOX; Ziad Ghanem

"Did I want to become a designer? My primary school report for 1983 said, 'Keen on drawing'. My goal was always artistic freedom. Tolerance for art but strictness with its realization and completion. Do what you want, but do it properly. I transform my ideas into 3D objects, graphics, whatever. I don't look to ready-made graphics for inspiration – usually too derivative. Like perfectly dressed people. No inspiration – because they're slaves to the media. Taste is linked to knowledge. How can you have taste if you've never tasted? Design is emotion – proof that you live and breathe your design. I love the physical craft of creating. Taking a mistake, a chance element – a coffee stain, a dead fly – and weaving it into the design. Creators should take their experiments more seriously. Everything starts with a prototype. Now the baby has to learn to walk – and never stop learning."

»Ob ich Designer werden wollte? In meinem ersten Schulzeugnis (1983) stand: ›Er zeichnet eifrig‹. Ich habe schon immer nach künstlerischer Freiheit gestrebt. Toleranz für die Kunst, aber absolute Strenge in deren Umsetzung und Fertigstellung. Mach, worauf du Lust hast, aber bring es zu Ende. Meine Ideen wandle ich in 3D-Objekte, Grafiken, Illustrationen oder Sonstiges um. Ich lasse mich nicht von vorgefertigen Grafiken inspirieren, weil sie meist nichts Neues bringen. Wie bei perfekt gekleideten Menschen. Inspiration gleich Null, weil sie zu medienhörig sind. Geschmack hat mit Wissen zu tun. Wie soll man Geschmack haben, wenn man nie geschmeckt hat? Design ist Gefühl – beweise, dass du dein Design lebst. Ich liebe das Handwerk. Ein Fehler, ein Zufallselement, das bewusst im Design umgesetzt wird. Schöpfer sollten ihre Experimente ernster nehmen. Alles fängt mit einem Prototyp an. Jetzt soll das Baby laufen lernen – und ein Leben lang dazulernen.«

«Est-ce que je voulais devenir graphiste? Mon bulletin de primaire de 1983 dit ›Intéressé par le dessin‹. Mon but a toujours été la liberté artistique. La tolérance pour l'art mais la rigueur dans sa réalisation et son exécution. Fais ce que tu veux, mais fais-le bien. Je transforme mes idées en objets en 3D, en créations graphiques, etc. Je ne m'inspire pas de graphismes tout faits – généralement trop peu originaux. Comme des gens parfaitement habillés. Pas d'inspiration – parce qu'ils sont esclaves des médias. Le goût est affaire de connaissances. Comment avoir du goût si on n'a jamais goûté? Le graphisme, c'est l'émotion – la preuve que vous le vivez et le respirez. J'aime l'activité physique de la création. Se saisir d'une erreur, d'un élément de hasard – une tache de café, une mouche morte – et l'intégrer au graphisme. Les créateurs devraient prendre leurs expérimentations plus au sérieux. Tout commence par un prototype. Maintenant le bébé doit apprendre à marcher – et ne jamais cesser d'apprendre.

Top:
Project: "Hamansutra.com"
fashion card book, 2005
Client: Self

Above left:
Project: "Alva" and "Ruben"
T-Shirt designs, 2004
Client: Self

Above right:
Project: "Kickz in CO-OP
with Hamansutra" track-
suit for national basketball
team promotional material, 2003
Client: Kickz Sportswear

Following page:
Project: "Sutraismus"
collage artwork, 2004
Client: Ziad Ghanem

KIM HIORTHØY

"No approach approach"

This is Real Art
17c Clerkenwell Road
London EC1M 5RD
UK
T +44 207 253 218 1
george@thisisrealart.com
www.thisisrealart.com

Biography
1973 Born in Trondheim, Norway
1991–1994 Studied at the Trondheim Art Academy
1994/95 Studied at the School of Visual Arts, New York
1995/96 Studied at the Trondheim Art Academy
1999–2001 Studied at the Royal Danish Academy of Fine Art, Copenhagen

Professional experience
1996+ Independent freelance designer

Recent exhibitions
2004 "Manifesta 5", San Sebastian
2005 "Early Works", Standard Gallery Oslo; "NADA Art Fair", Miami; "Nieves Books", Rocket Gallery, Tokyo
2006 "Art, Life and Confusion – The 47th October Salon", ICA/Belgrade Culture Centre; "Another Day Full of Dread", Galerie Juliette Jongma, Amsterdam

Clients
Drag City; Factory Films; MTV Europe; Rune Grammofon; Smalltown Supersound; Vice Records

CAVAN HUANG

"My goal is to create compelling motion-based visuals that enhance the way we communicate, challenge the way we look and design, and reinterpret our experiences of space."

Cavan Huang
148 Smith Street, apt. 3
Brooklyn, NY 11201
USA
T +1 646 512 121 2
cavdesign@gmail.com
www.cavanthology.com

Biography
1977 Born in Toronto, Canada
1997–2000 Studied history and urban planning, McGill University, Montreal
2003–2005 Studied graphic design, Rhode Island School of Design, Providence

Professional experience
2000/01 Multimedia/web designer, Rompus Interactive, Toronto
2001/02 Creative Director, Colorshadow Communications, Toronto
2003–2005 Instructor, Rhode Island School of Design, Providence
2005+ Distributed Media Designer, Time Warner, New York

Recent exhibitions
2004 "Graphic Design Triennial Exhibition", Rhode Island School of Design, Providence
2006 "Spoken with Eyes", Davis Design Museum, University of California, Sacramento

Recent awards
2003 Best Multimedia Design, Applied Arts Magazine, Toronto
2004 Best Multimedia Design, Summit Creative Awards, Toronto
2006 Nominated as 1 of 25 emerging designers, Step Inside Design magazine, New York

Clients
Canadian International Autoshow; CNN; General Electric; Rogers Sportsnet; Time Warner; Toshiba

"City and film are two words that describe my inspirations and approach to graphic design. I look to create challenging spatial experiences, shared by many, that continue to evolve and expand over time. There's something beautiful about the inexhaustible variety of details cities have to offer: lights, traffic, sounds, people. I love how cities are designed with a sufficient level of complexity in order to sustain interest, without becoming chaotic or unmanageable. There is hardly any wasted or unused space. Motion pictures share a lot in common with cities, and are particularly great at portraying them too. In a single scene, you can experience the magnitude of a metropolis, then zero in on the stories and characters of a specific street corner."

»Stadt und Film sind zwei Begriffe, die meine Inspirationsquellen und meinen Zugang zum Grafikdesign kennzeichnen. Ich versuche, anspruchsvollanregende räumliche Erlebnisse zu schaffen, die von vielen Menschen geteilt werden und die sich mit der Zeit weiter entwickeln und erweitern. Die unerschöpfliche Vielfalt von Elementen und Erscheinungen, die Städte zu bieten haben, ist etwas sehr Schönes: Lichter, Verkehr, Geräusche, Menschen. Ich mag die Art, in der Städte vielgestaltig angelegt sind, ohne chaotisch oder unkontrollierbar zu werden. Es gibt in ihnen kaum Brachen oder ungenutzte Flächen. Filme haben vieles mit Städten gemeinsam und eignen sich außerdem auch hervorragend um diese zu porträtieren. In nur einer einzigen Szene kann man sowohl die Größe einer Metropole darstellen, um dann auf die Geschichten und die Charaktere einer ganz bestimmten Straßenecke zu fokussieren.«

«Ville et film sont deux mots qui décrivent bien mes sources d'inspiration et mon approche du graphisme. Je cherche à créer des expériences spatiales délicates qui soient partagées par le plus grand nombre et continuent d'évoluer et de s'étendre dans le temps. L'inépuisable variété de détails qu'offrent les villes a quelque chose de magnifique: éclairage, circulation, sons, personnes. J'aime comment les villes sont constituées de façon suffisamment complexe pour soutenir l'intérêt sans pour autant devenir chaotiques et ingérables. L'espace perdu ou inutilisé est quasi-inexistant. Les films ont beaucoup de points communs avec les villes et savent aussi les montrer de façon magistrale. En une seule séquence, on peut ressentir l'immensité d'une mégapole avant de plonger dans les intrigues et sur les personnages d'un coin de rue particulier. »

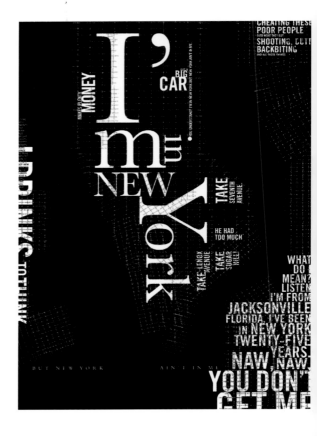

Page 157:
Project: *"Dusk" typographic concrete poem,* 2003
Client: *Self*

Previous page left:
Project: *"The Conversation"
film poster,* 2003
Client: *Self*

Previous page right:
Project: *"Harlem Document
No. 3"
typographic composition,* 2003
Client: *Self*

Top:
Project: *"Looking Closer"
exhibition poster,* 2003
Client: *Self*

Above left:
Project: *"The Street Drunks –
Series 8,2"
visual transcription,* 2004
Client: *Self*

Above right:
Project: *"The Street Drunks –
Series 8,3"
visual transcription,* 2004
Client: *Self*

YANG HUANG

"Graphic design is a '+' ?!"

HuangYang & Associates
F2 E6 East Industry District
OCAT Loft
Shenzhen 518 053
China
T +86 755 862 327 26
huangyangdesign@163.com
www.huangyangdesign.com

Biography
1971 Born in Sichuan, China
1993 Graduated from the Sichuan Fine Art College
1995–2000 Art Director, Sims Advertising Co. Ltd, Shenzhen
2001 Founded own studio HuangYang & Associates in Shenzhen

Recent exhibitions
2005 "The Asian Poster", Track 16 Gallery, Los Angeles; "INCHINA 2005", 20-person invitational exhibition on Chinese graphic design, Shenzhen
2006 "Extraordinary, Non-Commercial", Art Design Exhibition, Shenzhen

Recent awards
2003 Silver Medal and Excellence Award, Shenzhen Design Exhibition
2004 Gold Award, Mohawk Show 5, USA
2005 Bronze Medal and Excellence Award, Graphic Design in China (GDC05) Exhibition

Clients
Antalis; BSF; CGWS; Huawei; Phoenix; Ping An Life; SSO; SZMG; SZTV; TTF; U8; Urbanus; World Union

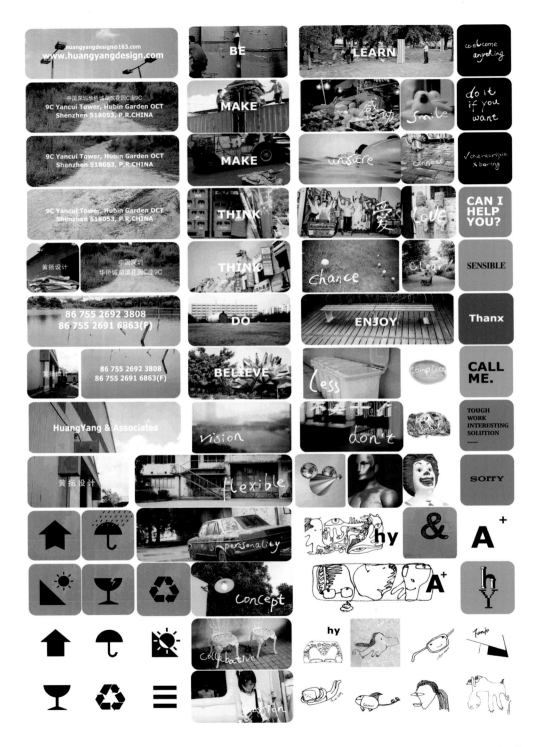

"Today, it seems that graphic design exists everywhere around us, and with the distinct effect of relevancy, it can be related to everything. We call this 'plus effect'. If this '+' can act as magical an effect as '1+1=2', then it is good graphic design. But it's a pity that this kind of situation is rare."

»Grafikdesign begegnet uns heute in allen Bereichen des täglichen Lebens und kann – mit der spezifischen Wirkung ihrer Relevanz – auf alles und jedes bezogen werden. Wir nennen das den ›Pluseffekt‹. Wenn dieses ›+‹ mit dem gleichen Zauber wirkt wie ›1+1=2‹, ist das Ergebnis gutes Grafikdesign. Leider kommt das aber nur selten vor.«

«Aujourd'hui, le graphisme semble exister tout autour de nous et peut parler de tout à condition qu'il soit abordé avec la pertinence nécessaire. Nous appelons cela 'l'effet plus'. Si ce '+' a un effet aussi magique que dans '1+1=2', alors le graphisme est bon. Mais, c'est dommage, ce type de situation est rare.»

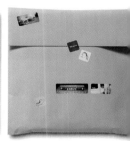

Previous page:
Project: "HuangYang & Associates" stationery identity (stickers), 2003
Client: Self

Top left and right:
Project: "HuangYang & Associates" stationery identity (envelopes), 2003
Client: Self

Above right:
Project: "In China" notebook for "China Graphic Design" invitational exhibition, 2005
Client: Shenzhen Culture Bureau, Shenzhen Graphic Design Association

Following page top left:
Project: "Nike" promotional design for paper company, 2003
Client: Tai Tak Takeo Fine Paper Co.

Following page top right:
Project: "Sony" promotional design for paper company 2003
Client: Tai Tak Takeo Fine Paper Co.

Following page bottom:
Project: "In China" poster for "China Graphic Design" invitational exhibition, 2005
Client: Shenzhen Culture Bureau, Shenzhen Graphic Design Association

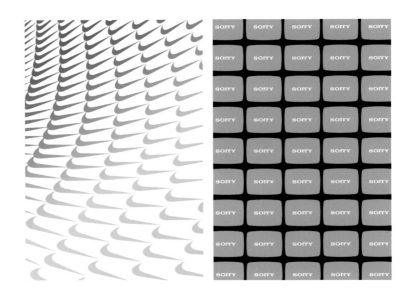

ANGUS HYLAND

"Simplicity allowing for occasional complexity."

Angus Hyland
Pentagram Design Ltd
11 Needham Road
London W11 2RP
UK
T +44 207 229 347 7
hyland@pentagram.co.uk
www.pentagram.com

Biography
1963 Born in Brighton, England
1982–1986 Studied media and production design, London College of Printing
1987/88 Studied graphic design, Royal College of Art, London

Professional experience
1988 Founded his own studio
1998+ Director, Pentagram
2001 Edited "Pen and Mouse: Commercial Art and Digital Illustration"
2003 Edited "Hand to Eye: Contemporary Illustration"
2005+ Consultant Creative Director, Laurence King Publishing, London

Recent exhibitions
2001/02 "Picture This", touring exhibition, The British Council
2001–2004 "Book Corner", touring exhibition, The British Council
2002/03 "D&AD's 40th anniversary exhibition", Victoria & Albert Museum, London
2004 "Pentagram–a world of typography", Klingspor-Museum, Offenbach; "Ballpoint", Pentagram Gallery, London; "Communicate: Independent British Graphic Design since the Sixties", Barbican Art Gallery, London
2005 "Handmade", Museum für Gestaltung, Zurich

Recent awards
2002 Awarded an Honorary Master of Arts by The Surrey Institute of Art and Design
2003 Award, Food & Beverage Awards (FAB); Award, Tokyo Type Directors Club; Award, Festival international de l'Affiche et des Arts graphiques
2004 Award, Warsaw Poster Biennale; Winner of Distinctive Merit, Art Directors Club; Winner, I.D. Annual Design Review

Clients
Asprey; BBC; BMP; British Council; British Museum; Canongate Books; Cass Art; Crafts Council; DDB; Documenta 11; Dorling Kindersley; EAT; EMI; Garrard; Getty Images; Nokia; Penguin Books; Phaidon; Sage; Shakespeare's Globe; The Sage Gateshead; Verso; Victoria & Albert Museum

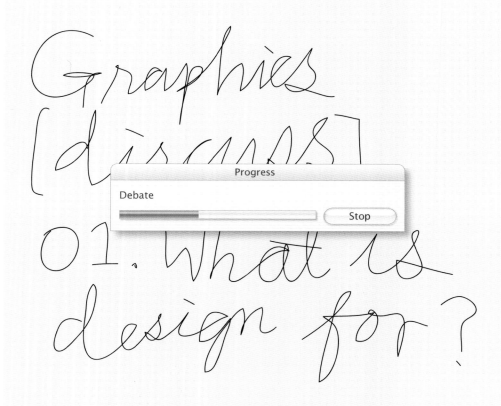

Graphics
[discuss]

Progress

Debate

[Stop]

01. What is design for?

TUESDAY 8 JUNE 2004 7PM   HOSTED BY CREATIVE REVIEW EDITOR PATRICK BURGOYNE. THE FIRST TALK IN THE [DISCUSS] SERIES FEATURES RICK POYNOR AND MICHAEL BIERUT. HELD AT PENTAGRAM DESIGN, 11 NEEDHAM ROAD, LONDON. W11 2RP.

"I follow a simple methodology. I am commissioned to come up with ideas and design solutions. These solutions are usually visual (pictures and words), and occasionally they are either only pictures or only words. Before I start, I often write a proposal that allocates time and resources in stages that include research, concept and artwork. This rational process is made in parallel to an intuitive one: creativity – which is governed by no rules. I do not know where it comes from."

»Meine Vorgehensweise ist ganz einfach: Ich werde beauftragt, Ideen und Designlösungen vorzulegen. Dabei handelt es sich für gewöhnlich um Kombinationen aus Bildern und Texten, manchmal aber auch nur aus Bildern oder nur aus Texten. Vor dem eigentlichen Entwerfen schreibe ich oft ein Konzept, das die Arbeitsvorgänge zeitlich und inhaltlich in die Phasen Recherche, Entwurf und Ausführung aufteilt. Dieser rationale Prozess wird von einem intuitiven und kreativen begleitet, der keinen Regeln unterworfen ist. Ich weiß nicht, woher er kommt.«

«Je suis une méthodologie simple. On me demande d'apporter des idées et des solutions graphiques. Ces solutions sont généralement visuelles (images et mots) et ne comportent parfois que de l'image ou que du texte. Avant de commencer, je rédige souvent une proposition dans laquelle je partage le temps et les ressources imparties entre les diverses étapes du processus créatif: recherche, conceptualisation et réalisation. Ce développement rationnel du projet va de pair avec un développement intuitif: la créativité – qui n'obéit à aucune règle. Je ne sais pas d'où elle vient.»

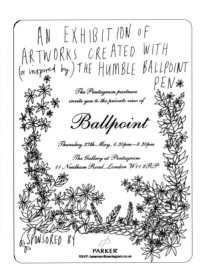

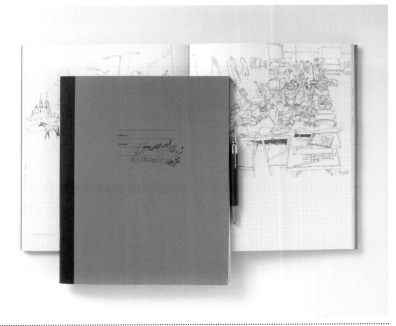

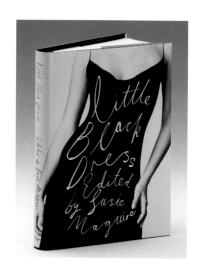

It is not for the purpose of reviving old or making new rules that these facsimiles have been reproduced. One might as well try to provide models for unalterable fashions in garments, houses, furniture, or decoration. However pleasing a new fashion may be, that pleasure does not entirely suppress the desire for change, and that desire was never greater than it is now. / Less is more. Catalogues, posters, advertisements of all sorts. Believe me, they contain the poetry of our epoch. / Build a book like a body moving in space and time, like a dynamic relief in which every page is a surface carrying shapes, and every turn of a page a new crossing to a new stage of a single structure. / A photograph neither lies nor tells the truth. Colour is a creative element, not a trimming ... The printed surface are taken in by seeing, not by reading. The more nonsensical, the stranger and more meaningless the letter, the more useful it is to the artist. / Being an exponent of form the artist's personal task is to form. ... Clarity is the mark of our age. / Contrast is the mark of our age. / I AM TYPE. / All the old fellows stole our best ideas. / Type production has gone mad, with its senseless outpouring of new types. ... Only in degenerate times can 'Personality' (opposed to the nameless masses) become the aim of human development. / Contrast is perhaps the most important element in all modern design. / A layout man should be simply with good photography. He should perform acrobatics when the pictures are bad. / Simplicity of form is never a poverty, it is a great virtue. / Artist a noun and design is a noun and also a verb. / Typography is an art, good typography is art. / Art in any form is a projected emotion using visual tools. ... The study of typography must include a study of the meaning of 'text' / Typography fostered the modern idea of individuality but it destroyed the medieval sense of community and integration. / Type can be a tool, a toy and a teacher. / Everything under the sun is art! / Communication should be entertaining. / You read best what you read most." / In order for language to function, signs must be isolable one from another (otherwise they would not be repeatable). At every level (phonetic, semantic, syntactic, and so on) language has its own laws of combination and continuity, but its primary material is constructed of irreducible atoms (phonemes for spoken language, and for written, signs ...) ... Language is a hierarchical combination of bits."

I AM THE LEADEN ARMY THAT CONQUERS THE WORLD:

I AM TYPE

12

This is
a poster.

___Primarily it serves the purpose
of promoting a lecture on graphic
design by Angus Hyland at the
Exeter Faculty of Arts, University
of Plymouth on Friday April 28th,
2006 at 1.30pm.
___Subsequently this poster can
become a memento of the event,
an object of desire in its own right,
or it can simply be disposed of.
___Furthermore, it fulfils an
egocentric objective to be entered
into design competitions.

RYOJI IKEDA

*"'Less is more' (Mies van der Rohe).
'More is more' (David Tudor)."*

Ryoji Ikeda
info@forma.org.uk
www.ryojiikeda.com

Biography
1966 Born in Gifu, Japan
1990+ Developing artistic career as a DJ
1993–1995 Worked as an audio and visual producer
1995–2003 Member of Japanese artist collective Dumb Type

Professional experience
1996+ Through a series of solo albums "+/-" (1996), "0°C" (1998) and "matrix" (2000), Ikeda has pioneered a minimal world of electronic music. His seventh album, "dataplex", was released in 2005
1999+ Working with electronic composer/visual artist Carsten Nicolai on the collaborative project "cyclo."
2000 Created the "matrix" sound installation for the Millennium Dome, London
2000+ Using digital technologies, Ikeda has developed and toured a series of audiovisual concerts, including "formula" (2000–2006), "C4I" (2004+) and his most recent work, "datamatics" (2006+)
2001 Worked with architect Toyo Ito on the sound design for an architectural installation that tours Europe, New Zealand and Japan
2002 Ikeda's "db" installation became part of ICC's permanent collection in Tokyo
2004 Composed music for "Wear", a performance by Frankfurt Ballet choreographed by William Forsythe
2005 Exhibited a collaborative project at the Mori Art Museum, Tokyo, with the artist Hiroshi Sugimoto
2005+ Ikeda's latest project, "datamatics", is a new series of works that includes audiovisual concerts, installations and publications

Recent exhibitions/concerts
2002 "cyclo.", Architectural Association, London; "formula [ver.1.0]", La Villette, Paris
2003 "spectra II", Göteborg Biennial; "formula [ver.2.1]", Auditorium Parco della Musica, Rome
2004 "C4I", Centre Pompidou, Paris/Serralves Museum of Contemporary Art, Porto/YCAM, Yamaguchi; "spectra [for Terminal 5, JFK]", JFK Airport, New York
2005 "db", ICC, Tokyo; "data.spectra" and "spectra II", Australian Centre for the Moving Image, Melbourne
2006 "spectra II", MIT, Massachusetts; "datamatics [prototype]", Sónar, Barcelona; "formula [ver.2.3]" and "C4I", Barbican Art Gallery, London; "datamatics [prototype]", Turbine Hall, Tate Modern, London; "C4I" and "datamatics [prototype]", Tokyo International Forum

Recent awards
2001 Golden Nica Prize for digital music, Ars Electronica, Linz
2003 Shortlisted for World Technology Award, World Technology Network, New York

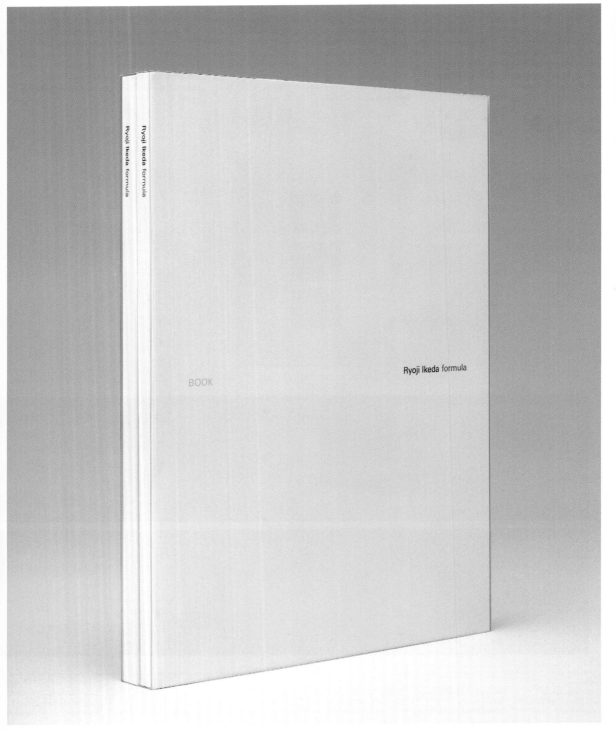

BOOK

Ryoji Ikeda formula

HIDEKI INABA

"I will do what I want to do.
I can only say that for the time being."

Hideki Inaba Design
Hanegi no mori 09
1–21–23, Hanegi, Setagaya
Tokyo 156–0042
Japan
T +81 3 332 117 66
user@hidekiinaba.com
www.hidekiinaba.com

Biography
1971 Born in Shizuoka, Japan
1993 Degree in science and
engineering, Tokai University,
Japan

Professional experience
1997 Freelance graphic
designer, Tokyo
1997–2001 Art Director,
+81 Magazine, Tokyo

1997+ Art Director,
GASBOOK series, Tokyo
2001+ Art Director, SAL
free magazine, Tokyo
2004 Art Director, Fashion
News Magazine, Tokyo;
Founded Hideki
Inaba Design

Recent exhibitions
2004 "NEWLINE", Rocket,
Tokyo/Soso, Sapporo
2005 "NEWLINE2", Trico,
Tokyo/Soso, Sapporo

Clients
+81 Magazine; Beams; GAS-
BOOK/GAS; Idn; Kenzo; Levi
Strauss; National Art Center,
Tokyo; Nike; NTT; Relax; SAL;

Shift; Sony Computer Enter-
tainment; Sony Music; United
Arrows; Victor Entertainment;
Walt Disney; Wella; WWD for
Japan

"For designers, circumstances are getting better as clients have come to realize that they need groundbreaking design and strategy to advertise their services and products. As a result, designers put their all into how they can break through to the next design stage. I think we are always wondering what we should do to surprise people. But, designers don't always have to surprise people, I think. I just don't care about what medium I choose as long as it's new and interesting and I'd like to work with clients who, hopefully, understand creativity and design."

»Die Auftragslage hat sich für Grafikdesigner verbessert, weil viele Auftraggeber inzwischen erkannt haben, dass sie bahnbrechende Werbegrafiken und Strategien brauchen, um ihre Dienstleistungen und Produkte zu vermarkten. Das hat dazu geführt, dass Grafiker sich heute mächtig ins Zeug legen, um immer innovativere Entwürfe zu kreieren. Ich glaube, wir alle fragen uns ständig, was wir tun können, um die Menschen zu überraschen. Das müssen wir aber gar nicht immer, finde ich. Mir ist egal, welches Medium ich nutze, so lange es neu und interessant ist, und ich arbeite gerne mit Kunden, die – hoffentlich – Kreativität und Design gegenüber aufgeschlossen sind.«

«La situation des graphistes s'améliore parce que les clients ont finalement compris qu'il leur fallait une stratégie et une présentation révolutionnaires pour promouvoir leurs services et leurs produits. En conséquence, les graphistes se démènent pour trouver le moyen de bouleverser les choses en place et d'avancer. Selon moi, nous sommes toujours en train de nous demander ce que nous devrions faire pour surprendre les gens. Mais je ne pense pas pour autant que les graphistes doivent tout le temps surprendre. En fait, peu m'importe le moyen d'expression que je choisis, tant qu'il est nouveau et intéressant, et j'aimerais travailler avec des clients qui comprennent ce que sont la créativité et le design. »

Previous page:
Project: *"NEWLINE"*
graphic artwork, 2004
Client: *Self*

Above:
Project: *"Relax No. 101"*
magazine artwork, 2005
Client: *Magazine House*

Following page top:
Project: *"E2-E4 2001"*
CD artwork, 2001
Client: *Electric SAL*

Following page bottom:
Project: *"NEWLINE"*
graphic artwork, 2004
Client: *Self*

NEWLINE NEWLINE NEWLINE
NEWLINE NEWLINE NEWLINE
NEWLINE NEWLINE NEWLINE
NEWLINE NEWLINE NEWLINE
NEWLINE NEWLINE NEWLINE
NEWLINE NEWLINE NEWLINE
NEWLINE NEWLINE NEWLINE
1. SOSOCAFE/札幌　NEWLINE
2. GALLERY ROCKET®/東京　E
NEWLINE NEWLINE NEWLINE
NEWLINE NEWLINE NEWLINE
NEWLINE NEWLINE NEWLINE

Atmosphere

INFORMATION

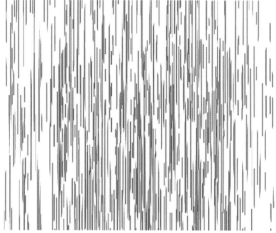

Pullin' the lun fire.
Throwin' records
out the window.
'Cause but the floor.
'Cause we don't
want 'em no more.
Burst-Helvetica

vious page left:
oject: "NEWLINE-Burst
lvetica Movie"
phic artwork sequence, 2004
ent: Self

Previous page right:
Project: *"Atmosphere 00"*
magazine design, 2002
Client: *Gas As I/F*

Above:
Project: *"NEWLINE-Burst
Helvetica"*
graphic artwork, 2004
Client: *Self*

INKAHOOTS

"Will we rise up against it,
or lay down beside it?"

Inkahoots
239 Boundary Street
West End
Queensland 4101
Australia
T +61 7 325 508 00
mail@inkahoots.com.au
www.inkahoots.com.au

Design group history
1990 Founded in Brisbane, Australia, as a community access screenprinting collective, working with unions, activists, grass roots political organisations and artists 1994+ Becomes a dedicated, multidisciplined design studio focusing on community, cultural and progressive commercial clients Partners: Robyn McDonald (b. 1958, Melbourne, Australia) and Jason Grant (b. 1971, Blenheim, New Zealand)

Clients
Anti-Discrimination Commission; Arc Biennial; Arts Queensland; Bankside Gallery; Children by Choice; Colourised Festival; Crime & Misconduct Commission; Domestic Violence Resource Centre; Eco Domo; Ecological Engineering; Family Planning Assoc.; Feral Arts; Foresters ANA; Fusions; Historic Houses Trust; Kooemba Jdarra; Legal Aid; Murriimage; Needle & Syringe Program; Queensland Community Arts Network; Queensland Prostitution Licensing Authority; Queensland Theatre Company; Raw Space Gallery; Red Connect; Social Action Office; State Library; Tenants Union; Village Twin Cinema; Youth Advocacy Centre

"Logos, Pathos, Ethos, Alliteration, Antithesis, Climax, Epizeuxis, Metanoia, Polysyndeton, Allusion, Apophasis, Conduplicatio, Eponym, Metaphor, Procatalepsis, Amplification, Aporia, Diacope, Exemplum, Metonymy, Anacoluthon, Aposiopesis, Dirimens Copulatio, Expletive, Onomatopoeia, Scesis Onomaton, Anadiplosis, Apostrophe, Distinctio, Hyperbaton, Oxymoron, Sententia, Analogy, Appositive, Enthymeme, Hyperbole, Parallelism, Simile, Anaphora, Assonance, Enumeratio, Hypophora, Parataxis, Symploce, Antanagoge, Asyndeton, Epanalepsis, Hypotaxis, Parenthesis, Synecdoche, Antimetabole, Catachresis, Epistrophe, Litotes, Personification, Understatement, Antiphrasis, Chiasmus, Epithet, Metabasis, Pleonasm, Zeugma."

»Logos, Pathos, Ethos, Alliteration, Antithese, Klimax, Epizeuxis, Metanoia, Polysndeton, Allusion, Apophasis, Conduplicatio, Eponym, Metapher, Prokatalepsis, Amplifikation, Aporia, Diakope, Exempel, Metonym, Anakoluthon, Aposiopesis, Dirimens Copulatio, Expletiv, Onomatopöie, Skesis Onomaton, Anadiplosis, Apostroph, Distinktion, Hyperbaton, Oxymoron, Sententia, Analogie, Appositiv, Enthymeme, Hyperbel, Parallelismus, Simile, Anaphora, Assonanz, Enumeratio, Hypophora, Parataxis, Symploke, Antanagogie, Asyndeton, Epanalepsis, Hypotaxis, Parenthese, Synekdoche, Antimetabolie, Katachese, Epistroph, Litotes, Personifikation, Understatement, Antiphrase, Chiasmus, Epithet, Metabasis, Pleonasmus, Zeugma.«

«Logos, Pathos, Éthique, Allitération, Antithèse, Climax, Epizeuxe, Métabole, Polysyndète, Allusion, Apophase, Conduplication, Éponyme, Métaphore, Procatalepsis, Amplification, Aporie, Diacope, Exemple, Métonymie, Anacoluthe, Aposiopèse, Dirimens Copulatio, Explétif, Onomatopée, Scesis Onomaton, Anadiplose, Apostrophe, Distinction, Hyperbate, Oxymore, Sentence, Analogie, Appositive, Enthymème, Hyperbole, Parallélisme, Simili, Anaphore, Assonance, Énumération, Hypophyge, Parataxe, Symploque, Antanaclase, Asyndète, Épanalepse, Hypotaxe, Parenthèse, Synecdoque, Antimétabole, Catachrèse, Épiphore, Litote, Personnification, Antiphrase, Chiasme, Épithète, Métabole, Pléonasme, Zeugma. »

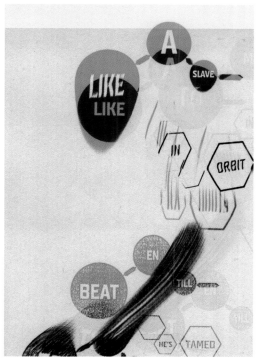

Previous page:
Project: *"Influence Series – John Berger" poster, 2006*
Client: *Red Connect/Inkahoots*

Left:
Project: *"Youth & Education 2006" theatre program/poster, 2006*
Client: *Queensland Theatre Company*

Right:
Project: *"Influence Series – Bob Dylan" poster, 2006*
Client: *Red Connect/ Inkahoots*

Following page top left:
Project:
"www.inkahoots.com.au" screen grabs from website menu that generates over 4,000 random poems/statements, 2005
Client: *Self*

Following page top right:
Project: *"Grow and Prosper" poster using official government propaganda to condemn Australia's new industrial relations and anti-terrorism legislation, 2006*
Client: *Self*

Following page bottom:
Project: *Stills from video projected artwork, 2005*
Client: *Self*

INTRO

"Style through process and development"

The Intro Partnership LLP
42 St John Street
London EC1M 4DL
UK
T +44 207 324 324 4
intro@intro-uk.com
www.introwebsite.com

Design group history
1988 Co-founded by Katy Richardson and Adrian Shaughnessy in London, England

Recent exhibitions
2004 "I See Music", ICA, London; "Communicate: Independent Graphic Design since the Sixties", Barbican Art Gallery, London
2005 "onedotzero9" film festival, ICA, London
2006 "Born Free", Victoria & Albert Museum, London; "Reflected Message", Victoria & Albert Museum, London

Recent awards
2002 Best Advertising Campaign, Insurance Times; Shortlisted for Best Designed Exhibition Catalogue, AXA Art Newspaper
2003 Best Music Video online, Interactive Music Awards; Silver Pencil for Outstanding Direction, D&AD Awards; Best TV Commercial, Music Week Creative and Design Awards
2004 Best TV Commercial, Music Week Creative and Design Awards; Yellow Pencil for Integrated Communication, D&AD Awards; Robert Horne Group Award, London Shout Award
2005 Winner, Creative Review Survey of Creativity, The Annual 2005; Shortlisted, Editorial Design Award, Design Week Awards
2006 Shortlisted, Print Design Award, Design Week Awards; Shortlisted for "The Snow Queen", British Animation Awards

Clients
ATC Management; BBC; British Council; BSkyB; Camden Arts Centre; cchm:ping; Christian Aid; Close Premium Finance; Department for Education & Skills; EMI Group; Grey London; Hawksmere; Kingstreet Tours; London Development Agency; McCann Erickson London; MTV Networks Europe; NHS Modernisation Authority; Nike; Nokia; Penguin Books; PhysioFirst; Quadrangle Consulting; Royal Academy of Music; Royal Philharmonic Orchestra; Sony BMG; SQ Productions / BBC; The National Art Collection Fund; Victoria & Albert Museum; Virgin Records; Warner Music; YO! Sushi; Young Vic Theatre Company

English Next

BRITISH COUNCIL

David Graddol

"Our approach is simple, we listen to the client, and devise a solution accordingly. As each brief is different and all clients are individuals, the resulting process generates un-formulaic design. The design process is an ongoing discourse from client to agency, and ideas grow organically, often leading to far more interesting areas than present at the initial pitch stage. Thus, we have no house style, and no off-the-shelf solutions."

»Unsere Vorgehensweise ist einfach: Wir hören uns an, was ein Auftraggeber von uns will und erarbeiten dann eine dem entsprechende Lösung. Da jeder Auftrag und jeder Kunde verschieden sind, entstehen stets individuelle Designs. Der Entwurfsprozess vollzieht sich im ständigen Dialog zwischen dem Auftraggeber und der Agentur. Die Ideen wachsen organisch und führen uns oft in viele interessante Bereiche, die am Anfang gar nicht absehbar waren. Deshalb haben wir keinen spezifischen Designstil und bieten auch keine vorgefertigten Lösungen.«

«Notre façon de travailler est très simple : nous écoutons le client et nous lui trouvons une solution. Chaque dossier étant différent et tous les clients étant des individus, le processus créatif qui est alors lancé génère un graphisme qui n'obéit à aucune formule mais au rythme du dialogue qui s'instaure entre le client et l'agence. Les idées germent de façon organique et nous emmènent souvent dans des sphères plus intéressantes que ce qui était prévu dans la présentation initiale. Voilà pourquoi nous n'avons ni style maison, ni solutions toutes faites. »

Previous page:
Project: *"English Next"* booklet, *2006*
Client: *British Council*

Above left:
Project: *"Pan Gasol"* basketball retail campaign, *2005*
Client: *Nike EMEA*

Above right:
Project: *"Lebron James"* basketball retail campaign, *2005*
Client: *Nike EMEA*

Following page:
Project: *"Kobe Bryant"* basketball retail campaign, *2005*
Client: *Nike EMEA*

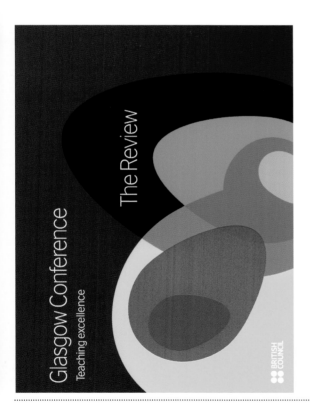

Top left:
Project: "Broadcast: Tender Buttons" CD cover, 2006
Client: Warp Records

Centre right:
Project: "Camden Arts Centre" courses leaflet, 2006
Client: Camden Arts Centre

Above:
Project: "Glasgow Conference" souvenir booklet, 2004
Client: British Council

Following page top:
Project: "Bath International Music Festival 06" poster, 2006
Client: Bath International Music Festival

Following page bottom:
Project: "10th Anniversary Festival" title sequence, 2006
Client: onedotzero

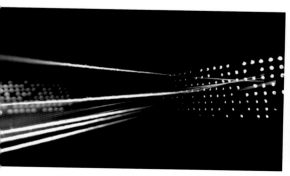

KESSELS-KRAMER

*"Just be honest.
Is it something you really like?"*

KesselsKramer
Lauriergracht 39
1016 RG Amsterdam
The Netherlands
T + 31 20 530 106 0
church@kesselskramer.com
www.kesselskramer.com

Design group history
1996 Co-founded by Erik Kessels and Johan Kramer in Amsterdam, The Netherlands
1997 Matthijs de Jongh joined as Strategy Director; Pieter Leendertse joined as Production Director
1998 Engin Celikbas joined as Managing Director
1996 Tyler Whisnand (b. 1968) joined as Creative Director
1996 Dave Bell (b. 1970) joined, becoming Creative Director in 2001

2006/07 "KK outlet: 10 years of KesselsKramer's work on show" exhibition at the Kunsthal Rotterdam

Founders' biographies
Erik Kessels
1966 Born in The Netherlands
1983–1986 Trained at St Lucas Technical College, Boxtel
1986–1991 Art Director, Ogilvy & Mather, Eindhoven and Amsterdam
1991–1993 Art Director, Lowe, Kuiper & Schouten, Amsterdam
1994 Art Director, Chiat Day, London
1995 Art Director, GGT, London
1996 Co-founder, Kessels-Kramer, Amsterdam
Johan Kramer
1964 Born in Utrecht, The Netherlands
1979/80 Butcher Trade School, Brunswick, Germany
1980–1982 Studied at Ozu Film School, Bombay
1984–1986 Copywriter, FHV/BBDO, Amsterdam
1986–1991 Copywriter, PMSvW/Young & Rubicam, Amsterdam
1994 Copywriter, Chiat Day, London
1995 Copywriter, GGT, London
1996 Co-founder, Kessels-Kramer, Amsterdam
2005 Left KesselsKramer

Clients
Absolut Vodka; AllAbout.co.jp; Amsterdam Uit Buro; Bavaria Beer; Britvic; The Hans Brinker Budget Hotel, Amsterdam; Hier climate project; I amsterdam; Ilse.com; MTV Japan; Reaal Insurance; Shampoo Planet; SNS Bank; Trussardi; Unilever; United Biscuits

WOMEN inc.

300 vrouwen met lef – 24 en 25 september 2005
Beurs van Berlage Amsterdam – www.women-inc.nl
theater, debat, muziek, speeddating, documentaire, workshop, lezing, feest, film, fotografie

"So many tools and devices to choose from in order to design your poster campaign or house style or end title or website. But where is the idea? Do you have a compelling rationale behind that super cool typeface? Is the dynamic logo and exploding tagline really the best choice for a brand of cookies? Maybe it is. Nobody knows better than you. And you should listen to yourself, to your doubts and your sense of reality. Take the time to be honest and realistic, only then you will be more relevant and understandable. Most often these days, ideas get lost in the kerning."

»Es gibt ein Riesenangebot an Programmen und Anwendungen, mit denen du die neue Plakatkampagne oder den Hausstil, einen Abspann oder ein Internetportal gestalten könntest. Aber wo ist die zündende Idee? Hast du die zwingende Logik für deine supercoole Schrifttype? Sind das dynamische Logo und der auffällige Werbeslogan wirklich die beste Lösung für diese bestimmte Sorte von Keksen? Vielleicht nicht. Niemand weiß das besser als du. Und du solltest auf dich selbst hören, auf deine Zweifel und dein Gefühl für Realität. Nimm dir Zeit, ehrlich und realistisch zu sein, denn nur dann wirst du auch relevant und verständlich sein. Nur allzu oft verlieren sich Ideen heutzutage in Unterschneidungen.«

«Il y a tant d'outils et d'instruments parmi lesquels choisir pour concevoir une campagne d'affichage, un style de déco, un gros titre, ou un site Internet. Mais l'idée, où se trouve-t-elle? Existe-t-il un exposé raisonné et implacable derrière cette police super cool? Le logo dynamique et la ligne d'accroche explosive sont-ils la meilleure option pour une marque de biscuits? Peut-être bien. Personne ne le sait mieux que toi. Et tu devrais t'écouter, écouter tes doutes et ton sens des réalités. Prends le temps d'être honnête et réaliste; ce n'est qu'alors que tu seras plus pertinent et compréhensible. Le plus souvent, ces temps-ci, les idées se perdent dans le crénage.»

SCOTT KING

"I keep trying, because I can't do anything else."

Scott King
c/o Herald Street Gallery
2 Herald Street
London E2 6JT
UK
T +44 208 980 396 8
info@scottking.co.uk
www.scottking.co.uk

Biography
1969 Born in East Yorkshire, England
1988–1992 Studied graphic design, University of Hull

Professional experience
1993–1996 Art Director, i-D Magazine, London
2001/02 Creative Director, Sleazenation magazine, London

Recent exhibitions
2005 "Other People's Projects", White Columns, New York; "Regarding Terror: The RAF Exhibition", Kunst-Werke, Berlin/Neue Galerie, Graz; "Herald Street & The Modern Institute", GBE, New York; "Inaugral", Herald Street, London; "Art Statements", Galleria Sonia Rosso, Basle; "Bridge Freezes Before Road", Barbara Gladstone Gallery, New York; "So klappt's/Modelle des Gelingens", Künstlerhaus Mousonturm", Frankfurt; "Post No Bills", White Columns, New York; "What Now?/Et maintenant?", CRAC Alsace, Altkirch; "Lee Brilleaux Memorial Bench", White Columns, New York
2006 "And On To The Discotheque Comrade?", Centre d'Art Contemporain, Fribourg; "Oh! Pylon Heaven", Galleria Sonia Rosso, Turin; "Objects of Yesterday and Today", Gallery Édouard Manet, Gennevilliers; "Information", Bortolami Dayan, New York; "And The Pylons Stretched For Miles", Herald Street, London; "Che Guevara: Revolutionary and Icon", Victoria & Albert Museum, London; "Defamation of Character", PS 1, New York; "Conversation Pieces", Centre d'Art Contemporain Genéve, Geneva; "People", Museo d'Arte Contemporanea Donna Regina, Naples

Recent awards
2002 Nomination for Sleazenation magazine cover, D&AD

Clients
Benetton; Earl Brutus (Island Records); Diesel; Institute of Contemporary Arts, London; Malcolm McLaren; The Michael Clark Dance Company; Morrissey (Sanctuary Records); Pet Shop Boys (Parlophone); Selfridges; Sleazenation; Smirnoff; Sony Music UK; Suicide; Suizide (Blast Fist)

VOGUE

AUG

6

**EXPERT TIPS
ON HOW
TO GET THAT
TALIBAN LOOK
THIS SUMMER**

Scott King 193

"My approach has always been to try and 'use' graphic design (as opposed to trying to 'do' graphic design). For the last five years, I've tried to use it to make art. Sometimes this makes sense and it works; sometimes I feel trapped by what I know about graphic design. I still use the tools of graphic design, but the context within which my work is presented is different. Now I make a version of what I did before, with similar internal concerns: those of the reduction of a language. Ultimately, it means I don't usually have to speak to anyone in 'marketing', which is all I ever wanted really."

»Ich versuche immer, Grafikdesign zu ›nutzen‹ statt zu ›machen‹. In den letzten fünf Jahren habe ich mich bemüht, Kunst zu schaffen. Mitunter macht das Sinn und funktioniert, aber manchmal fühle ich mich in meinem Wissen über Grafikdesign gefangen. Ich verwende immer noch die gleichen Werkzeuge wie beim Grafikdesign, präsentiere meine Arbeiten aber inzwischen in einem anderen Kontext. In Abwandlungen mache ich das Gleiche wie früher, mit der gleichen Intention: die Bild- und Formensprache zu reduzieren. Letztlich bedeutet das, dass ich in den meisten Fällen mit niemandem vom ›Marketing‹ mehr sprechen muss. Und das ist es, was ich mir schon immer gewünscht habe.«

«J'ai toujours essayé d''utiliser' le graphisme (par opposition à essayer de 'faire' du graphisme). Ces cinq dernières années, j'ai essayé de l'utiliser pour faire de l'art. Parfois ma démarche est sensée et elle fonctionne; parfois je me sens pris au piège par ce que je sais du graphisme. J'utilise encore les outils de création graphique mais le contexte dans lequel mon travail est présenté est différent. Je réalise aujourd'hui une variation de ce que je faisais dans le passé, autour des mêmes interrogations: celles qui concernent la réduction d'un langage. Au bout du compte, ça signifie surtout que je n'ai plus besoin de parler à des gens du 'marketing', ce qui est en fait ce que j'ai toujours voulu.»

Page 193:
Project: "How I'd Sink Vogue"
graphic art work, 2007
Client: Self

Previous page left:
Project: "Never Trust a Hippie"
letterpress print, 2005
Client: Bortolami Dayan

Previous page right:
Project: "The Oppressed"
exhibition installation, 2006
Client: Galleria Sonia Rosso

Above (all images):
Project: "Stalky" photocopies
(4 from a series of 12), 2006
Client: Galleria Sonia Rosso

CHRISTIAN KÜSTERS

"Collaboration + context + concept = visual communication = CHK"

CHK Design
8 Flitcroft Street
London WC2H 8DL
UK
T +44 207 836 200 7
mail@chkdesign.com
www.chkdesign.com

Biography
1966 Born in Oberhausen, Germany
1993 BA (Hons) Graphic Design, London College of Printing
1995 MFA, Yale University School of Art, New Haven
1996 Research trip to Tokyo (Yale University Travel Fellowship)

Professional experience
1993 Lecturer at Yale School of Art, New Haven/Central Saint Martins College of Art & Design, London/Antwerp Citype conference/London College of Printing/Camberwell College of Arts, London
1995 Founded CHK Design, London
1996 Founded Acme Fonts (Digital Typefoundry), London
1997 Art Director and designer, Booth-Clibborn Editions, London
1998 Art Director and designer, Black Dog Publishing, London
1999–2006 Art Director, AD Architectural Design magazine, London
2002 Co-curated and co-designed "Design Now – Graphics", Design Museum, London
2002+ Art Director, MAKE magazine, London
2004+ Art Director, Miser & Now magazine, London

Recent exhibitions
2005 "Making History: LCC and the School of Graphic Design", London College of Communication
2006 "Spoken with Eyes", Sacramento Art Directors and Artists Club, Davis Design Museum, University of California, Sacramento

Clients
Academy Editions; Alexander McQueen; Architectural Association; Black Dog Publishing; Booth-Clibborn Editions; Design Museum London; Football World Cup; Institute of Contemporary Arts; Laurent Delaye Gallery; Milch Gallery; Museum für Gegenwartskunst, Zurich; Open; Sergison Bates; Thames & Hudson; Vespa; Yale School of Architecture

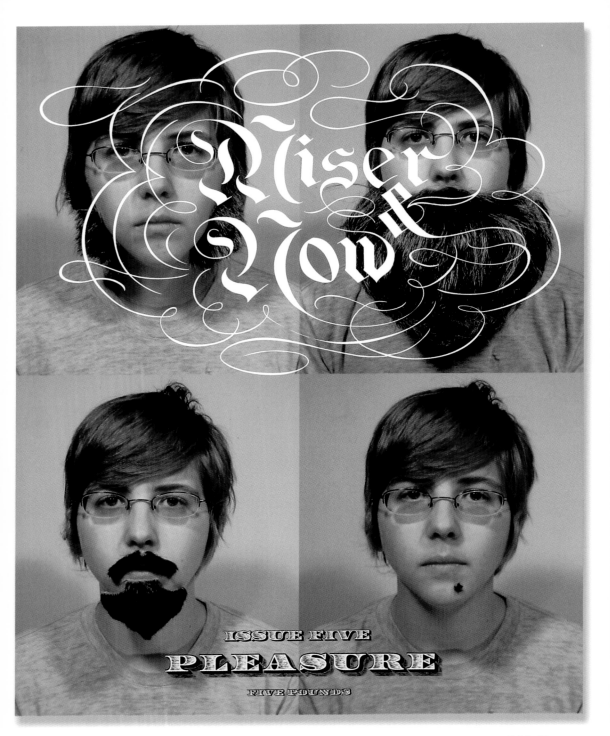

Miser Now

ISSUE FIVE
PLEASURE
FIVE POUNDS

"Graphic Design is a collaborative effort. One needs to make the most of this by learning from all those involved in the different aspects of any particular project. It is necessary to look at a project and ask questions about its context. Where is it coming from (similar to the way some architects work, visual communicators should analyse the given parameters of a project and then react to them and work with them as a tool or concept) and, to some extent, where is it going? These parameters help in learning and adapting different ways of working as well as clarifying one's own position. In an ideal world, this would result in a completely new way of working – conceptually as well as visually. Practically, however, that hardly ever happens. If it does, it is very hard work – but well worth it. The result is (at its best) a new and surprising way of communication."

»Grafikdesign ist eine Gemeinschaftsarbeit. Man muss das Beste daraus machen, indem man von allen lernt, die an den verschiedenen Aspekten eines Projekts beteiligt sind. Man muss sich einen Auftrag anschauen und Fragen zum Kontext stellen. Woher kommt er? (Ähnlich wie ein Architekt sollte der ›visuelle Kommunikator‹ die vorgegebenen Parameter eines Projekts analysieren, um dann darauf einzugehen und sie als Werkzeuge oder Konzepte zu verwenden.) Und – bis zu einem gewissen Grad – wohin führt der Auftrag? Durch die Antwort auf diese Fragen lernt man dazu, kann seine Arbeitsweise verändern und die eigene Position klären. In einer idealen Welt würde das zu einer – konzeptionell wie visuell – ganz neuen Arbeitsweise führen. In der Praxis passiert das allerdings kaum. Wenn doch, ist das harte Arbeit, die sich aber lohnt. Das Ergebnis ist (bestenfalls) eine neue und überraschende Art der Kommunikation.«

« La création graphique est un effort collectif. Il faut profiter de ce travail pour apprendre autant de choses que possible de tous les autres acteurs impliqués dans les différentes étapes de chaque projet. Il est capital de bien regarder le projet et de poser des questions sur son contexte. D'où vient-il (comme le font certains architectes, les responsables de la communication visuelle devraient analyser les paramètres imposés d'un projet puis y réagir en les utilisant comme outils ou comme concepts) et, dans une certaine mesure, où va-t-il ? Ces paramètres aident à apprendre et à adapter différentes méthodes de travail ainsi qu'à clarifier sa propre position. Dans un monde parfait, cette méthodologie devrait déboucher sur une toute nouvelle façon de travailler – aussi bien conceptuellement que visuellement. Dans la pratique, cependant, ça n'arrive que rarement. Si c'est le cas, c'est au prix d'un dur labeur – mais qui en vaut la peine. Ce qui en résulte est (au mieux) une manière nouvelle et surprenante de communiquer. »

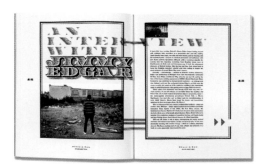

Previous page:
Project: *"Miser & Now – issue 5" magazine cover*, 2005
Client: *Keith Talent Gallery*

Top (both images):
Project: *"Miser & Now – issue 5" magazine spreads*, 2005
Client: *Keith Talent Gallery*

Above (both images):
Project: *"Miser & Now – issue 1" magazine spreads*, 2003
Client: *Keith Talent Gallery*

Following page (all images):
Project: *"Architectural Environments" campaign*, 2004
Client: *Sony Playstation*

JÜRG LEHNI

"Join the effort!"

Jürg Lehni
Agnesstr. 28
8004 Zurich
Switzerland
T +41 76 332 007 7
juerg@scratchdisk.com
www.scratchdisk.com

Biography
1978 Born in Lucerne, Switzerland
1998 Department of Information Technology and Electrical Engineering, Swiss Federal Institute of Technology Zurich (ETH)
1999–2002 Studied interaction design & new media at Hyper-Werk in Basel and the School of Art and Design in Lausanne (ECAL)
2002–2004 Postgraduate studies at the School of Art and Design in Lausanne (ECAL)
2002–2006 Independent designer/artist in Zurich
2006+ Designer, Sony SET Concept Laboratory in Tokyo

Recent exhibitions
2001 "Kunst 2000", Zurich; "Stealing Eyeballs", Künstlerhaus, Vienna
2002 "Viper 02", Basel; "Transmediale 02", Berlin; "Claude Monet bis zum digitalen Impressionismus", Fondation Beyeler, Basel
2003 "Mursolaici", Centre Culturel Suisse, Paris; "Robotergestützter Graffitikurs, Lektion 1–4", Galerie Wieland, Berlin; "Signes des Écoles d'art", Centre Pompidou, Paris; "Lee 3 Tau Ceti Central Armory Show", Villa Arson, Nice; "Tourette's II", Gallery W139, Amsterdam
2004 "Fresh Type", Museum für Gestaltung, Zurich; "When Robots Draw", Kunstmuseum, Solothurn; "Work from Switzerland / Czech Republic 21st International Biennale of Graphic Design", The Moravian Gallery, Brno; "Detox", Kunsthall, Bergen (Hektor)
2005 "Detox", Kunstnernes Hus, Oslo; "You Are Here", Design Museum, London; "Rita + Hektor", Tensta Konsthall, Stockholm; "Generator.x", Kunsthallen, The National Museum of Art, Architecture and Design, Oslo
2006 "Landscape/Portrait", Information Gallery, Tokyo; "Autoportrait", By Trico, Fukuoka, Japan; "Work from Mars / Czech Republic 22nd International Biennale of Graphic Design", The Moravian Gallery, Brno

Recent awards
2000 Work grant of the City and Canton of Lucerne
2001 Award, Swiss Federal Competition of Design; Award, New Talent Competition, Milia 2001
2003 Award, Swiss Federal Competition of Design
2005 Award, Sitemapping.ch project grant
2006 Award, Swiss Federal Competition of Design

Clients
Sony

"Although my main background is computer programming, I primarily work within the field of design. My self-initiated work originates from reflections about tools, the computer and the way we work with and adapt to technology. I like the results of technology failing or not being able to keep up with its promises. The first generation of affordable personal computers was very promising, bringing a vast amount of possibilities for exploration and play into the living room, while remaining easy to understand and manageable. Computers like the Commodore VC-20 or the C-64 had a strong influence on me when I was younger. I learned to program computers early. Later I studied electronic engineering at the ETH in Zurich before I changed direction and a few transitions later ended up at a proper art school: ÉCAL (École Cantonale d'Art de Lausanne). I often work together with people from other backgrounds: graphic designers, artists, typographers and engineers. These collaborations are very inspiring and facilitate projects that would not be possible by only focusing on a topic on my own."

»Ich bin zwar gelernter Programmierer, arbeite aber hauptsächlich im Bereich Design. Meine eigenen Projekte entwickeln sich aus meinem Nachdenken über Programmanwendungen, den Computer und die Art und Weise, in der wir mit Technik arbeiten und uns ihrer bedienen. Die erste Generation kostengünstiger PCs war äußerst vielversprechend und brachte vielfältige Möglichkeiten der Informationsbeschaffung und Computerspiele in die Wohnzimmer, blieb dabei aber verständlich und leicht zu bedienen. Computer wie der Commodore VC-20 oder C-64 haben mich in jungen Jahren stark geprägt. Schon früh lernte ich zu programmieren. Später studierte ich Elektronik an der ETH Zürich, bevor ich umsattelte und etliche Stadien später in einer richtigen Kunstakademie landete, der École Cantonale d'Art de Lausanne (ÉCAL). Oft arbeite ich mit anderen Fachleuten zusammen – Grafikern, Künstlern, Typografen, Ingenieuren. Das ist immer sehr anregend und erleichtert die Erarbeitung von Projekten, die nicht realisierbar wären, wenn ich mich nur auf mein eigenes Thema konzentrieren würde.«

«Bien que je sois particulièrement compétent en matière de programmation informatique, je travaille principalement dans le domaine du design. Mon travail personnel prend sa source de réflexions sur les outils, l'ordinateur et la manière dont nous travaillons avec la technologie et dont nous nous adaptons à elle. J'aime ce que ça donne quand la technologie a des ratés ou ne parvient pas à tenir ses promesses. La première génération d'ordinateurs personnels à un prix abordable était très prometteuse et ouvrait un vaste champ de possibilités ludiques tout en restant accessible et maniable. Des ordinateurs comme le Commodore VC-20 ou le C-64 ont eu une grande importance pour moi quand j'étais plus jeune. J'ai appris à programmer des ordinateurs très tôt. Plus tard, j'ai étudié l'ingénierie électronique à l'ETH de Zurich avant de bifurquer, et quelques virages plus tard je me suis retrouvé dans une vraie école d'art: l'ÉCAL (École Cantonale de Lausanne). Je travaille souvent avec des gens d'horizons différents: des graphistes, des artistes, des typographes et des ingénieurs. Ces collaborations sont très stimulantes et facilitent l'accomplissement de projets que je n'aurais pas su mener à bien dans mon coin.»

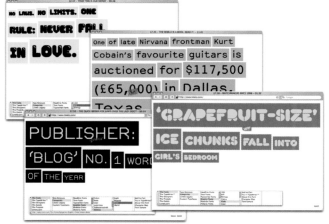

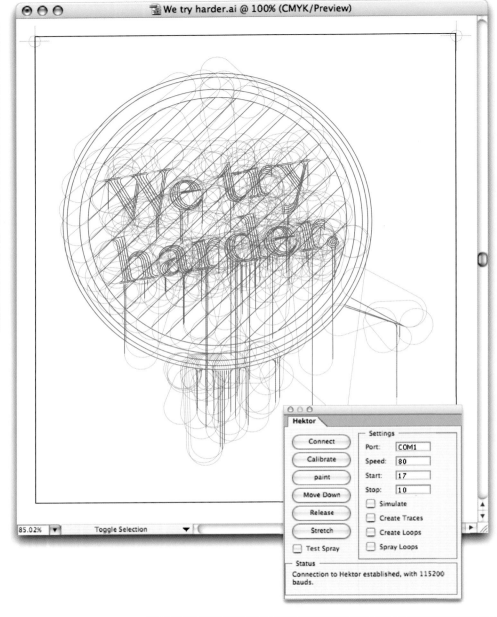

85.02% ▼ Toggle Selection ▼

Hektor

Connect
Calibrate
paint
Move Down
Release
Stretch
☐ Test Spray

Settings
Port: COM1
Speed: 80
Start: 17
Stop: 10
☐ Simulate
☐ Create Traces
☐ Create Loops
☐ Spray Loops

Status
Connection to Hektor established, with 115200 bauds.

Page 201:
Project: *I. D. Magazine cover showing the use of the "Hektor Interface", a spray-paint output device for computers, 2004*
Client: *I. D. Magazine*

Previous page left:
Project: *Examples of automatically rendered type specimens for which text is dynamically drawn from various online sources and databases, 2004*
Client: *Lineto.com*

Previous page right:
Project: *"The+TypeWriter" online design application embedded in the Lineto.com website, that lets visitors try out fonts, create designs and send the results by email, 2004*
Client: *Lineto.com*

Above:
Project: *"Hektor" motion paths for the wall-painting "We Try Harder", automatically calculated by Hektor's software (based on Scriptographer.com, a scripting plugin for Illustrator). Realized using "Hektor",*

"We Try Harder" was Cornel Windlin's contribution to the "Public Affairs" exhibition, Kunsthaus Zurich, 2002
Client: *Self*

TOMMY LI

"Chinese people need more humour."

Tommy Li
Design Workshop Ltd
Room 2401, Honour Centre
6 Sun Yip Street
Chai Wan
Hong Kong
T +852 283 463 12
info@tommylidesign.com
www.tommylidesign.com

Founder's biography

1960 Born in Hong Kong
1983 Diploma of Graphic Design, Hong Kong Polytechnic
1990 Founded the Tommy Li Design Workshop Ltd, Hong Kong

Recent exhibitions

2002 "Superwoman", Hong Kong Poster League Episode II; "HKDA 02 Poster Biennial", Hong Kong; "The Living Heritage" poster exhibition, Hong Kong; Shenzhen CIS Poster Exhibition, Shenzhen
2003 "No War" Invitational Poster Art Exhibition, Shenzhen; "5th Bienal de Design de Macau – Judges Exhibition", Macau; "Tianjin Invitational Poster Exhibition", Tianjin; "China International Poster Biennial", Hangzhou; "Taipei International Poster Exhibition", Taipei; "15th Hong Kong Print Awards Exhibition", Hong Kong; "Bad – Tommy Li Poster Decode", Guangzhou; "HKDA 03 Members Show", Hong Kong
2004 "Insideout 8" Designers' Show, Hong Kong; "Igniting the Flame: 40 Years of Design@PolyU", Hong Kong; "10th National Art Invitational Exhibition", China; "Building Hong Kong redwhiteblue", Design Infinity Exhibition Series 4, Hong Kong; "3rd International Poster Biennial", Ningbo; "1st Shenzhen International Cultural Industry Fair", Shenzhen; "Design aGain", HKDA 04 Members Show, Hong Kong; "Reading is…" Invitational Poster Exhibition, Hong Kong; "Hong Kong International Poster Triennial", Hong Kong
2005 "Hong Kong Good Dong Xi" Invitational Poster Exhibition, Hong Kong; Hebei; Hong Kong Week Exhibition, Hebei; "Black & White", MTR ART-tube, Hong Kong; "In China" joint exhibition, Shenzhen
2006 "Supertrader: Hong Kong, 40 Years of Trade", Hong Kong Convention and Exhibition Centre; "Hong Kong Designers Association Members Show", One IFC & Taikoo Place, Hong Kong

Recent awards

2001 Gold Award (x2), New York Art Directors Club; Gold Award (x3) and Excellence Award (x4), Asia Graphics Awards
2002 Award (x48), 2nd International Chinese Graphic Design Competition; Excellence Award (x2), Tokyo Type Directors Club
2003 Judges Award, Shenzhen 03 Show, Shenzhen
2004 "Outstanding Alumni", Hong Kong Polytechnic University
2005 Gold Award, Hong Kong Print Awards; Judges Award, HKDA 05 Awards; 2005 Distinguished Designs from China, Hong Kong Design Centre
2006 Distinctive Merit, New York Art Directors Club; Merit, Hong Kong Print Awards

Clients

Art Promotion Office; Beijing Aquarium; Beijing Jefen Fashion Design; Casablanca Disco & KTV, Delhi; China International Marina Club; China Motion Telecom Development; Chinoiserie, Singapore; Chow Sang Sang Holdings International; Cinta Rasa Sayang Hotel; Coca-Cola; Culture Club, Singapore; Ebony Videotheque, Indonesia; Fu Gar International; Guangzhou Antin Cosmetics; Hilton Hotel; Honeymoon Dessert Limited; Hong Kong (Chek Lap Kok) International Airport; Hong Kong Design Centre; Hong Kong Dragonair Airlines; Hong Kong Post Office; Hong Kong Telecom CSL; Inspiring Fascination; J. J. Mohoney's Disco; Jun & Peace; Konew Financial Express; Kowloon Canton Railway; Ma Belle Jewelry Boutique; Maxim's Caterers; Mayland Group; Metro Broadcast Corporation; Metro Publishing HK; Mr. Li Peking Cuisine; MTR; One2Free Personal Communications; PCC Skyhorse; Plant International Beauty Holdings; Queen Plaza Hotel, Toronto; Queens Konditorei; Red Apple Furniture; Red Taps International; Sanli International Garment Co.; Smartone; Sociedade De Turismo E Diversoes De Macau; Startillate TV; Wai Yuen Tong Medicine; Zhuhai Yesterday Time

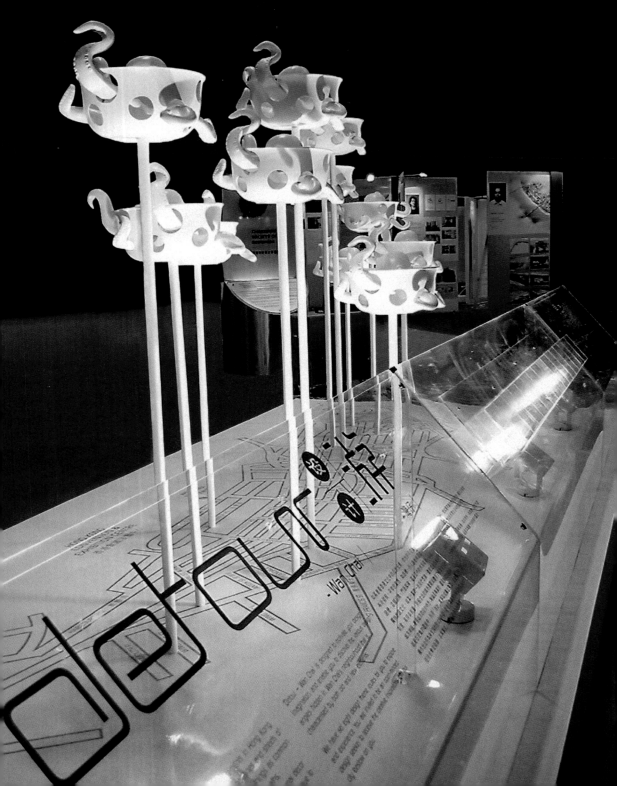

"With regard to the manner and style of graphic design, the main difference between Hong Kong and China is that the latter's output is too heavily stressed, too serious, too corporate, too political. High-quality, original design does not come easily. My approach, 'More Humour: More Impact', sounds at first playful, free and easy. But, if you study carefully, some serious and important messages and concepts can be found. I believe concepts are very important, sometimes even more than the techniques in design."

»Was Art und Stil des Grafikdesigns angeht, so liegt der Hauptunterschied zwischen Hong Kong und China darin, dass die Arbeiten aus China mit zu viel Nachdruck und Ernsthaftigkeit gestaltet und allzusehr auf Industriekonzerne und Politik ausgerichtet sind. Qualitätvolles originelles Design kommt nicht von ungefähr. Mein Motto: ›mehr Humor, mehr Wirkung‹ klingt zunächst spielerisch, frei und leicht. Wenn man aber näher hinschaut, kann man einige ernsthafte und wichtige Botschaften und Konzepte entdecken. Ich halte Konzepte für sehr wichtig, manchmal sogar für wichtiger als die Technik des Entwerfens.«

«Concernant le style et la manière de la création graphique, la principale différence entre Hong Kong et la Chine est que la production chinoise est trop lourdement accentuée, trop sérieuse, trop institutionnelle, trop politique. La qualité et l'originalité graphique ne viennent pas tout seuls. Ma devise, 'plus d'humour, plus d'impact', peut sembler badine, gratuite et facile, mais à y regarder de plus près, elle peut aussi être porteuse de messages et de concepts importants, parfois même davantage que les techniques graphiques.»

Previous page:
Project: *"Detour – Wan Chai"*
exhibition installation, 2004
Client: *Hong Kong Design Centre*

Above:
Project: *"Handmade Dessert"*
designs for eating utensils, 2002
Client: *Handmade Dessert Limited*

Following page top:
Project: *"Heromoism"*
poster, 2005
Client: *Tommy Li Solo Exhibition@MTR ARTtube*

Following page bottom:
Project: *"Handmade Dessert"*
business cards, 2002
Client: *Handmade Dessert Limited*

LUST

"Although we are technically Generation X, we feel more part of Generation Random."

LUST
Dunne Bierkade 17
2512 BC The Hague
The Netherlands
T +31 70 363 577 6
lust@lust.nl
www.lust.nl

Design group history
1996 Co-founded by Jeroen Barendse and Thomas Castro in Utrecht, The Netherlands
1999 Dimitri Nieuwenhuizen joined as a partner
2000 LUST moved into the historical house of the Dutch master Paulus Potter in The Hague
2005 Research Fellowship at Leeds Metropolitan University, LSx Leeds Unknown project

Founders' biographies
Jeroen Barendse
1973 Born in Poeldijk, The Netherlands
1991–1993 Studied graphic design, Academy of Arts, Utrecht
1993–1995 Studied graphic design, Academy of Arts, Arnhem

1998/99 Involved with Werkplaats Typografie, Arnhem
1999+ Lecturer in graphic design, Academy of Arts, Arnhem
Thomas Castro
1967 Born in Queson City, Philippines
1987–1990 Studied psychology and fine art, University of California
1991–1993 Studied graphic design, Academy of Arts, Utrecht
1993–1995 Studied graphic design, Academy of Arts, Arnhem
1995–1996 Worked for the Barlock design company, The Hague
2002+ Lecturer in graphic design, Academy of Arts, Arnhem
2003+ Member of the Commission for Design, Nether-

lands Foundation for Visual Arts, Design and Architecture
Dimitri Nieuwenhuizen
1971 Born in Bergen op Zoom, The Netherlands
1991–1993 Studied industrial design, Delft University of Technology
1993–1997 Studied man and activity, Design Academy, Eindhoven
1996 Founded Studio ZOAB
2003+ Lecturer in Interaction Design, Academy of Arts, Utrecht

Recent exhibitions
2002 "On Track", NAi, Rotterdam
2003 "Presentation Atelier HSL, Architecture Biennale Rotterdam", NAi, Rotterdam
2004 "Artworks", Buitenhof 37, The Hague; "Innovative Communication Experience",

Gallery 90SQM, Amsterdam; "Best Dutch Book Designs Exhibition", Stedelijk Museum, Amsterdam; "Inbetween", OAP, NAi, Rotterdam
2005 "Look Right, (Look Left)", Leeds Metropolitan University; "Dutch Resource", International Poster Exhibition, Chaumont; "Halte Brussel (Trainstop Brussels)", Brussels
2006 "Interactivity 06", The Hague; "Look Left, Look Right", Leeds; "Unknown Territory", Leeds
2007 "Generation Random", solo exhibition, The Hague; "Post More Bills", Los Angeles

Recent awards
2003 Best Dutch Book Design Award, Foundation Best Designed Books, Amsterdam

2004 Award of Excellence, 10th Annual Interactive Exhibition, Communication Arts; Winner, Exhibition and Experience Design, Dutch Designprijzen, Amsterdam
2005 Best Annual Report Design, Grafische Cultuurstichting, Amstelveen

Clients
Atelier HSL; Episode Publishers; Huis Marseille: Foundation for Photography; Leeds Metropolitan University; LOOS; Museum Boijmans van Beuningen, Rotterdam; Pages Magazine; Palmboom & Van den Bout; Stimuleringsfonds voor Architectuur; Stroom Den Haag; TodaysArt; TPG Post; TU Delft; VU

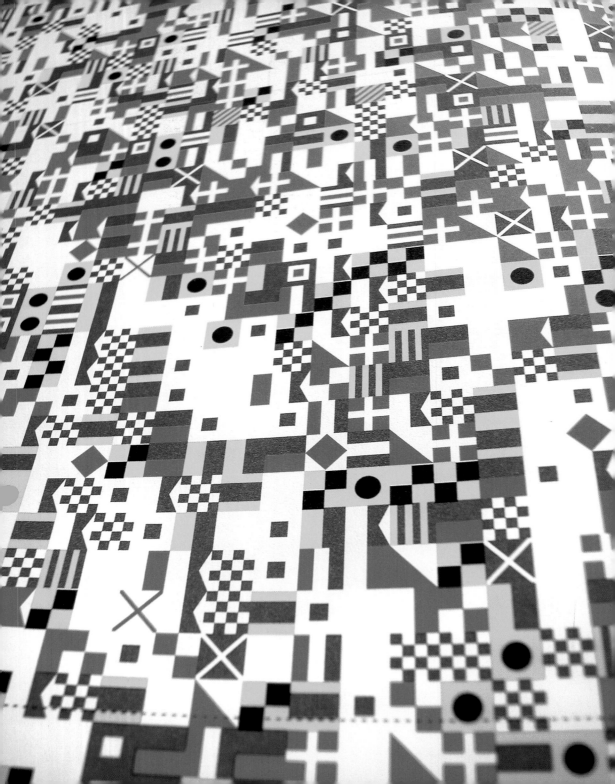

"LUST is a graphic practice that tries to map out new terrains for graphic design, for software, and for new audiences. LUST works in a variety of media, including printed materials, interactive installations and architectural graphics. LUST considers design as a process. Each design stems from a concept that results from extensive research. In the course of its existence, LUST has developed a design methodology described as process-based or generative-systems based. This entails developing an analytical process which ultimately leads to something that designs itself."

»Das Grafikbüro LUST versucht für das Grafik-design, für Software-Programme und für deren Benutzer neue Anwendungsgebiete zu erschließen. LUST arbeitet mit verschiedenen Medien, unter anderem mit Druckerzeugnissen, interaktiven Instal-lationen und Architekturzeichnungen. LUST fasst Design als Prozess auf. Jeder Entwurf wird nach einem auf gründlichen Recherchen beruhenden Kon-zept entwickelt. Im Lauf seiner Tätigkeit hat LUST eine Designmethode entwickelt, die man als prozess-orientiert oder als generativ bezeichnen kann. Dazu gehört ein analytischer Vorgang, aus dem letzten Endes etwas entsteht, das sich selbst gestaltet.«

«LUST est un bureau de création graphique qui tente de cartographier de nouveaux territoires pour le graphisme, les logiciels et de nouveaux publics. LUST travaille dans un grand nombre de disciplines, notam-ment imprimés, installations interactives ou représen-tations graphiques architecturales. LUST considère le graphisme comme un procédé. Chaque création tire son origine d'un concept, lui-même né de recherches approfondies. Au cours de son existence, LUST a déve-loppé une méthodologie du graphisme fondée sur le procédé ou sur les systèmes génératifs. Elle exige de développer une méthode analytique qui finit par donner un objet artistiquement autonome.»

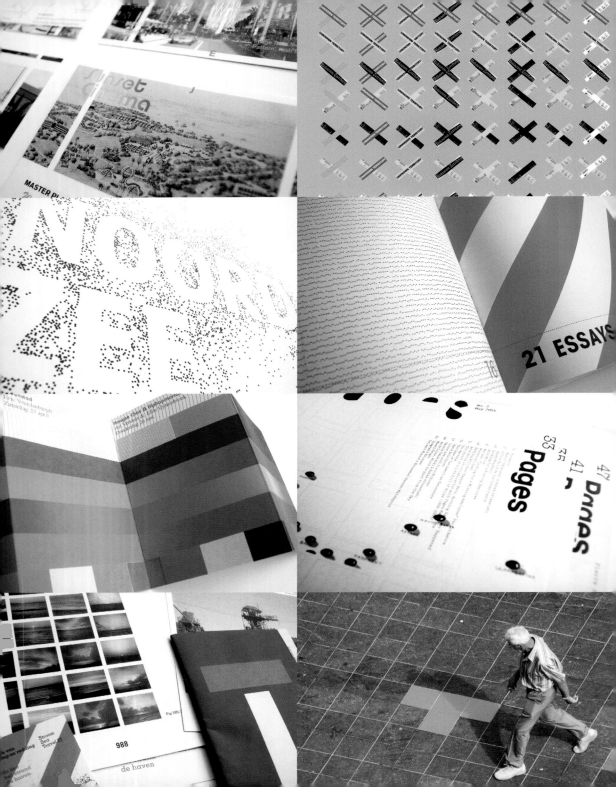

M-A-D

"Design is what matters most during the creative process and what matters least at the finish."

M-A-D
237 San Carlos Ave
Sausalito, CA 94965
USA
T +1 415 331 102 3
info@madxs.com
www.madxs.com

Design group history
1989 Co-founded by Erik Adigard and Patricia McShane in Sausalito, California, USA

Founders' biographies
Erik Adigard
1953 Born in San Francisco, USA
1976–1979 Studied communication, semiotics and fine art, France
1987 B. F. A. Graphic Design, California College of Arts and Crafts, Oakland
1996–1998 Design Director, Wired Digital, San Francisco
2000 Taught new media at California College of Arts and Crafts (CCAC)
Patricia McShane
1953 Born in Brazzaville, Congo
1972–1975 Studied fine art and photography at San Francisco University
1987 B. F. A. Graphic Design with Distinction, California College of Arts and Crafts, Oakland

Recent exhibitions
2000 "National Design Triennial", Cooper-Hewitt National Design Museum, New York
2001 "Sundance Film Festival"; "010 101: Art in Technological Times", San Francisco Museum of Modern Art
2002 "Design, 1975–2000", Denver Art Museum, Denver; "Chronopolis", Parc de la Villette, Paris
2003 "The Art of Design", San Francisco Museum of Modern Art
2005 "Value Meal: Design and (Over)Eating", Center for Architecture, New York; "Experimentadesign", Lisbon Biennale
2006 "Spoken with Eyes", Davis Design Museum, University of California, Sacramento
2007 "Alumni at the Centennial", Oliver Arts Center, Oakland

Recent awards
2000/01 Nomination, National Design Award
2002 Nomination, Rockefeller Foundation New Media Fellowship
2003 Outstanding Achievement Award, HOW Self-Promotion Annual; Best 100 nomination, AIGA; WADC Award
2004 Grown in California Award, AIGA

Clients
ABC/Disney; Absolut; Adobe; Alcatel; Amnesty International; AOL; California College of Arts; Chevron; Chiat Day; CNET; Daimler Benz; Hotwired; IBM; International Design Conference in Aspen; Levi Strauss; Lotus; Macromedia; Microsoft; MTV; New York Times; Ogilvy Mather; SF AIDS Foundation; SFMOMA; Sony; Time Magazine; Vogue; Weiden & Kennedy; Wired Digital; Wired Magazine; Ziff Davis

"Our strategy is to focus on the synergies between business, culture and technology, while exploring and exploiting the changes as they happen around us."

»Unsere Strategie besteht darin, uns auf die Synergien zwischen Wirtschaft, Kultur und Technik zu konzentrieren, wobei wir die Veränderungen, die sich in unserem Umfeld vollziehen, analysieren und nutzen.«

«Notre stratégie est de nous concentrer sur les synergies entre commerce, culture et technologie en explorant et exploitant les changements qui interviennent autour de nous.»

Previous page:
Project: *"Fuelicide" poster, 2003*
Client: *AIGA*

Above left:
Project: *"Dorito Project" installation for "Value Meal: Design and (Over)Eating" exhibit, 2004*
Client: *Saint-Étienne International Design Biennale*

Above right:
Project: *"Who Is Watching the Watchers?" tote bag, 2004*
Client: *Computers, Freedom and Privacy Conference*

dollarman

right turn

curve

curvy

road kill

mediahandicap

spinner

crossing of life

back to nature

crumble

fuelicide

no entry

self carrier

airman

family car

freeway

Above:
Project: "Signal Signifier"
font/range of people
symbols, 2003
Client: Typebox Foundry

M/M (PARIS)

"We are reaching the point when we realize that we have created a language. In the beginning we formulated questions and their answers, now we use this language that we have built."

M/M (Paris)
5–7, rue des Récollets
75 010 Paris
France
T +33 1 4036174 6
anyone@mmparis.com
www.mmparis.com

Founders' biographies
Michael Amzalag
1968 Born in Paris, France
1988–1990 studied at the École
Nationale Supérieure des Arts
Décoratifs, Paris
Mathias Augustyniak
1967 Born in Cavaillon,
France
1991 MA Graphic Design and

Design group history
1992 Co-founded by Michael
Amzalag and Mathias
Augustyniak in Paris, France

Art Direction, Royal College
of Art, London

Recent exhibitions
2002 "Restart: Exchange &
Transform", Kunstverein,
Munich; "Design Now:
Graphics", Design Museum,
London
2003 "No Ghost Just A Shell",
Roda & Carlos de la Cruz,
Key Biscayne; "M/M (Paris)
Nine Posters and a Wallpaper",
Le Rectangle, Lyon; "Utopia
Station", Venice Biennale;

"M/M goes to Tokyo", Ginza
Graphic Gallery, Tokyo
2004 "M/M (Paris) Antigula",
Ursula Blickle Foundation,
Kraichtal; "M/M (Paris)
Antigone", Rocket Gallery,
Tokyo and CNEAI, Chatou;
"Tokyo TDC 2004", Ginza
Graphic Gallery, Tokyo
2005 "M/M (Paris) Utopia of
Flows, Air de Paris/Art Posi-
tions", Art Basel, Miami Beach;
"Posters", Stedjelik Museum,
Amsterdam
2006 "M/M (Paris) Haunch of

Venison/Venison of Haunch",
Haunch of Venison, London;
"M/M (Paris) Malaga", Insaa
Art Space, Seoul; "Writing in
Strobe", Dicksmith Gallery,
London

Clients
Anna Molinari; Balenciaga;
Björk; Blumarine; Calvin
Klein; CDDB Théâtre de Lori-
ent; Celluloid Dreams; Centre
Georges Pompidou; EMI
Music France; ENSAF; Frog;
Givenchy; Grand Compagnie;

Hermès; i-D Magazine; Jil
Sander; Louis Vuitton;
Madonna; Mercury; One Lit-
tle Indian Records; Palais de
Tokyo; Pirelli; Pittimagine
Discovery Foundation; Popu-
lism; Purple; Schirmer/Mosel;
Siemens Arts Program; Sony
BMG UK Ltd; Stella McCart-
ney; The Republic of Desire;
Virgin Music France; Vitra;
Vogue Paris; Yves Saint Lau-
rent Beauté; Yohji Yamamoto

KAREL MARTENS

"It's a matter of common sense and instinct."

Karel Martens
Monumentenweg 21A
6997 AG Hoog-Keppel
The Netherlands
km@werkplaatstypografie.org

Biography

1939 Born in Mook en Middelaar, The Netherlands
1961 Commercial Art and Illustration Degree, School of Art and Industrial Art, Arnhem

Professional experience

1961+ Freelance graphic designer specializing in typography
1977+ Taught graphic design at Arnhem School of Art; Jan van Eyck Academie, Maastricht; School of Art, Yale University, New Haven, Connecticut
1998 Founded the ArtEZ typography workshop with Wigger Bierma for postgraduate education in Arnhem (programme received MA status in 2006)
1999 Designed the façade of the printing company Veenman in Ede – a commission from Neutelings Riedijk Architecten in collaboration with the writer K. Schippers
2005 Designed the glass façades of the new part of the building for the Philharmonie Haarlem

Recent exhibitions

1999 Nominations for Rotterdam Design Prize, Museum Boijmans Van Beuningen, Rotterdam; "Mooi maar goed" (Nice but Good), Stedelijk Museum, Amsterdam; "Type On the Edge: The Work of Karel Martens", The Yale University Art Gallery, New Haven, Connecticut
1999–2002 "Roadshow of Dutch Graphic Design", Institut Néerlandais, Paris/Villa Steinbeck, Mulhouse/Musée des Beaux-Arts de Valence/Maryland Institute College of Art, Baltimore/ADGFAD/Laus 01, Barcelona/Erasmushuis, Djakarta/Design Center Stuttgart/Gallery AIGA, New York
2004 "Mechanic Exercises", University of Seoul

Recent awards

1996 Dr A. H. Heineken Prize for Art, The Netherlands
1997 Nomination, Rotterdam Design Prize
1998 Gold Medal, World's Best Book Design Award, Leipzig Book Fair
1999 Nomination for the design of the façade of the Veenman printing works, Ede, Rotterdam Design Prize

Clients

Amstelveen; Apeldoorn; City of Arnhem; Artez; Bibliotheek TU Delft; Bureau Rijksbouwmeester; De Architecten Cie; De Haan; De Nijl Architecten; Drukkerij Romen en Zonen; Drukkerij SSN; Drukkerij Thieme; Filmhuis Nijmegen; Fonds voor Beeldende Kunsten; Frienden Holland; Geertjan van Oostende; Gelderse Cultuurraad; Hoogeschool voor de Kunsten; Jan van Eyck Academie; Juriaan Schrofer; Katholiek Documentatie Centrum; Keppelsch ijzergieterij; Kluwer Publishing; Konduktor Elektro; KPN Nederland; Manteau Publishing; Ministry of Finance; Ministry of Justice; Ministry WVC; Museum Boijmans van Beuningen; NAi Publishers; Nederlandse Staatscourant; Nel Linssen; Neutelings Riedijk Architecten; Nijmeegs Museum 'Commanderie van St. Jan'; Nijmeegse Vrije Akademie; Paul Brand Publishing; PTT Kunst en Vormgeving; Rijksmuseum Kröller-Müller; Simeon ten Holt; Stedelijk Museum Amsterdam; Collectie Stichting Altena – Boswinkel; Stichting Holland in Vorm; Stichting Joris Ivens; Stichting Leerdam; Stichting Nijmeegse Jeugdraad; Stichting Oase; Stichting Post-Kunstvakonderwijs; Stiftung Museum Schloss Moyland; SUN Publishing; Te Elfder Ure; Tijdschrift Jeugd en Samenleving; Van Lindonk Publishing; Van Loghum Slaterus; Vereniging Rembrandt; Wolfsmond; World Press Photo

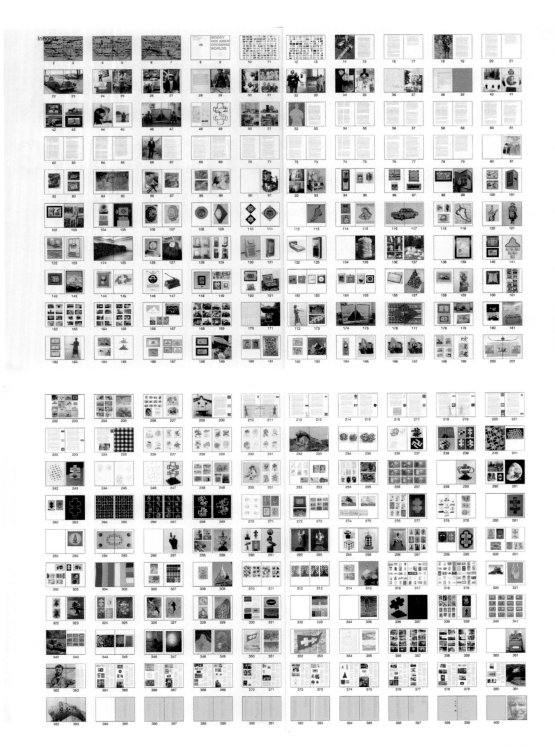

"Somewhere there is a box with the right answer. It's about finding this box and the key to open it. The only thing you have to do is to make it Blue. Or Brown. Or Sienna. Or green. Or Cerise. Or Cobalt. Or Cyan. Or Dark blue. Or Dark brown. Or Dark green. Or Indigo. Or Pink. Or Grey. Or Violet. Or Gold. Or Goldenrod. Or Lavender Blush. Or Lemon. Or Magenta. Or Bright turquoise. Or Maroon. Or Mauve. Or Midnight Blue. Or Mint Green. Or Moss Green. Or Navy blue. Or Orange. Or Pale Blue. Or Red-violet. Or Pale Sandy Brown. Or Pastel Green. Or Prussian blue. Or Purple. Or Red. Or Royal Blue. Or Salmon. Or Sandy brown. Or Scarlet. Or School bus yellow. Or Sea Green. Or Sepia. Or Silver. Or Spring Green. Or Steel Blue. Or Terracotta. Or Ultramarine. Or Vermilion. Or Blue-violet. Or Yellow perhaps. Or keep it as it is."

»Irgendwo existiert eine Kiste mit der richtigen Antwort. Man muss die Kiste sowie den dazugehörigen Schlüssel nur finden und den Inhalt der Kiste dann blau färben, oder braun, oder siennabraun, oder grün, oder kirschrot, oder kobaltblau, oder grünlichblau, oder dunkelblau, oder dunkelbraun, oder indigoblau, oder rosa, oder grau, oder violett, oder goldfarben, oder lavendelblau, oder zitronengelb, oder magentafarben, oder helltürkis, oder nachtblau, oder minzgrün, oder moosgrün, oder marineblau, oder orange, oder himmelblau, oder rotviolett, oder sandfarben, oder lindgrün, oder preußischblau, oder lila, oder rot, oder königsblau, oder lachsrosa, oder scharlachrot, oder postautogelb, oder meergrün, oder sepiabraun, oder silberfarben, oder stahlblau, oder ultramarinblau, oder zinnoberrot, oder blaulila, oder vielleicht gelb. Oder man lässt alles, wie es ist.«

«Il existe quelque part une boîte avec la bonne réponse. Il s'agit de trouver cette boîte et la clé qui l'ouvre. Il suffit pour cela de la faire bleue. Ou brune. Ou Terre de Sienne. Ou verte. Ou cerise. Ou cobalt. Ou cyan. Ou bleu foncé. Ou brun foncé. Ou vert foncé. Ou indigo. Ou rose. Ou grise. Ou violette. Ou dorée. Ou cuivrée. Ou lavande. Ou citron. Ou magenta. Ou turquoise vif. Ou marron. Ou mauve. Ou bleu nuit. Ou vert menthe. Ou vert mousse. Ou bleu marine. Ou orange. Ou bleu pâle. Ou rouge violet. Ou brun sable clair. Ou vert pastel. Ou bleu de Prusse. Ou pourpre. Ou rouge. Ou bleu roi. Ou saumon. Ou brun sable. Ou écarlate. Ou jaune bus d'école. Ou vert d'eau. Ou sépia. Ou argentée. Ou vert tendre. Ou bleu acier. Ou ocre rouge. Ou bleu outremer. Ou vermillon. Ou bleu violet. Ou jaune peut-être. Ou de la laisser comme elle est. »

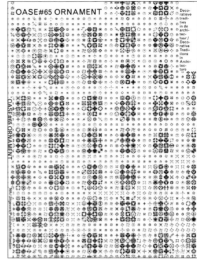

Top left:
Project: *"OASE #63 – Country-side" architectural journal, 2004 (in collaboration with Aagje Martens)*
Client: *Stichting Oase and NAi Publishers*

Top centre:
Project: *"OASE #64 – Landscape and Mass Tourism" architectural journal, 2004 (in collaboration with Radim Pesko)*
Client: *Stichting Oase and NAi Publishers*

Top right:
Project: *"OASE #65 – Ornament-Decorative Traditions in Architecture" architectural journal, 2004 (in collaboration with Felix Weigand)*
Client: *Stichting Oase and NAi Publishers*

Above left:
Project: *"OASE #68 – Home Land" architectural journal, 2005 (in collaboration with Jeff Ramsey)*
Client: *Stichting Oase and NAi Publishers*

Above centre:
Project: *"OASE #69 – Positions / Shared Territories in Historiography & Practice" architectural journal, 2006 (in collaboration with Layla Tweedy-Cullen)*
Client: *Stichting Oase and NAi Publishers*

Above right:
Project: *"OASE #71 – Urban Formation & Collective Spaces" architectural journal, 2006 (in collaboration with Aagje Martens)*
Client: *Stichting Oase and NAi Publishers*

ME COMPANY

"Emotional Efflorescence"

Me Company
14 Apollo Studios
Charlton Kings Road
London NW5 2SA
UK
T +44 207 482 426 2
meco@mecompany.com
www.mecompany.com

Design group history
1985 Me Company founded by Paul White in London
2001 Chromasoma was created to run as a sister company to Me Company

Founder's biography
Paul White
1959 Born in England
Trained as graphic designer and illustrator

Recent exhibitions
2001 "Luminous", G8 Gallery, Tokyo
2002 "Luminous", Visionaire Gallery, New York/Spielhaus Morrison Gallery, Berlin
2003 "Summer", Spielhaus Morrison Gallery, Berlin
2004 "Communicate: Independent British Graphic Design Since the Sixties, Barbican Art Gallery, London

Clients
Absolut Vodka; Adidas; Apple; Björk; BT; Cacharel; Citizen K; Dave Clarke; Escentric Molecules; Ford GSK; Garrard; Hello Kitty; Jaeger-LeCoultre; Kenz; Lancome; L'Oréal; Mercedes; Nike; Nurofen; Patrick Cox; Renault; Trash Palace; Visionaire; V Magazine

"Emotional efflorescence, the unfolding images of objects impossible to otherwise see. Technology gets us to where the eye cannot penetrate. We find the concept of understanding the world through computer-aided devices compellingly vital and relevant. Or if you like, we like to think of these instruments as prostheses for our eyes."

»Emotionales Aufblühen – sich entfaltende Bilder von Objekten, die man ansonsten gar nicht sehen kann. Die Technologie bringt uns dahin, wohin das Auge nicht vordringen kann. Wir finden die Vorstellung, die Welt durch computergestützte Mittel verstehen zu können, überzeugend vital und relevant. Wir nennen diese Mittel gerne Prothesen für unsere Augen.«

« Floraison émotionnelle, lorsque s'épanouissent les images d'objets autrement impossibles à voir. La technologie nous emmène là où l'œil ne peut pénétrer. Le concept de comprendre le monde à travers des instruments informatiques nous semble crucial et pertinent. Ou si vous préférez, nous aimons considérer ces instruments comme des prothèses pour nos yeux. »

Previous page:
Project: *"XSi"*
brand/identity/packaging/splash screen design for XSi V4.0, 2005
Client: *Softimage XSi*

Above:
Project: *"Snowflakes"*
editorial design, 2003
Client: *Numero*

Following page top:
Project: *"Magic"*
stills from an 18-frame lenticular animated print, 2006
Client: *Visionaire*

Following page bottom:
Project: *"Eden"*
editorial design, 2006
Client: *Numero*

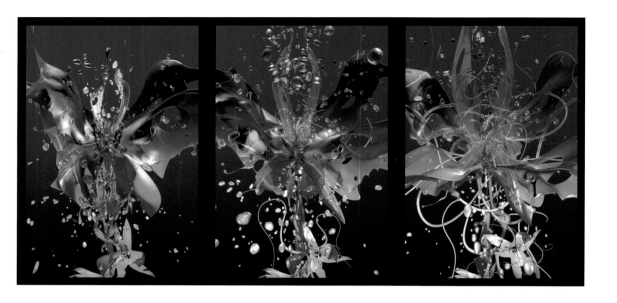

MEVIS & VAN DEURSEN

"As designers we need to be able to find or respond to things that are relevant to us."

Mevis & van Deursen
Geldersekade 101
1011 EM Amsterdam
The Netherlands
T +31 20 623 609 3
mevd@xs4all.nl

Design group history
1987 Co-founded by Linda van Deursen and Armand Mevis in Amsterdam, The Netherlands

Founders' biographies
Linda van Deursen
1961 Born in Aardenburg, The Netherlands
1981/82 Academie voor Beeldende Vorming, Tilburg
1982–1986 Studied fine art, Gerrit Rietveld Academy, Amsterdam
2001+ Head of the Graphic Design Department at the Gerrit Rietveld Academy

Armand Mevis
1963 Born in Oirsbeek, The Netherlands
1981/82 Academie St. Joost, Breda
1982–1986 Studied fine art, Gerrit Rietveld Academy, Amsterdam
2002+ Design critic at the Werkplaats Typografie workshop

Recent exhibitions
2000 "Best Book Designs", Stedelijk Museum, Amsterdam; "Mevis & Van Deursen", Zagrebacki Salon, Zagreb
2002 "Design Now: Graphics", Design Museum, London; "Dát was vormgeving – KPN Art & Design", Stedelijk Museum, Amsterdam; "Best Book Designs", Stedelijk Museum, Amsterdam
2004 "Mark", Stedelijk Museum, Amsterdam
2005 "Recycled Works: Mevis & Van Deursen", Nagoya; "The European Design Show", Design Museum, London; "Dutch Resource", Chaumont
2006 "Grafist 10", Istanbul; "Graphic Design in the White Cube", International Biennale of Graphic Design, Brno

Recent awards
1997 Nomination, Design Award, Rotterdam; Best Book Design, Amsterdam
1998 I. D. Forty (40 Best Designers Worldwide); Best Book Design, Amsterdam
1999 Best Book Design, Amsterdam; Nomination, Theatre Poster Award
2000 Best Book Design, Amsterdam; Nomination, Theatre Poster Award
2001 Winner of competition to design the graphic identity of "Rotterdam, Cultural Capital of Europe 2001"
2002 Best Book Design, Amsterdam

Clients
Artimo Foundation; Bureau Amsterdam; Gastprogrammering Het Muziektheater; Museum Boijmans Van Beuningen; NAi Publishers; Netherlands Design Institute; Ludion, Gent/Amsterdam; Stedelijk Museum Bureau Amsterdam; Stichting Fonds voor Beeldende Kunst, Vormgeving en Architectuur; Uitgeverij 010; Thames & Hudson; TPG Post; Viktor & Rolf; Walker Art Center

"As a studio we mainly design posters, catalogues and identities for cultural institutions. We don't believe in conventions. Design should reflect contemporary cultural developments. In the future, we will have a better understanding of our world through information. We will even have more access to information through the effect of globalization, new media, cheaper printing techniques and so on. Graphic designers are desperately needed in this development. Their work is the most significant expression of our time… I think the condition for making good work, though, is to find a client who at least lives in the same world as you."

»In unserem Studio gestalten wir hauptsächlich Plakate, Kataloge und Corporate Identities für Kulturinstitutionen. Wir glauben nicht an Konventionen. Design sollte zeitgenössische kulturelle Entwicklungen spiegeln. In Zukunft werden wir unsere Welt aufgrund von Informationen besser verstehen. Wir werden sogar infolge der Globalisierung Zugang zu noch mehr Informationen, zu neuen Medien, billigeren Drucktechniken, etc. bekommen. Für diese Entwicklungen werden Grafiker dringend gebraucht. Ihre Arbeit ist der bedeutendste Ausdruck unserer Zeit … Ich denke aber, dass man – um gute Arbeit zu leisten – einen Auftraggeber finden muss, der zumindest in der gleichen Welt wie man selber lebt.«

«En tant que studio, nous créons principalement des affiches, des catalogues et des chartes pour des institutions culturelles. Nous ne croyons pas aux conventions. Le graphisme doit refléter la manière dont la culture contemporaine évolue. Dans l'avenir, nous comprendrons mieux notre monde grâce à l'information. Nous aurons même de plus en plus accès à cette information sous l'effet de la mondialisation, des nouveaux médias, des techniques d'impression plus abordables, etc… Les graphistes sont d'une importance cruciale dans cette évolution. Leur travail est l'expression la plus marquante de notre époque… Je pense toutefois que pour faire du bon travail il faut trouver un client qui, au moins, vive dans le même monde que soi. »

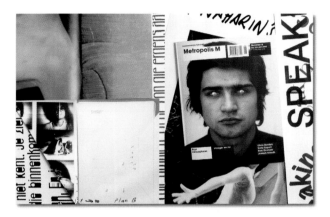

Previous page:
Project: *"Spring & Summer 2003"* invitation (out of a series of 700 unique invitations), 2002
Client: *Viktor & Rolf*

Above:
Project: *"Mevis & van Deursen – Recollected Works "* catalogue spreads, 2005

Client: *Mevis & van Deursen*

Following page top:
Project: *"ABCDE Viktor & Rolf"* magazine, 2003
Client: *Artimo*

Following page bottom:
Project: *"Geert van Kesteren – Why Mister Why?"* catalogue, 2004
Client: *Artimo*

ABCDE-MAGAZINE:

VIKTOR&ROLF
PAR VIKTOR ET ROLF

★★★★★★★★★★
PREMIÈRE DÉCENNIE

EUR 15 / D, I   EUR 18 / F   GBP 10 / UK

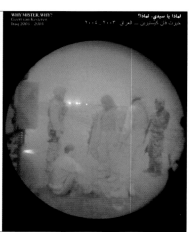

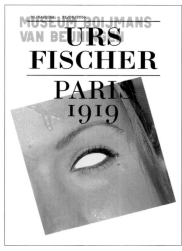

BB—TYPE
SPECIMEN

Previous page top left:
Project: *"Rirkrit Tiravanija"*
exhibition invitation, 2005
Client: *Museum Boijmans Van Beuningen*

Previous page top right:
Project: *"Urs Fischer"*
exhibition invitation, 2005
Client: *Museum Boijmans Van Beuningen*

Previous page bottom:
Project: *"Spring & Summer 2003" invitations (out of a series of 700 unique invitations), 2002*
Client: *Viktor & Rolf*

Above:
Project: *"BB-Type Specimen" museum identity logotypes, 2003*
Client: *Museum Boijmans Van Beuningen*

MUTABOR DESIGN

"Mutabor is derived from Latin and, roughly translated, means 'I'm going to change'."

Mutabor Design
Grosse Elbstr. 145B
22 767 Hamburg
Germany
T +49 40 399 224 0
info@mutabor.de
www.mutabor.de

Design group history
Mid-1990s Graphic design magazine Mutabor is launched at Muthesius University in Kiel
1998 The co-founders Heinrich Paravicini and Johannes Plass turn the Mutabor design and magazine team into a design agency. Mutabor Design is founded
2000+ Heinrich Paravicini and Johannes Plass serve as jury members of national design awards, give university speeches and attend design conferences; obtains the German ADC membership

Founders' biographies
Heinrich Paravicini
1971 Born in Göttingen, Germany; grew up in Paris

1991–1997 Studied communication design at Muthesius University, Kiel
1996 Academic design research project together with Johannes Plass in California
1994–1997 Worked as a graphic designer in Kiel, Munich and Paris
Johannes Plass
1970 Born in Osnabrück, Germany
1992–1997 Studied communication design at Muthesius University, Kiel
1996 Academic design research project together with Heinrich Paravicini in California
1994–1997 Worked as a graphic designer in Kiel, Hamburg and Munich

Recent awards
2000 German prize for Communication Design
2001 Most Beautiful German Book Award, Stiftung Buchkunst; Winner, Hamburg Design Award; Merit, Art Directors Club New York; Finalist (Shortlisted), German Corporate Design Award; First Prize, German Corporate Magazine of the Year; Awards for Typographic Excellence (x3), Type Directors Club New York
2002 Awards (x3), Type Directors Club New York; Distinctive Merit Art Directors Club New York; Silver medal and Bronze medal (x2), Art Directors Club Germany; Shortlisted (x2), D&AD Awards

2003 Award, Type Directors Club New York; Honour Award (x5) and Bronze Medal, Art Directors Club Germany; Red Dot Award; Hamburg Design Award
2004 Type Directors Club New York, Award for Trade Fair Identity; Art Directors Club Germany, Honour Award for Trade Fair Identity; DDC German Designers Club award; Red Dot Award; IF Award (x2); Most Beautiful German Book Award; Gold Award, OPI Office Product International
2005 Award, Type Directors Club New York; Honour Award, Art Directors Club Germany
2006 Honour Award and

Bronze Medal, Art Directors Club Germany

Clients
Adidas; Audi; BMW; Bulthaup; Classen Papier; Coremedia; Distefora Holding; Greenpeace; Hoffmann & Campe Editions; Ision Internet; International School Of New Media, Lübeck; Kunsthalle, Kiel; Media Lab Europe; Panasonic Germany; Premier Automotive Group; Ravensburger Editions; Sanford Rotring; S.Oliver Group; Sinner Schrader; Universal Music; VW

"True to our principles, we don't just observe what's happening and developing on the international design scene; we try to find new creative approaches of our own within our projects. In addition to traditional fields of business such as brand identity, corporate environment and editorial design, Mutabor puts its faith in innovative branding concepts that are designed to open up future markets for brands. It is a brand identity agency whose primary focus point is brand innovation in consulting and creation. With its 30-strong team of designers, Mutabor is interested in clients for whom design trends and innovations are relevant."

»Getreu unserem Grundsatz beobachten wir nicht nur das Geschehen und die Entwicklungen in der internationalen Designszene, sondern wir versuchen bei unseren Projekten auch, eigene neue, kreative Wege zu gehen. Zusätzlich zu den traditionellen Tätigkeitsbereichen wie Markenbildung, Unternehmenskultur und Layouten von Publikationen setzt Mutabor auf innovative Marketingkonzepte, die für Markenprodukte neue Absatzmärkte erschließen. Mutabor ist eine beratende und ausführende Markenbildungsagentur mit Schwerpunkt Markeninnovation. Mutabor ist an Auftraggebern interessiert, denen Designtrends und -innovationen wichtig sind.«

«Fidèles à nos principes, nous ne nous contentons pas d'observer ce qui se passe et ce qui change sur la scène du graphisme international; nous essayons de trouver pour chacun de nos projets une démarche créative nouvelle. Parallèlement à ses interventions dans les secteurs d'activité traditionnels comme l'identité visuelle, l'environnement institutionnel et le graphisme publicitaire, Mutabor se consacre à des concepts de création d'imagerie novateurs destinés à ouvrir la voie des nouveaux marchés aux marques. Nous sommes une agence spécialisée dans l'identité visuelle, dont le principal objectif est l'innovation dans le conseil et la création. La trentaine de créatifs de Mutabor s'intéresse aux clients qui apprécient les tendances et les innovations graphiques à leur juste valeur. »

 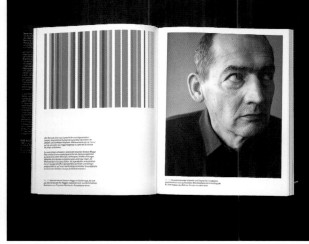

Previous page:
Project: *"Hans-Peter Feldmann"*
exhibition poster, 2005
Client: *Kunsthalle zu Kiel*

Above (both images):
Project: *"Bulthaup Perspectives"*
imagebook, 2004
Client: *Bulthaup*

Above left:
Project: "Golf Loves Europe –
Europe Loves Golf" photo
catalogue, 2006
Client: Volkswagen

Above right (both images):
Project: "Audi" stand design
for Detroit Motorshow, 2006
Client: Audi

Mutabor Design   239

HIDEKI NAKAJIMA

"To create a completely new style of design with my own two hands."

Nakajima Design
Kaiho Bldg-4F
4–11, Uguisudani-cho
Shibuya-ku
Tokyo 150–0032
Japan
T +81 3 548 917 57
nkjm-d@kd5.so-net.ne.jp

Biography
1961 Born in Saitama, Japan
Self-taught

Professional experience
1988–1991 Senior Designer, Masami Shimizu Design Office, Tokyo
1992–1995 Art Director, Rockin'on, Tokyo
1995 Established Nakajima Design

Recent exhibitions
1994 "Tokyo Visual Groove", PARCO, Tokyo
1998 "Japan Graphic Design Exhibition", Paris; Art Exhibition for Seiko's Neatnik, Tokyo
2000 "Graphic Wave 2000", Ginza Graphic Gallery, Tokyo
2001 "Takeo Paper Show 2001"; "Graphisme(s)", Paris; "Typo-Janchi", Seoul; "032c's The Searching Stays With You", Berlin and London
2004 "Nakajima Design Exhibition", Guandong Museum of Art
2006 "Hideki Nakajima: Clear in the Fog", Ginza Graphic Gallery, Tokyo; "Clear in the Fog II", Art Zone, Kyoto

Recent awards
1995–2000 Gold Award (x5) and Silver Award (x7), The Art Directors Club, New York
1999 Tokyo ADC Award
2000 Best Book Design, 19th International Biennale of Graphic Design, Brno
2001 Good Design Award, Chicago Athenaeum
2003 Kodansha Prize for Book Design
2004 Wang Xu Prize, 3rd International Poster Biennial, Ningbo
2006 Judges' Prize, Type Directors Club Awards

Clients
Avex Trax; Code; Hong Kong Arts Centre; Issey Miyake; Levi Strauss Japan; Nestlé Japan; PARCO; Rockin'on; Sony Music; The National Museum of Modern Art, Tokyo; Toshiba-EMI Warner Music

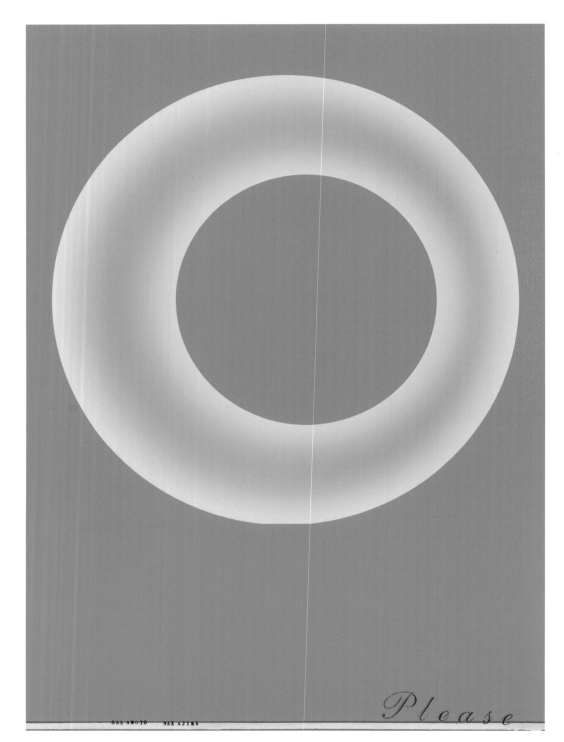

SAKAMOTO   NAKAJIMA

Please

"Year after year, people claim that creativity in design has reached its limits. However, the reality is that new designs are produced every year. I myself would like to pursue the possibility of design, and create a completely new style – a style that no one has ever seen – all by myself."

»Jahr für Jahr wird immer wieder behauptet, dass das Grafikdesign an die Grenzen seiner Kreativität gestossen sei. Andererseits werden aber jedes Jahr neue Designs geschaffen. Ich selbst würde gerne noch weitere Designpotenziale erforschen und einen ganz neuen Stil kreieren – und zwar ganz alleine.«

«Année après année, les gens assurent que la créativité graphique a atteint ses limites. Il est pourtant tout aussi vrai que de nouveaux graphismes sont créés chaque année. J'aimerais personnellement continuer à explorer le potentiel du graphisme et créer un style complètement nouveau – un style que personne n'a jamais vu – tout seul. »

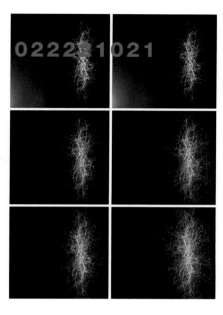

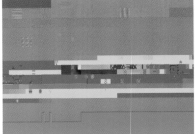

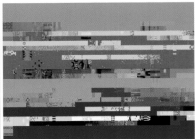

Top left:
Project: "Ryuichi Sakamoto/04"
CD cover, 2004
Client: Warner Music, Japan

Top right:
Project: "Ryuichi Sakamoto/05"
CD cover, 2005
Client: Warner Music, Japan

Above:
Project: "Phut Cr@ckle Tokyo
[K]: Sl@yre & The Feminite
Stool" CD cover, 2005
Client: Sublime Records

PHILIP O'DWYER

*"Use the pages of a sketchbook
to fill a digital world. Write some lines
of computer code to draw a poster."*

Philip O'Dwyer
Studio 16
5 Durham Yard
London E2 6QF
UK
T +44 207 033 374 1
philip@philipodwyer.com
www.philipodwyer.com

Biography
1974 Born in Dublin, Ireland
1992–1995 Studied graphic
design, Limerick School of
Art & Design
1995–1996 Studied communication design, Central Saint
Martins College of Art &
Design, London

Professional experience
1996–1997 Freelance designer,
Wired (UK) magazine
1996–1997 Art Director,
Raise magazine
1997–2004 Creative Director,
State Design, London
(co-founded with Mark
Hough and Mark Breslin)
2004/05 Interaction Designer at
Imagination Limited, London

Recent exhibitions
2004 "Communicate: Independent British Graphic Design
since the Sixties", Barbican Art
Gallery, London
2005 "Measc", Bristol
2006 "Transvision", Victoria &
Albert Museum, London,
"onedotzero10", touring exhibition, Institute of Contemporary Arts (ICA), London/Cen-
tro Recoletta, Buenos Aires/
Red Dot Design Museum, Singapore; "B-nest Exhibition",
Shizuoka
2007 "Shizuoka Contents
Valley Festival", Shizuoka

Recent awards
2004 Interaction Design
Award, DISS2004 Boston
(shortlisted)

Clients
Futurelab; Girl's Day School
Trust; Imagination; Laurence
King Publishing; The Light
Surgeons/Geffrye Museum;
MaoWorks; Mixed Media
(Japan); Networks; Olivia
Morris Shoes; onedotzero;
Polar Produce; Soundtoys;
Turner Entertainment Net-
works

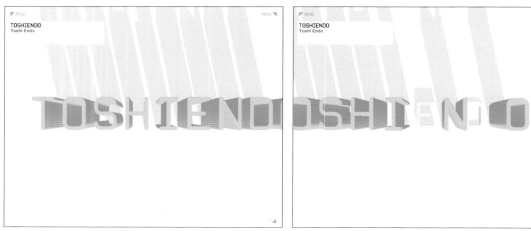

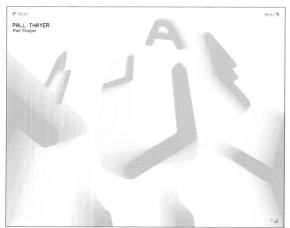

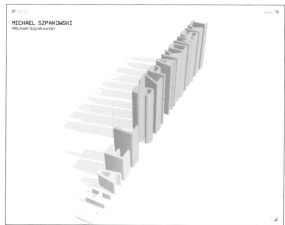

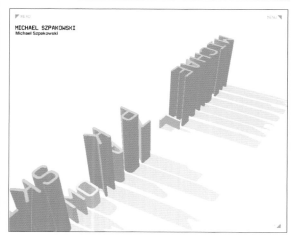

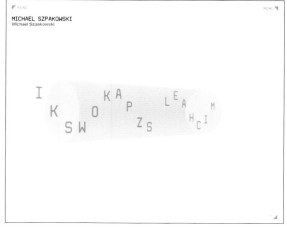

"Create a new world with its own strange landscape, physics, atmosphere. Re-imagine a 'real' object as an information structure. Work too fast and do it all over again many times. Be inspired by the past, by anonymous craft. Make a word into a toy."

»Eine neue Welt mit seltsamen Landschaften und einer ganz eigenen Natur und Atmosphäre schaffen. Ein ›reales‹ Objekt als Informationsstruktur neu erfinden. Zu schnell arbeiten und alles mehrfach nochmal machen. Sich von Vergangenem, von Werken unbekannter Handwerker inspirieren lassen. Aus einem Wort ein Spielzeug machen.«

«Créer un monde nouveau doté de ses propres paysages, lois physiques et atmosphères étranges. Transposer un objet 'réel' en une structure informative. Travailler trop vite et tout recommencer plusieurs fois. Être inspiré par le passé, par le savoir-faire anonyme. Changer un mot en jouet.»

Previous page:
Project: *"Soundtoys Journal" website, 2006*
Client: *Soundtoys*

Top (all images):
Project: *"Soundtoys Journal" website, 2006*
Client: *Soundtoys*

Above (all images):
Project: *"Trans_Vision" generative animation/ installation, 2006*
Client: *Victoria & Albert Museum/onedotzero*

Following page (all images):
Project: *"onedotzero_select dvd" DVD covers and label, 2003– 2006*
Client: *onedotzero*

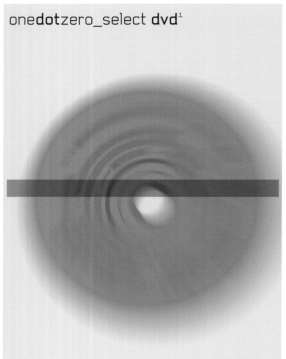

onedotzero_select **dvd**[1]

onedotzero_select **dvd**[3]

adventures in moving image

onedotzero_select **dvd**[4]

adventures in moving image

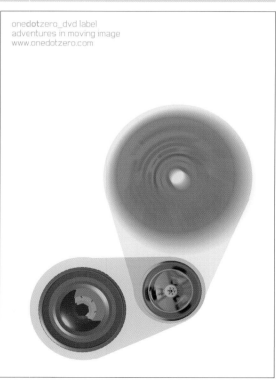

one**dot**zero_dvd label
adventures in moving image
www.onedotzero.com

GABOR PALOTAI

"Design is a way of discussing life."

Gabor Palotai Design
Västerlånggatan 76
11129 Stockholm
Sweden
T +46 8 248 818
design@gaborpalotai.com
www.gaborpalotai.com

Biography
1956 Born in Budapest,
Hungary
1975–1980 Studied graphic
design, National Academy
of Arts, Crafts and Design,
Budapest
1981 Moved permanently to
Stockholm
1981–1983 Studied at the Royal
Swedish Academy of Fine
Arts, Stockholm
1982/83 Studied at the
Beckmans School of Design,
Stockholm

Professional experience
1983–1990 Art Director and
graphic designer for advertising agencies
1988 Established Gabor Palotai
Design
1991–2001 Visiting professor at
various design schools in
Stockholm

Recent exhibitions
2000+ "Moderna Formen",
Nationalmuseum, Stockholm
2001 "The Year of the
Architecture", Grafikens Hus,
Mariefred
2002 "Maximizing the Audi-
ence", solo exhibition, C3,
Budapest; "Vision", Kunsthalle,
Budapest
2003 "European Design
Biennial", London;
"Dissonanzia", Milan
2003–2006 "Scandinavian
Design Beyond the "Myth"
touring exhibition, Berlin/
Milan/Ghent/Prague/Buda-
pest/Copenhagen/Oslo/
Gothenburg/Vigo/La Coruna/
New York
2005 "Designed in Sweden",
Museum of London; "The
Hungarian House of Photo-
graphy", Budapest

Recent awards
1984–2001 Working scholarship (x5), Arts Grants Commit-
tee, Stockholm; Excellent
Swedish Design Award (x18);
Received numerous awards
including The Golden Egg
Award and nominations by
the Swedish Advertising Federation; Coredesign, Stockholm
2003 Red Dot Award (x3)
2005 Red Dot Award
2006 The Swedish Golden Egg
Award; The Swedish Book Art
Award; Nomination for the
Design Award of the Federal
Republic of Germany

Clients
Arvinius Förlag; Eniro;
Ericsson; Hennes & Mauritz;
IKEA; KF; Maritime Museum
of Stockholm; Museum of
Architecture, Stockholm;
Museum of Science and Tech-
nology, Stockholm; National-
museum, Stockholm; Posten;
Postgiro; Restaurant Anna-
khan; Röhsska Museet; SAS;
Skandia; Swedens Economical
Museum; Telia; V & S Group

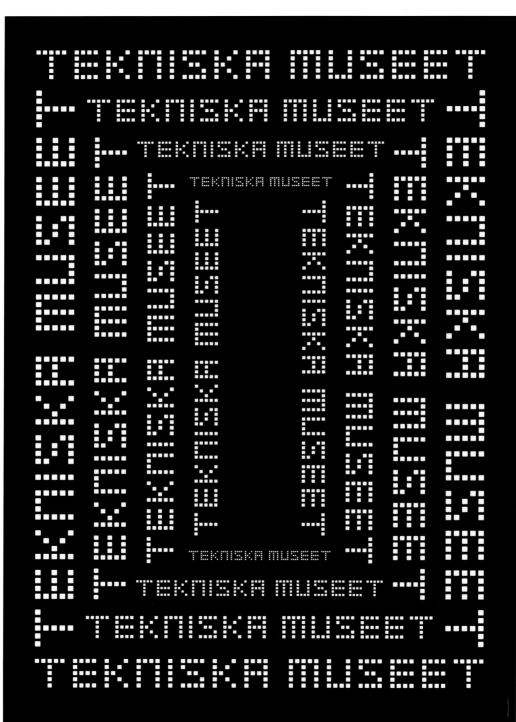

"To quote Gaetano Pesce, 'I believe that death makes us all alike, and that being alive means to be different. The objects that surround us during the short time of our existence should help us enjoy that prerogative'… In two sentences Pesce summarizes an important meaning of life, and at the same time gives a kind of answer to the questions: What is identity? How can I be happy in life? What is design? He says that identity comes from not adopting a culture, but by being fair to oneself through differentiation. Furthermore, that design is a means to design identities with. And designers should help create diversity. On every level of life, from companies to individuals, design should make you enjoy life but if possible also pose questions about life. In fact design is a way of discussing life."

»Ich zitiere Gaetano Pesce: ›Ich glaube, der Tod macht uns alle gleich. Also bedeutet leben, sich zu unterscheiden. Die Dinge, mit denen wir uns während unserer kurzen Lebenszeit umgeben, sollten uns helfen, dieses Privileg zu genießen.‹ … In zwei Sätzen fasst Pesce einen wesentlichen Sinn des Lebens zusammen und gibt zugleich Antworten auf die Fragen: Was bedeutet Identität? Was ist Glück? Was ist Design? Seiner Meinung nach, entsteht Identität nicht dadurch, dass man eine Kultur kopiert, sondern dadurch, dass man sich einen eigenen Stil schafft. Für ihn ist Design ein Mittel zur Gestaltung von Identitäten. Und Designer sollten zum Entstehen von Vielfältigkeit beitragen. Auf jeder Ebene des Lebens – vom Unternehmen bis zum Individuum – sollte Design die Lebensfreude fördern, dabei aber möglichst auch Fragen über das Leben stellen. Design ist also eigentlich eine Art Diskussion über das Leben.«

«Comme a dit Gaetano Pesce: ›Je pense que la mort fait de nous tous des semblables et qu'être vivant signifie être différent. Les objets qui nous entourent pendant notre brève existence devraient nous aider à profiter de cette prérogative'… Il résume en deux phrases un important aspect de la vie tout en donnant une amorce de réponse aux questions: Qu'est-ce que l'identité? Comment puis-je être heureux dans la vie? Qu'est-ce que le design? Il dit que l'identité naît lorsqu'on n'adopte pas une culture mais que l'on reste fidèle à soi-même par la différenciation. Il dit aussi que le design est un moyen de créer des identités. Et que les créateurs devraient vous faire profiter de la vie mais aussi, si possible, vous pousser à vous interroger sur la vie. En fait, le design est un moyen de parler de la vie.»

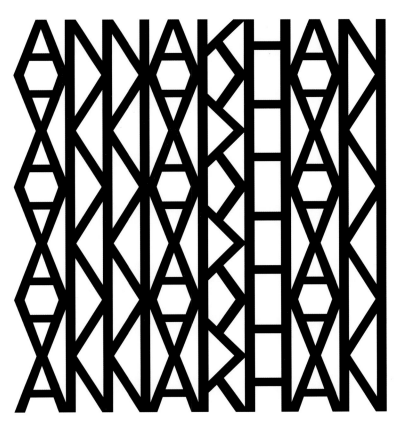

Previous page:
Project: *"Tekniska Museet"*
graphic identity (poster), 2002
Client: *Tekniska Museet*
*(Museum of Science and
Technology), Stockholm*

Above:
Project: *"Annakhan"*
graphic identity (logotype), 2002
Client: *Restaurant Annakhan*

Following page top left:
Project: *"Scandinavian Design
Beyond the Myth"*
exhibition poster, 2003
Client: *Nordic Council of
Ministers*

Following page top right:
Project: *"Made in Sweden"*
exhibition poster, 2003
Client: *Svenska Form (Swedish
Society of Craft and Design)*

Following page bottom left:
Project: *"Estonia"*
exhibition poster, 2006
Client: *The Maritime Museum,
Stockholm*

Following page bottom right:
Project: *"Swedish Graphic
Designers"*
poster/book design, 2004
Client: *Arvinius Förlag*

SCANDINAVIAN DESIGN BEYOND THE MYTH

**SKANDINAVISCHES DESIGN
JENSEITS DES MYTHOS
7. NOV. 2003 – 29. FEB. 2004**

S M
B Kunstgewerbemuseum
Staatliche Museen
zu Berlin

MADE IN SWEDEN

The (un)importance of nationality
Designforum Svensk Form, Skeppsholmen
12 juni – 24 augusti 2003

estonia
estonia
estonia
estonia
estonia

SJÖHISTORISKA MUSEET

30.04.2005 – 3.09.2006

SWEDISH GRAPHIC DESIGNERS 2004

SWEDGED

ARVINIUS FÖRLAG

RINZEN

"We exploit play as the genesis for creating alternate or heightened realities, fed through a filter of graphical simplicity."

Rinzen Australia
PO Box 1729
New Farm
Queensland 4005
Australia
T +61 439 668 112
they@rinzen.com
www.rinzen.com

Design group history
2000 Founded by Steve and Rilla Alexander, Adrian Clifford, Craig Redman and Karl Maier

Founders' biographies
Steve Alexander
1973 Born Ipswich, Australia
1991 BVA Fine Art, University of South Queensland
1992–1994 Studied graphic design, Queensland College of Art

Rilla Alexander
1974 Born in Brisbane, Australia
1992–1994 Studied graphic design, Queensland College of Art
Adrian Clifford
1975 Born in Maffra, Australia
1994–1996 Studied graphic design, Queensland College of Art
Craig Redman
1978 Born in Gloucester, Australia

1996–1998 Studied graphic design, Queensland College of Art
Karl Meier
1978 Born in Gold Coast, Australia
1996–1998 Studied graphic design, Queensland College of Art

Recent exhibitions
2000 "We are the World", Brisbane; "RMX/A Visual Remix Project", Brisbane/Berlin

2001 "Rinzen Presents RMX Extended Play", Sydney/ Brisbane/Berlin; "All about Bec", Sydney; "Kitten", Melbourne
2004 "Neighbourhood", Berlin; "Place", Barcelona
2004/05 "Psy(k)é/Off the Wall", Paris
2005 "Are You My Home?", Hamburg
2006 "In the Milky Night", Berlin/Sydney

Clients
Absolut Vodka; Bebike; Black + White; Blue; Brisbane Marketing; DC Comics; Die Gestalten Verlag; Family/ Empire/Pressclub; Kitten; Mooks; Mushroom; Nylon; Stussy; The Face; Toy2R; Vogue; Warner; Wink Media; Wired

"As an Australian design and art collective, we are best known for our collaborative and illustrative approach, creating utopian alternative realities and other worlds. Utilizing a process of play to follow our fancies into the visual wilderness, we strive to be cheerful but not ironic, spontaneous but not haphazard, and inclusive but not derivative."

»Als australisches Designer- und Künstlerkollektiv sind wir am bekanntesten für unsere gemeinschaftliche, illustrative Arbeitsweise. Wir schaffen utopische Wirklichkeiten und neue Welten. Wir gehen spielerisch vor, um unseren Einfällen je nach Lust und Laune in das Dickicht der Bilder zu folgen. Wir streben nach Humor, aber nicht nach Ironie, nach Spontanität, aber nicht nach Planlosigkeit, nach Vollkommenheit, aber nicht nach Zweitklassigkeit.«

«Collectif australien d'art et de design, nous sommes surtout connus pour notre approche illustrative et collaborative, qui nous permet de créer des réalités utopiques alternatives et d'autres mondes. Nous utilisons des procédés ludiques pour poursuivre nos caprices dans les méandres de la jungle visuelle et nous nous efforçons de rester gais sans ironie, spontanés mais pas désordonnés et touche-à-tout sans nous disperser.»

Previous page:
Project: *"Dryads"*
room design, 2005
Client: *Volkswagen*

Top:
Project: *"Torbjorn" and "Viking"*
T-shirt designs, 2004
Client: *2k by Gingham*

Above:
Project: *"Under Bifrost"*
large-scale installation, 2003
Client: *Queensland Art Gallery*

Following page top:
Project: *"The Incredible Strand"*
album cover, 2005
Client: *The Incredible Strand*

Following page bottom left:
Project: *"Kong"*
poster design, 2006
Client: *Kong Shop and Gallery*

Following page bottom right:
Project: *"The Scare"*
album cover, 2005
Client: *The Scare*

254   **Rinzen**

RUIZ+ COMPANY

"Concept: Direct message that makes you reflect and that is robust and effective."

ruiz+company
C/Zamora 45, 5°2a
Barcelona 08 022
Spain
T +34 93 253 178 0
estudio@ruizcompany.com
www.ruizcompany.com

Design group history
1993 Founded by David Ruiz and Marina Company in Barcelona, Spain

Founders' biographies
David Ruiz
1960 Born in Barcelona, Spain
1977–1980 Studied at Escola Elisava de Barcelona
1985–1986 Advertising creative, Art Director and graphic designer for RCP Saatchi & Saatchi, Publis and GGK
1987–1992 Art director and Creative Director, Bassat Ogilvy & Mather
1997 Appointed member of AGI (Alliance Graphique Internationale)
Marina Company
1967 Born in Buenos Aires, Argentina
1986 Escola Llotja de Barcelona

Recent exhibitions
2005 "Red Dot Awards communication design", Essen; "Art Directors Club of Europe", London
2006 "El Sol: Festival publicitario Iberoamericano", San Sebastian; "Best Pack", Barcelona; 47th International Advertising Festival, Cannes

Recent awards
2001–2004 Red Dot Award (x5), Essen
2004 Best of the Best, Red Dot Award for Communication Design, Essen
2001/02 FAB Award Trophy for Packaging, London
1998–2006 Gold Award (x 4), Best Pack, Spain
1995 Gran Prix, Gold Sun and Silver Sun Awards, San Sebastian Festival
1991–2006 Bronze Laus Award (x 16)
1991–2006 Silver Laus Award (x 10)
1991–2006 Gold Laus Award (x 5)
2006 Silver Lion, Cannes International Festival

Clients
Adidas; Antonio Miró; ; Barcelona City Council; Barcelona Provincial Government; Camper; Canal Metro; Canal Plus; Canal Satélite Digital; Catalunya Radio; Chocolat Factory; City TV; Coca-Cola; Cruz Verde; Cruz Roja (Spanish Red Cross); Damm; Danone; Diesel; Euskal Telebista; Frigo; Habitat; Illa Diagonal; Levi's; Martini; Nike; RCR; RENFE (Spanish Railways); San Miguel; Seat; Smart; Sony Music; TV3; VW

BCN DESIGN WEEK

BETTER
DESIGN
=
BETTER
BUSINESS

Del 6 al 10 de novembre de 2006
Del 6 al 10 de noviembre de 2006

Places limitades
Fes la teva inscripció a: www.bcd.es
Més informació: bcd@cambrabcn.es

Plazas limitadas
Haz tu inscripción en: www.bcd.es
Más información: bcd@cambrabcn.es

D=B

"Without a concept, there's nothing. Having found the concept, it's a question of communicating this in the clearest and most succinct way possible, paying attention to the objectives, the target and the requirements of the briefing and always in agreement with the client. Nothing superfluous or that can't be justified – everything for a reason and everything with a function. There's no room here for 'I like it', 'I don't like it': only whether 'it's effective' or not."

»Ohne Konzept geht nichts. Wenn man ein Konzept gefunden hat, geht es darum, es so klar und knapp wie möglich zu vermitteln, dabei die Ziele und Anforderungen des Auftrags im Blick zu behalten und immer in Abstimmung mit dem Kunden zu arbeiten. Es darf nichts geben, was überflüssig oder ungerechtfertigt ist. Alles muss einen Grund und eine Funktion haben. Es gibt keinen Spielraum für ein ›das mag ich‹ oder ›das mag ich nicht‹, nur für ein ›es funktioniert‹ – oder eben nicht.«

« Sans concept, il n'y a rien. Une fois le concept trouvé, il s'agit de le communiquer de la façon la plus claire et succincte possible en gardant toujours à l'esprit les objectifs, la cible et les exigences du *brief*, et en accord avec le client. Rien de superflu ou qui puisse être justifié – tout doit avoir une raison et tout doit avoir une fonction. Pas de place ici pour 'j'aime bien, je n'aime pas' : seul compte de savoir si c'est 'efficace' ou pas. »

Previous page:
Project: *"Better Design = Better Business" poster, 2006*
Client: *BCD Design Week*

Top:
Project: *"01, 02, 03" packaging for Swell iced teas, 2004*
Client: *Evasa*

Above:
Project: *"Fresh Produce" jeans packaging, 2005*
Client: *Cooked in Barcelona*

Following page top left:
Project: *"Your Product, Here" catalogue, 2004*
Client: *Palau de la Música*

Following page top right:
Project: *"Fresh Fruit" packaging for Swell fruit juices, 2003*
Client: *Evasa*

Following page bottom:
Project: *"Team" corporate identity for production company, 2004*
Client: *RCR Films*

258   *ruiz+company*

PALAU DE LA MÚSICA,
ELS CONCERTS,
ELS NEGOCIS,
ELS CONGRESSOS,
LES PRESENTACIONS,
LES CONVENCIONS,
LES RECEPCIONS,
LES CONFERÈNCIES,
ELS DINARS I SOPARS,
LES EXPOSICIONS,
LES CELEBRACIONS.

STEFAN SAGMEISTER

"Trying to touch the heart of the viewer."

Sagmeister Inc.
222 West 14th Street
Suite 15a
New York, NY 10011
USA
T +1 212 647 178 9
info@sagmeister.com
www.sagmeister.com

Biography
1962 Born in Bregenz, Austria
1982–1986 Studied graphic design, University of Applied Arts, Vienna
1986–1988 Studied communication design, Pratt Institute, New York (as a Fulbright Scholar)

Professional experience
1983/84 Designer, ETC. Magazine, Vienna
1984–1987 Designer, Schauspielhaus, Vienna
1987/88 Designer, Parham Santana, New York
1988/89 Designer, Muir Cornelius Moore, New York
1989 Art Director, Sagmeister Graphics, New York
1989/90 Art Director, Sagmeister Graphics, Vienna
1991–1993 Creative Director, Leo Burnett (Hong Kong Office)
1993 Creative Director, M&Co, New York
1993+ Principal of Sagmeister Inc. in New York

Recent exhibitions
2000 "Design Biannual", Cooper-Hewitt National Design Museum, New York
2001 "Stealing Eyeballs", Künstlerhaus, Vienna; Solo exhibition, Gallery Frédéric Sanchez, Paris
2002 Solo exhibition, MAK, Vienna
2003 Solo exhibition, Museum für Gestaltung, Zurich, Switzerland; Solo exhibition, DDD Gallery, Osaka / GGG Gallery, Tokyo
2004 Solo exhibition, Kook min University, Seoul; Solo exhibition, KISD Gallerie, Cologne; Solo exhibition, Czech Design Center, Brno; Solo exhibition, Zumtobel Lounge, Lichtturm, Berlin; Solo exhibition, SVA gallery, New York; Solo exhibition, Les Silos, Chaumont; Solo exhibition, Czech Design Center, Prague
2005 Solo exhibition, Bratislava
2006 Solo exhibition, Centro, Mexico City

Recent awards
Has won over 200 design awards including four Grammy nominations and gold medals from The New York Art Directors Club and the D&AD plus:
1999 Best of Show, I. D. Magazine
2000 Gold Medal, Poster Biannual, Brno; Gold Medal, Warsaw Poster Exhibition
2001 Chrysler Design Award; Best of Show, I. D. Magazine
2002 Grand Prix, TDC Tokyo; Gold Award, The Golden Bee, Moscow
2003 Gold Award, The One Show, New York; Best of Show, Brno Poster Biennale
2004 Grammy, National Academy of Recording Arts
2005 National Design Award, USA
2006 National Design Award, USA

Clients
Aiga Detroit; Anni Kuan Design; Booth Clibborn Editions; Business Leaders for Sensible Priorities; Capitol Records; Chaumont;.copy Magazine; Dai Nippon Printing Company; The Guggenheim Museum; Museum für Gestaltung Zurich; Neenah Paper; Rhino; Warner Bros.; Warner Jazz; Zumtobel AG

"Having spent many years designing for the music industry – CD covers for the Rolling Stones and Aerosmith, books for Lou Reed and the Talking Heads – we decided five years ago to open up the scope of our work and concentrate on four areas: 25% of our work now consists of design for the art world, such as books and publications for galleries and museums, another 25% takes place within the scientific community (we just designed a popular science magazine), and a further 25% for social causes like TrueMajority, a group that seeks to cut Pentagon spending and move the savings over to education. The rest of our work is spent on design for corporations. We never wanted to grow the studio, and are now exactly the same size we were when starting out 13 years ago: myself, Matthias Ernstberger and an intern. Like before, I am still concerned with design that has the ability to touch the viewer's heart and continue to find it extremely difficult to achieve."

»Nachdem wir viele Jahre für die Musikindustrie gearbeitet hatten – CD-Cover für die Rolling Stones und Aerosmith, Bücher für Lou Reed und die Talking Heads – beschlossen wir vor fünf Jahren, unser Arbeitsfeld zu vergrößern und uns auf vier Themenbereiche zu konzentrieren. Ein Viertel unserer Arbeiten sind heute Designs für die Kunstszene (darunter Bücher und Kataloge für Galerien und Museen), ein Viertel bewegt sich in der Welt der Wissenschaften (wir haben gerade eine beliebte naturwissenschaftliche Zeitschrift neu gestaltet), und ein Viertel unserer Zeit arbeiten wir an gesellschaftlich-sozialen Themen, zum Beispiel für TrueMajority (USA), eine Gruppe, die erreichen will, dass das Budget des Pentagons gekürzt und die eingesparten Gelder für Bildung ausgegeben werden. Den Rest der Zeit arbeiten wir für Unternehmen. Wir wollten das Büro nie vergrößern und sind heute noch genau so viele wie vor dreizehn Jahren, als wir anfingen: Matthias Ernstberger, ein Praktikant und ich. Nach wie vor bemühe ich mich darum, Entwürfe zu schaffen, die das Herz des Betrachters rühren, und finde das immer noch so schwer zu erreichen wie eh und je.«

«Après avoir passé de nombreuses années à créer des compositions graphiques pour l'industrie musicale – des jaquettes de CD pour les Rolling Stones et Aerosmith, des livres pour Lou Reed et les Talking Heads – nous avons décidé il y a cinq ans d'ouvrir notre champ d'action dans quatre directions : 25% de notre travail est réalisé à destination du monde de l'art (livres et revues d'art pour des galeries et des musées), un autre quart est consacré à la communauté scientifique (nous venons de créer une maquette pour un célèbre magazine scientifique) et 25 autres pour-cent concernent des causes sociales comme TrueMajority, un groupe qui tente d'obtenir que les crédits alloués au Pentagone soient consacrés à l'éducation. Le reste de notre travail consiste en commandes institutionnelles. Nous n'avons jamais cherché à développer le studio, qui n'est pas plus gros aujourd'hui que lorsque nous l'avons fondé il y a 13 ans, Matthias Ernstberger, un stagiaire et moi. Comme avant, je m'intéresse au graphisme qui a la capacité d'atteindre le cœur de celui qui le regarde et je continue à trouver que c'est très difficile à réussir. »

Previous page:
Project: *"Trying to look good limits my life"/"Starting a charity is surprisingly easy"* billboards and magazine spreads, 2004–2006
Clients: *Art Grandeur Nature/Copy Magazine*

Above left:
Project: *"Zumtobel AG" annual report (back cover)*, 2002
Client: *Zumtobel AG*

Above right:
Project: *"Zumtobel AG" annual report (inside page)*, 2002
Client: *Zumtobel AG*

Following page top left:
Project: *"Sagmeister in Chaumont" poster*, 2004
Client: *Chaumont Festival*

Following page top right:
Project: *"Sagmeister in Zurich" poster*, 2003
Client: *Museum für Gestaltung, Zurich*

Following page bottom:
Project: *"Douglas Gordon: The Vanity of Allegory" catalogue*, 2005
Client: *Guggenheim Berlin*

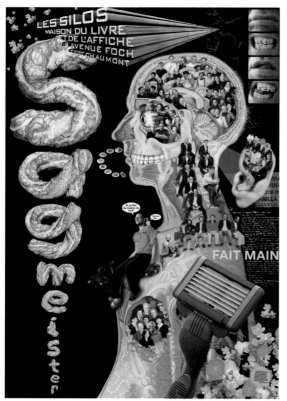

PETER SAVILLE

"For others, to others"

Peter Saville
25–31 Ironmonger Row
London EC1V 3QN
UK
T +44 207 253 433 4
peter@petersavillestudio.com
www.petersaville.com

Biography
1955 Born in Manchester, England
1978 BA (Hons) Graphic Design, Manchester Polytechnic

Professional experience
1979–1991 Founding Partner and Art Director, Factory Records, Manchester
1981–1983 Art Director, Dindisc (Virgin Records), London
1983–1990 Established his own studio, Peter Saville Associates, London
1990–1993 Partner, Pentagram Design, London
1993/94 Creative Director, Frankfurt Balkind, Los Angeles
1995–1998 Established London office for German communications agency Meire und Meire
1999 Co-founded multidisciplinary new media project, SHOWstudio, with photographer Nick Knight
2000/01 Co-curator SHOWstudio with Nick Knight, London

Recent exhibitions
2003 "Peter Saville Show", Design Museum, London/Laforet, Tokyo
2004 "Peter Saville Show", Urbis, Manchester; "Communicate", Barbican Art Gallery, London
2005 "Peter Saville Estate", Migros Museum, Zurich
2006 "What Now", CRAC Alsace; "The Secret Public, The Last Days of the British Underground 1978–1988", Kunstverein, Munich

Recent awards
2005 Doctor of Arts Honoris Causa, Manchester Metropolitan University

Clients
ABC Television; Alexander McQueen; Audley; Balenciaga; Barbican Centre; Björk; Cacharel; Channel One; Christian Dior; Clements Ribeiro; CNN; Design Museum; Egg; Electronic; EMI Group; English National Opera; Estée Lauder; Everything But The Girl; Gagosian Gallery; Gay Dad; Givenchy; Goldie; Holland & Holland; Jil Sander; Joy Division; Kilgour; Kvadrat; London Records; Manchester City Council; Mandarina Duck; Marconi/Pres. Co; Mercedes Benz/Smart Car; Monaco; New Order; OMD; Paul Stolper Gallery; Pringle of Scotland; Pulp; Richard James; RTL; Selfridges; Sergio Rossi; Somerset House; Stella McCartney; Suede; The Hacienda; The Other Two; Viva Plus; WDR; ZDF

"Many young designers and students are now under the impression that graphic design is about self-expression…it isn't. Professional communications design is paid for by a commissioner in order to relay a specific message to an intended audience and this necessarily means that one works to a set brief. Self-generated work – free from such constraints – is closer to art than design. The zone that lies between art and design has become even less distinct in recent years as both practice and technology have fused what used to be clearly identifiable as separate media. You can, however, still make the distinction; if someone has commissioned a predetermined outcome it has to be considered design. Often graphic designers succumb to being more interested in technique rather than an organizing idea – the means rather than the end. This is a hobbyist tendency characteristic of the early stages of a career. Technology has also made the practice of graphic design quicker but also more complex, and not necessarily easier and with shorter deadlines there is less time to question principles. A designer really needs to ask about the agenda being addressed and the purpose of the work. Contemporary culture is constantly confronting us with a forest of misleading and often deceitful messages and a designer must retain some sense of purpose and moral value. Design has to have an inherent truth otherwise it becomes disingenuous decoration."

»Viele junge Grafiker und Grafikstudenten sind heute der Meinung, beim Grafikdesign gehe es um den Ausdruck der eigenen Persönlichkeit. Das stimmt nicht. Professionelles Grafikdesign wird von einem Auftraggeber bezahlt und soll einem definierten Publikum eine spezifische Botschaft übermitteln, was bedeutet, dass man festgelegte Vorgaben umsetzen muss. Entwürfe, die man aus eigenem Antrieb erstellt, sind eher Kunst als Design. Die Übergänge zwischen Kunst und Design sind in den letzten Jahren noch verschwommener geworden, weil in der Berufspraxis mit den heutigen technischen Mitteln die früher klaren Trennungen zwischen verschiedenen Medien zunehmend aufgehoben werden. Man kann aber immer noch sagen, dass eine Auftragsarbeit, bei der ein vorgegebenes Resultat erzielt werden muss, als Design zu gelten hat. Häufig erliegen Designer der Versuchung, sich mehr mit der Technik ihrer Designs als mit der Umsetzung von Inhalten – mehr mit den Mitteln statt dem Zweck – zu befassen. Die Computertechnik hat Arbeitsprozesse beschleunigt, aber auch verkompliziert, so dass die Arbeit des Grafikers nicht leichter geworden ist und er weniger Zeit hat, grundsätzliche Fragen zu stellen. Ein Designer sollte aber die Auftragsvorgaben und den Zweck eines Projekts hinterfragen. Die zeitgenössische Kultur konfrontiert uns ständig mit einem Wust von irreführenden, häufig sogar betrügerischen Informationen und ein Grafiker muss sich dabei seine grundlegenden Zielsetzungen und moralischen Werte bewahren. Grafikdesign muss innere Wahrhaftigkeit besitzen, wenn es nicht zur einfallslosen Dekoration verkommen soll.«

« Un grand nombre de jeunes graphistes et d'étudiants ont aujourd'hui l'impression que le graphisme est une question d'expression personnelle… C'est faux. Le graphisme publicitaire est rémunéré par un commanditaire pour transmettre un message particulier à un public ciblé, ce qui signifie nécessairement que l'on travaille selon un cahier des charges précis. Le travail personnel – libre de telles contraintes – est plus proche de l'art que du design. La zone qui s'étend entre art et design est devenue d'autant plus floue ces dernières années que la pratique et la technologie ont fait fusionner ce qui était auparavant deux disciplines distinctes et clairement identifiables. La distinction se fait pourtant toujours. Si le travail a été commandé dans un but prédéterminé il doit être considéré comme du design. Les graphistes succombent souvent à la tentation de s'intéresser davantage à la technique qu'à une idée structurante – aux moyens plutôt qu'à la fin. Il s'agit d'une tendance amateuriste caractéristique des premières étapes d'une carrière. La technologie a également rendu la pratique du graphisme plus rapide mais aussi plus complexe, avec des délais plus courts et moins de temps pour remettre les principes en question. Or un graphiste doit vraiment s'interroger sur la thématique abordée et sur le but de son travail. La culture contemporaine nous confronte constamment à une forêt de messages trompeurs et souvent déloyaux et un graphiste doit conserver un semblant de clairvoyance et de valeurs morales. Le graphisme doit être porteur d'une vérité intrinsèque, sinon il devient de la décoration fourbe. »

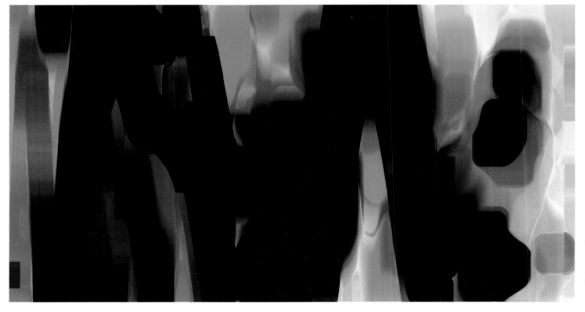

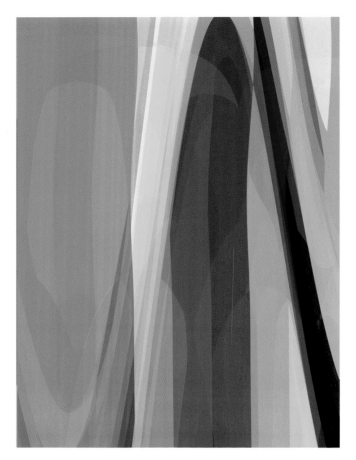

loop

Page 265:
Project: *"Suite for Adobe"*
special edition marketing poster,
2003 (in collaboration with
Howard Wakefield)
Client: *Adobe*

Previous page:
Project: *"Waste Painting #11*
En Suite" unique artwork, 2003
(in collaboration with Howard
Wakefield)
Client: *Paul Stolper Gallery*

Top:
Project: *"End of Year"*
Christmas card, 2005
(in collaboration with Howard
Wakefield and Sarah Parris)
Client: *Kvadrat*

Above:
Project: *"Loop"*
product information card, 2006
(in collaboration with Howard
Wakefield)
Client: *Kvadrat*

SCANDI-NAVIAN DESIGNLAB

"Challenging our clients' thinking and our own."

Scandinavian DesignLab
Amaliegade 5C, 3
1256 Copenhagen
Denmark
T +45 702 708 06
contact@
scandinaviandesignlab.com
www.
scandinaviandesignlab.com

Design group history
2004 Founded by Per Madsen, Anne-Mette Højland and Jesper von Wieding, based in Copenhagen, Denmark and Shanghai, China.

Partners' biographies
Per Madsen
1965 born in Denmark
1988 Studied graphic design, Danish Design School, Copenhagen
1988 Art Director, Zangenberg & Lembourn
1992 Founded Box Design

(Creative and Managing Director)
1999 Sold Box Design to Scandinavian Design Group/ Futurebrand (Creative Director/Partner)
2004 Founded Scandinavian DesignLab (Creative Director/ Partner)
Anne-Mette Højland
1967 born in Denmark
1993 MSc Marketing & General Management, Copen-hagen Business School
1997 Egmont Entertainment (Vice President Games)

1999 Jack Of All Games (Managing Director)
2001 TV-Shop Europe GmbH, Frankfurt (Vice President)
2003 Scandianvian Design Group (Account Director)
2004 Founded Scandinavian DesignLab (Account Director/Partner)

Recent exhibitions
2006 "Who am I?", Storm, Copenhagen; "Graphics in Fashion", Copenhagen City Hall; "Honey I'm Home", Danish Design Centre, Copen-

hagen; "Graphics in Fashion– Vol. 2", Copenhagen

Recent awards
2008 Voted The Danish Design Agency of The Year; The Danish Design Award; CLIO Award, Bronze Winner; EPICA Award, Bronze Winner; EUROBEST Award, Bronze winner; The Danish Arts Foundation Prize
2009 Voted The Danish Design Agency of The Year; Design-preis der Bundesrepublik Deutschland; CLIO Award,

Silver Winner; EUROBEST Award, Bronze winner; Creative Circle, Gold Award

Clients
Carlsberg, Lego, Nestlé, Bang & Olufsen, Visit Denmark, Bestseller, Yarpivo Russia, Toms Group, Sara Lee, Mannaz, Alectia, Velux, Paristexas, munthe plus simonsen, 1:1 Architects, Republique Theatre, Nørrebro Theatre, Dyhrberg Kern.

"We keep an open mind and adapt our approach, avoiding a standardized process, as every client's need is different… Our name reflects the style and working process we offer clients… Scandinavian = Pure, Simple, Fresh, Humour, Creativity, Functionality; DesignLab = Professionalism, Highest Level of Competence, Constant Development, In-depth Research, Finding the Right Solution, Respect for Details… but ultimately seeing the big picture."

»Wir wollen aufgeschlossen und unvoreingenommen bleiben und wandeln unsere Vorgehensweisen ab, um Routineabläufe zu vermeiden, da die Anforderungen jedes Auftraggebers anders sind … Unser Name reflektiert den Stil und die Arbeitsweise, die wir anbieten … Skandinavisch = klar, schlicht, frisch, humorvoll, kreativ, funktional. DesignLab = Professionalität, höchste Kompetenz, ständige Weiterentwicklung, gründliche Recherchen, Suche nach der richtigen Lösung, Respekt für Details – aber letztlich das Sehen des gesamten Bildes.«

«Nous gardons l'esprit ouvert et nous adaptons notre démarche en évitant les méthodes standardisées, car le besoin de chaque client est unique… Notre nom reflète le style et les méthodes de travail que nous proposons aux clients… Scandinave = pureté, simplicité, fraîcheur, humour, créativité, fonctionnalité; DesignLab = professionnalisme, compétence, recherche approfondie, trouver des solutions, respecter les détails… pour finir par voir l'image générale.»

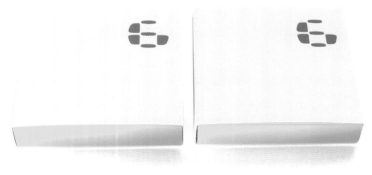

Top (all images):
Project: "Tomorrow #03"
trend publication, 2005
Client: Bestseller/Stylecounsel

Above:
Project: "Who Am I?"
promotion book, 2005
Client: 2pm modelmanagement

Following page (both images):
Project: "Graphics in Fashion 02"
images from exhibition, 2006
Fashion/Styling: Nikoline Liv
Andersen/Laura Baruël

SPIN

"We think about what we're going to do, and then we do it."

Spin
33 Stannary Street
London SE11 4AA
UK
T +44 207 793 955 5
post@spin.co.uk
www.spin.co.uk

Design group history
1992 Founded by Tony Brook and Patricia Finegan in London, England
1997 Warren Beeby (b. 1968) joined Spin having previously worked for Time Out magazine (1993–1997)

Founders' biographies
Tony Brook
1962 Born in Halifax, West Yorkshire, England
1978–1980 Foundation Course, Percival Whitley College of Further Education, Halifax
1980–1982 SIAD, Somerset College of Arts & Technology
1983–1987 Worked for Shoot That Tiger!, London
1987–1990 Worked for Icon, London
1990/91 Worked for SMS Communications, London

Patricia Finegan
1965 Born in Manchester, England
1985–1989 Studied design management, London College of Fashion
1989/90 Worked for Lynne Franks PR, London
1990–1992 Worked for PR Unlimited, London

Recent exhibitions
1998 "Powerhouse UK", Design Council, London; "onedotzero", ICA, London
1999 "onedotzero", ICA, London
2000 "onedotzero", ICA, London
2001 "Stealing Eyeballs", Künstlerhaus, Vienna; "Great Expectations" (Design Council), Grand Central Station, New York

2004 "Communicate: British Independent Graphic Design since the Sixties", Barbican Art Gallery, London
2005 "50 Posters", Spin Studio, London
2006 "Relics on Spirit", Aiap Gallery, Milan

Recent awards
1998 Silver, D&AD for Interactive Design; Silver New Media Award, I. D. Magazine; Global Top Forty nomination, I. D. Magazine
1999 Honourable Mention, D&AD for Typography
2001 Gold Award, Promax; Best Identity Development, Superbrand
2002 Silver D&AD Award, Cinema and TV Graphics
2003–2005 Nominations, D&AD for Posters, Books & Catalogues, Corporate Identity, Graphic Design and Advertising Typography; Distinctive Merit Award, Art Directors Club NY; Distinction, I. D. International Design Magazine for Identity Design
2006 Nomination, D&AD for Channel Identity; Broadcast Digital Awards–Best New Channel; D&AD Award for Graphic Design–Brochures & Catalogues

Clients
American Movie Channel; Amrita & Mallika; Artangel; Azman Architects; Bird's Eye View; British Council; British Documentary Film Foundation; Caruso St. John Architects; Central Office of Information; Channel 4; Christie's; D&AD; Deutsche Bank; Diesel; Discovery Chanel; Five; Foreign & Commonwealth Office; Greater London Authority; Haunch of Venison Gallery; Health Education Authority; Hilliard; Home Office; Hospital Group; John Brown Citrus Publishing; Rose of Kingston Theatre; Liberty; Levi Strauss & Co.; Makri; Mother; MTV; MTV 2; Nike; Orange; Precise Reprographics; Project 2; Richard Rogers Partnership; Sotheby's; Strategic Rail Authority; Tate Modern; The Photographers' Gallery; UBS Warburg; Unilever; University of Arts London; Vision-On Publishing; VH-1; Whitechapel Gallery

"We are excited by challenging thinking, imagery and typography. For us graphic design is about content, functionality, expression and the physical nature of the medium we are working in. A fundamental part of our approach is collaboration with our clients and with photographers, illustrators, programmers, typographers and animators. All we are ultimately interested in is the quality of the end result. Successful graphic design must have originality, relevance, clarity and an element of risk."

»Uns begeistern anspruchsvolle Gedanken, Bilder und typografische Lösungen. Für uns geht es beim Grafikdesign um Inhalte, Funktionalität, Ausdruckskraft und die physische Beschaffenheit des jeweiligen Mediums. Zu unserer Arbeitsweise gehört ganz grundlegend die Zusammenarbeit mit Auftraggebern, Fotografen, Zeichnern, Programmierern, Typografen und Animatoren. Alles, was uns letztlich interessiert, ist die Qualität des Endergebnisses. Gelungene Werbegrafiken müssen originell, relevant und klar sein – und auch ein bisschen was riskieren.«

« Nous sommes attirés par les ideés, les images et la typographie exigeantes. Pour nous, le graphisme est une affaire de contenu, de fonctionnalité, d'expression et dépend de la nature physique du moyen d'expression que nous employons. Notre démarche repose en grande partie sur la collaboration avec nos clients mais aussi avec les photographes, illustrateurs, programmeurs, typographes et animateurs. Tout ce qui compte pour nous, au bout du compte, c'est la qualité du produit fini. Pour avoir du succès, le graphisme doit être original, pertinent, clair et porteur d'un élément de risque. »

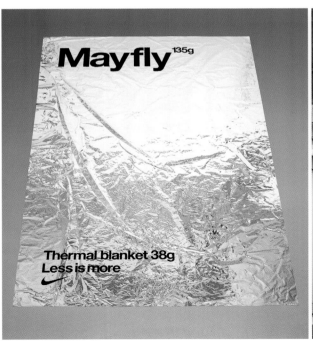

Page 277:
Project: *"More 4" television channel identity*, 2005
Client: *Channel 4*

Previous page top:
Project: *"Visuell" magazine spreads*, 2005
Client: *Deutsche Bank*

Previous page bottom left:
Project: *"Mayfly" poster/thermal blanket*, 2005
Client: *Nike*

Previous page bottom right:
Project: *"Changes of Mind" window graphics*, 2005
Client: *Haunch of Venison*

Top left:
Project: *"Jorge Pardo" catalogue*, 2005
Client: *Haunch of Venison*

Top right:
Project: *"Deutsche Börse Photography Prize" catalogue*, 2006
Client: *The Photographers Gallery*

Above:
Project: *"Dan Flavin" invitation*, 2005
Client: *Haunch of Venison*

VLADAN SRDIĆ

"Key terms: irony, cynicism, humour, advertising and subversive communication, visual-culture domination, exposure of social 'pollution'"

TheSign/Studio360
Kotnikova 34
1000 Ljubljana
Slovenia
T +386 31 847 261
vladan@thesign.org.uk
www.thesign.org.uk

Biography
1972 Born in Belgrade, Serbia
1989–1991 Studied at Schumatovačka School of Art, Belgrade
1993–1998 Studied graphic design at the Academy of Applied Arts, Belgrade

Professional experience
1998/99 Senior Designer, Preview Graphics, Vancouver
1994–1999 Art Director, Torpedo Theatre Company, Belgrade
1992/93 Art Director, STB Saatchi & Saatchi, Belgrade
1999–2001 Art Director, STB Saatchi & Saatchi, Ljubljana
2001–2005 Creative & Art Director, VF Young & Rubicam, Ljubljana
2005+ Creative & Art Director, TheSign/Studio360, Ljubljana

Recent exhibitions
2000 Solo Exhibition, Graficki Kolektiv Gallery, Belgrade; "Biennale Brno"; "SOF," Portoroz; "Magdalena Festival", Maribor; "Golden Drum Festival", Portoroz; "Golden Bee", Moscow; "Nagoya Design Do", Nagoya
2001 "8th International Triennial of the Political Poster", Mons; "SOF", Portoroz; "Magdalena Festival", Maribor; "Golden Drum Festival", Portoroz
2002 PICA; "Magdalena Festival", Maribor; "Golden Drum Festival", Portoroz
2003 Solo Exhibition, KCB Gallery, Belgrade; Solo Exhibition, Art Gallery Maribor; "Magdalena Festival", Maribor; "Golden Drum Festival", Portoroz; "1st Biennial of Visual Communication", Ljubljana
2004 "International Triennial of the Political Poster", Mons; "Golden Griffon", Belgrade; "Golden Drum Festival", Portoroz; EPICA
2005 Solo Exhibition, O3one Gallery, Belef Festival, Belgrade; "Golden Drum Festival", Portoroz; Group exhibition, Visual Arts Gallery, New York; "Exponto Festival", Ljubljana; "2nd Biennial of Visual Communication", Ljubljana; "Young Blood", Ljubljana/Prague
2006 Solo exhibtion, KUD France Preseren, Ljubljana; "Belef Festival", Belgrade

Recent awards
2000 Finalist, SOF; Finalist, Magdalena Festival; Honourable Mention, Nagoya Design Do
2001 2nd place, 5th Best Calendar Exhibition; Silver Prize, 10th SOF; Best Print Ad, Magdalena Festival; Graphic Design Award, May Exhibition; Silver Drumstick, Golden Drum Festival; Shortlist, EPICA
2002 Golden Griffon Award, Graficki Kolektiv
2003 1st Prize, Special Award, 6th Best Calendar Exhibition; Graphic Design Award, May Exhibition; Finalist, BRUMEN 03
2004 1st Prize, Mladina Magazine Contest; Finalist, EPICA; Golden Griffon Award
2005 Finalist, Golden MM 05; Finalist, BRUMEN 05
2006 Golden MM Award, GOLDEN MM 06; Griffon Award (x2), Graficki Koletiv; 1st Prize–PPAIA Creative Brief, Golden Drum Festival, Portoroz

Clients
Agency Ogilvy Imelda; Alfa Romeo; Allied Domecq; Band Vrooom; BAT; Belef 05; Difar; Domina Grand Media Hotel; Dusko Radovic Theatre; Fiat; FIFA; FormArt; Fabriano; Gorenje; Hairstyle Panjkovic; Inkam d.o.o.; Kvadart magazine; Magdalena Festival; MGLC Gallery; Ministry of Health of the Republic of Slovenia; Mladina magazine; P&G; Radio Television of Slovenia; Reckitt Benckieser; Rambo Amadeus; Saatchi & Saatchi Ljubljana; Sava Tyres; Sony; SonyEricsson; Sparkasse; Sport 2000; Studio Click; Sushimama; TheSign; Torpedo Theatre; Toyota; Vrooom; Vulco; Western Wireless

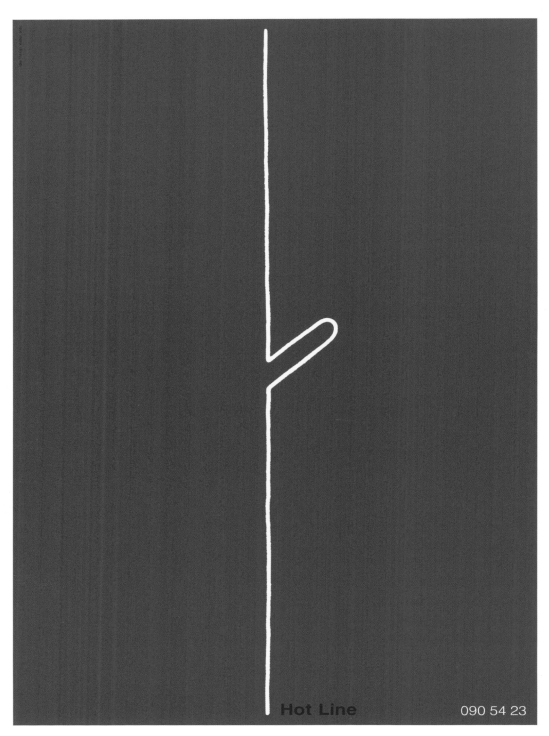

Hot Line 090 54 23

"My studio/office in Ljubljana (Slovenia) is known as TheSign/Studio360 and functions as a creative boutique offering solutions in the field of advertising, branding, graphic and web design, interior design and architecture. Our philosophy is to communicate in a fresh and sophisticated manner: simple, clever, efficient and always longing for a twist. With 10 years of experience and 100% dedication to work, I really try to create winning solutions that have an inherent flexibility. Our goal is a strong concept for our clients and we always aim to give the cause the dignity it deserves."

»Meine Agentur in Ljubljana (Slowenien) heißt TheSign/Studio360 und arbeitet als Kreativladen, der Designlösungen in den Bereichen Werbung, Markenentwicklung, Grafik- und Webdesign, Innenarchitektur und Architektur verkauft. Wir wollen auf neue, lebendige und raffinierte Weise einfach, clever und wirkungsvoll Inhalte vermitteln, immer auf der Suche nach dem besonderen Pfiff. Mit zehnjähriger Erfahrung und hundertprozentigem Einsatz versuche ich, optimale Lösungen mit eingebauter Flexibilität zu produzieren. Unser Ziel ist in jedem Fall ein starkes Konzept für unsere Kunden, und wir versuchen immer, Inhalte mit der Würde auszudrücken, die sie verdienen.«

« Mon studio/bureau de Ljubljana (Slovénie) s'appelle TheSign/Studio360 et fonctionne comme une boutique de création qui propose des solutions dans les secteurs de la publicité, de l'identité visuelle, du graphisme papier ou Web, de la décoration intérieure et de l'architecture. Notre philosophie est de communiquer de façon fraîche et élégante : simple, astucieuse, efficace et toujours en quête d'une impulsion. Riche de mes 10 ans d'expérience et de mon dévouement total à mon travail, j'essaie vraiment de créer des solutions optimales et intrinsèquement flexibles. Notre but est d'imaginer un concept fort pour nos clients et nous donnons toujours à leur cause la dignité qu'elle mérite. »

Previous page:
Project: *"Hot Line"*
print advertisement, 2001
Client: *Inkam D. O. O.*

Above:
Project: *"Ms Click"*
billboard, 2004
Client: *Belgrade Fashion Week*

Following page top:
Project: *"Petka"*
print advertisement, 2005
Client: *Difar D. O. O.*

Following page bottom left:
Project: *"International*
Car-free Day" postcard, 2004
Client: *Ministry of Health,*
Republic of Slovenia

Following page bottom right:
Project: *"Feel the Road"*
billboard, 2005
Client: *Fiat*

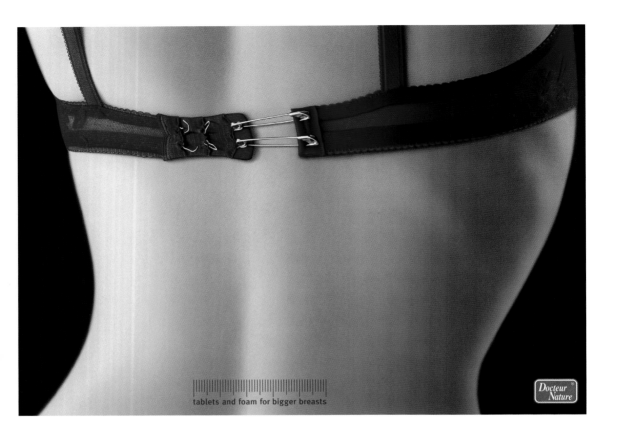

||||||||||||||||||||||||||||||||||||||||||||||
tablets and foam for bigger breasts

Docteur Nature ®

International Car-free Day 22. September 2004

FEEL THE ROAD

FIAT

SLAVIMIR STOJANOVIĆ

"Complicate simply."

Futro Studios
Poljanska Česta 8
1000 Ljubljana
Slovenia
T +386 1 430 274 1
slavimir@futro.si
info@futro.si
www.futro.si

Biography
1969 Born in Belgrade, Serbia (formerly Yugoslavia)
1984–1986 Studied graphic communications at the Design High School in Belgrade
1987–1992 Studied graphic design at the Academy of Applied Arts, Belgrade
1992/93 Studied graphic communications at HDK, Gothenburg

Professional experience
1993–1999 Regional Design Director at S Team Bates Saatchi & Saatchi Advertising Balkans
1999 Moved to Slovenia, working for Kompas Design and Arih Advertising
2003 Founded Futro in Ljubljana

Recent exhibitions
2003 "Pheno!man", Belgrade
2005 "Superinferior Project", Belgrade
2006 "Ghost Project", Beton Hala, Belgrade; "Good News", 03one Gallery, Belgrade; "Fiction", Fresh Caffe, Ljubljana

Recent awards
2003 Brumen Grand Prix for Best Design in Slovenia

2004 Gifon Grand Prix for Best Design in former Yugoslavia
2005 Brumen Grand Prix for Best Design in Slovenia; Golden Drum Silver Award for Print Ads
2006 Award, 2nd Biennial of Slovene Visual Communications

Clients
Abanka; Danone; Delo Revije; Droga Kolinska; Elektroncek Group; Gorenje; Kolosej; Modern Gallery Ljubljana; MTV Adria; Noviforum; Porsche Slovenia; Radio Television Slovenia; Rotovision; Studio Moderna; Telekom Slovenia

"Futro is a mobile creative service unit, where experimental and commercial work feed one another with endless inspiration producing work for clients worldwide. We are crossing boundaries between art, design, fashion, writing, publishing and corporate culture. We take our strong emotional experiences from the past and mix them with our visions of the future, adding a little twist in that combination of form and content which are then explored, processed and used in our commercial work."

»Futro ist ein mobiles kreatives Dienstleistungsunternehmen, in dem sich experimentelle und kommerzielle Arbeiten gegenseitig befruchten und das mit unerschöpflicher Inspiration und Fantasie für Kunden in aller Welt tätig ist. Wir überschreiten die Grenzen zwischen Kunst, Design, Mode, Schriftstellerei, Publizistik und Unternehmenskultur. Wir nehmen die gefühlsbeladenen Erlebnisse unserer eigenen Vergangenheit und mischen sie mit unseren Zukunftsvisionen. Die Mischung wird dann in Form und Inhalt leicht abgewandelt, untersucht, verarbeitet und fließt in unsere kommerzielle Arbeiten ein.«

«Futro est une unité de service créatif mobile, où travail expérimental et commercial se nourrissent l'un l'autre, et nous mettons cette symbiose créatrice féconde au service de clients du monde entier. Nous franchissons les frontières entre art, design, mode, écriture, édition et culture de l'entreprise. Nous tirons les leçons de nos fortes expériences émotionnelles passées et les fusionnons avec notre vision de l'avenir, avant d'ajouter un petit effet de torsion à cette combinaison entre forme et contenu, que nous analysons, transformons et utilisons ensuite dans notre travail commercial. »

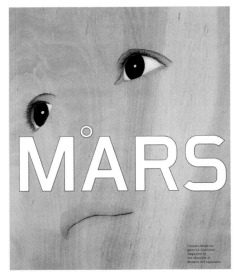

Page 285:
Project: "I Know Everything"
light for Futro, 2005
Client: Self

Previous page top (both images):
Project: "6ix Pack" book
(front and back covers), 2005
Client: DESSA

Previous page bottom (both images):
Project: "I Need" Futro
fanzine (Issue 007), 2004
Client: Self

Top (both images):
Project: "M'ars"
magazine (two issues), 2003
(in collaboration with Robert
Lucander and Marc Quinn)

Client: Museum of Modern
Art Ljubljana

STRANGE ATTRACTORS DESIGN

"We want to cast a new eye over what modernism rebelled against: the traditions of craft, calligraphy and ornamentation as cultural expression."

Strange Attractors Design
Paramaribostraat 18-I
2585 GN The Hague
The Netherlands
T +31 6 248 677 99
mail@strangeattractors.com
www.strangeattractors.com

Founders' biographies
Catelijne van Middelkoop
1975 Born in Alphen a/d Rijn, The Netherlands
1994–1996 Studied art history and archeology, University of Amsterdam
1996–2000 Studied graphic & typographic design, Royal Academy of Art, The Hague
2000–2002 MFA, Cranbrook Academy of Art
2003 Residency o-b-o-k/ Projekt Djurgårdsbrunn, Stockholm
2006 Faculty VIDE

Design group history
2001 Founded by Catelijne van Middelkoop & Ryan Pescatore Frisk in Bloomfield Hills (Cranbrook Academy of Art), USA
2006+ On the national board of directors of the Association of Dutch Designers (BNO)
Ryan Pescatore Frisk
1977 Born in Rochester, USA
1995–1999 BFA, The Savannah College of Art and Design
2000–2002 MFA, Cranbrook Academy of Art
2002 On-site Content Producer/Phototographer/Videographer, Britney Spears European Promo Tour
2003 Residency o-b-o-k/ Projekt Djurgårdsbrunn, Stockholm
2004/05 MA in Type Design, Royal Academy of Art, The Hague
2006 Faculty VIDE (Visual & Individual Design Experiences), The Hague

(Visual & Individual Design Experiences), The Hague
2006+ On the national board of directors of the Association of Dutch Designers (BNO)

Recent exhibitions
2003 82nd Annual and touring exhibition of the Art Directors Club New York; 49th Annual and touring exhibition of the Type Directors Club; "Dutch Design Prizes 2003", Amsterdam
2004 "ADC Young Guns 4" touring exhibition; "21st Biennale of Graphic Design", Brno; "Sidewalk Film Festival", Birmingham, Alabama; 50th Annual and touring exhibition of the Type Directors Club
2004+ "FiFFteen", touring FontFont exhibition by FSI FontShop International; "The Foreign Affairs of Dutch Design", touring exhibition by the BNO and the PresemelaFoundation
2005 51st Annual and touring exhibition of the Type

Directors Club; "Backstage 1", Museum De Beijerd, Breda; "Typophile Film Festival", TypeCon 2005, New York
2006 "Cut for Purpose", Museum Boijmans Van Beuningen, Rotterdam; "Graphic Design Day 2.0", Bologna

Recent awards
2003 Nomination, Dutch Design Awards; Certificates of Typographic Excellence TD49 (Type Directors Club); Distinctive Merit Award ADC82 (Art Directors Club NY)
2004 Judges Choice TDC2, International Type Design Competition; Selection ADC Young Guns 4
2005 Red Dot Award for High Quality in Communication Design; Certificates of Typo-

graphic Excellence TDC51 (Type Directors Club)
2006 Nomination, Design Award of the Federal Republic of Germany 2007; I. D. Forty

Clients
2+3D Polish Design Quarterly; Art + Commerce; City Centre Offices (Berlin); Cranbrook Academy of Art; FontFont/FSI FontShop International; Metropolitan LLC; Museum Boijmans Van Beuningen; o-b-o-k (studio of Laurie Haycock Makela & Ronald Jones); Oratai Sound Salon; Sage Publications; Stroom/Centre for Visual Arts & Architecture; Studio Dumbar; Vanity Fair; VIDE/Visual Individual Design Experiences

MARCH//16TH>>>19TH///2005
STRANGE ATTRACTORS DESIGN

/////BROADCASTING TONGUES//////
WORKSHOP////////////////////////
LECTURE//ASPKAT.EDU.PL
WWW.ASPKAT.EDU.PL
WWW.STRANGEATTRACTORS.COM////////:)

Broadcasting Tongues

//////////////KATOWICE///POLAND

///////////ASPKAT///ACADEMY//OF//FINE//ARTS

"Whether it takes the form of typography, type designs, posters, catalogues, digital animations, CD covers, or 3D installations, their work is a polemic against the depersonalizing effects of modernist typography and design. Such projects are often decried as being superficial, but that criticism misses the point. In today's visual cultures, the surface very often is the message. Strange Attractors are 'decorationalists' (I borrow the term from Denise Gonzales Crisp), who want to rediscover the potential of expressive ornamentation. They use the computer not just as an extension of the ordering brain, as Marshall McLuhan would say, but also as a true instrument of the expressive hand." (Max Bruinsma, first published in *I. D. Magazine*)

»Ob sie nun typografische Designs, Schrifttypen, Plakate, Kataloge, Computeranimationen, CD-Cover oder 3D-Installationen gestalten – ihre Arbeit stellt in jedem Fall eine Polemik gegen die unpersönliche Ausstrahlung modernistischer Typografien und Grafiken dar. Ihre Entwürfe werden oft als oberflächlich abgetan, die Kritik geht jedoch an der Sache vorbei. In der heutigen visuellen Kultur ist die Oberfläche nämlich vielfach schon der Inhalt. Strange Attractors sind ›Dekorationalisten‹ (der Begriff stammt von Denise Gonzales Crisp), die das Potenzial expressiver Ornamente neu entdecken wollen. Sie nutzen Computer nicht nur als Erweiterung des Ordnung schaffenden Kopfes, wie Marshall McLuhan sagen würde, sondern auch als Instrument der Ausdruck schaffenden Hand.« (Max Bruinsma, veröffentlicht im *I. D. Magazine*)

«Qu'il prenne la forme de typographie, de création de polices, d'affiches, de catalogues, d'animations numériques, de couvertures de CD ou d'installations en 3D, leur travail est une lutte contre les effets dépersonnalisants de la typographie et du design modernistes. De tels projets sont souvent accusés de superficialité mais cette critique est absurde. Dans la culture visuelle actuelle, la surface est très souvent le message. Les Strange Attractors sont des 'décorationnalistes' (j'emprunte ce terme à Denise Gonzales Crisp), qui veulent redécouvrir les potentialités de l'ornementation expressive. Ils n'utilisent pas seulement l'ordinateur comme une extension de leur commandes neuronales, comme dirait Marshall McLuhan, mais aussi comme un instrument fidèle entre les mains d'un créateur. » (Max Bruinsma, publié dans *I. D. Magazine*)

Previous page:
Project: *"Broadcasting Tongues"* poster/workshop announcement, 2005
Client: *ASPKAT/Academy of Fine Arts, Katowice*

Above (all images):
Project: *"Little Yellow Writing Hood" animated type specimen fairytale*, 2005
Client: *FSI/FontShop International/FontFont Library*

Following page top:
Project: *"Rotten Cocktails" album/CD cover design*, 2005
Client: *Boy Robot/City Centre Offices*

Following page bottom:
Project: *Jack of Hearts* series of invitations, 2005
Client: *Stroom – Centre for Visual Arts & Architecture, The Hague*

Top:
Project: *"Punkt" typeface/speci-men self-initiated project, 2005*
Client: *Self*

Above:
Project: *"Yesterday I Lost My Helvetica" invitation for "Fresh Talent 2006," 2006*
Client: *AIGA Chicago*

Following page top:
Project: *"BIG TYPE SAYS MORE" typographic instal-lation, 2006*
Client: *Museum Boijmans Van Beuningen, Rotterdam*

Following page bottom:
Project: *"Brunn" typeface/specimen, 2005*
Client: *Self*

STUDIO BOOT

"Dutch Design has been Made in Holland."

Studio Boot
Luijbenstraat 40
5211 BT 's-Hertogenbosch
The Netherlands
T +31 73 614 359 3
info@studioboot.nl
www.studioboot.nl

Founders' biographies

Petra Janssen
1965 Born in Deurne, The Netherlands
1988 Internship at Studio Dumbar in The Hague and in London
1989 Freelance projects for: Hard Werken, Rotterdam, Toon Michiels Ontwerp, 's-Hertogenbosch
1990 Graduates from the Royal Academy of Arts in 's-Herto-

Designgroup History

1993 Founded by Petra Janssen & Edwin Vollebergh in 's-Hertogenbosch, The Netherlands
1993 Studio renamed Studio Boot
1998+ Teacher and mentor at the Design Academy Eindhoven
1999–2005 Teacher at the Academy for Royal Arts, Sint-Joost
2005+ Member of board, Platform 21, a new design institute in Amsterdam

Edwin Vollebergh
1962 Born in 's-Hertogenbosch, The Netherlands
1988 Internship as a graphic design-illustrator at Samen-

genbosch and established her own studio "Gewoon Beginnen"

werkende Ontwerpers in Amsterdam working on Oilily account
1989 Designer at Oilily Studio, Alkmaar
1991 Graduated from Royal Academy of Arts in 's-Hertogenbosch
1998+ Teacher and Mentor at the Design Academy Eindhoven
1999–2003 Teacher at the Academy for Royal Arts, Sint-Joost

Recent exhibitions
2000 "Work from Holland", Brno
2001 "Holland Design, New Graphics", Barcelona

2001–2004 "Festival de Chaumont"
2002 "Hommage à Toulouse Lautrec", Centre Georges Pompidou, Paris
2004–2006 "The Foreign Affairs of Dutch Design", Beurs van Berlage, Amsterdam
2005 "3rd Poster Biennial ", Ningbo

Recent awards
2000 EPICA Award; Merit Awards (x2), Art Directors Club New York; Award and Nomination, Type Directors Club New York
2001 Merit Awards, Art Directors Club New York;

Nominations (x4), Festival de Chaumont
2004 Award and Nomination, Type Directors Club New York; Dutch Design Prize
2005 Silver Award (x2), ADCN; Bronze World Medal, New Yorker Festivals; Award, Festival de Chaumont
2006 PCM Award; ADEE Award; Esprix Award

Clients
City Theatre; Coca-Cola; Harry Kies Theater Productions; Malmberg Publishers; Nike; Oilily; Royal Dutch Mail; Royal Institute of the Tropics

"Studio Boot has nothing to do with boots, other than you can always walk in. We are a graphic design/ illustrative agency that creates strong images with an illustrative use of typography. We are always looking for new solutions. The variety of our clients reflects this approach to graphic design. We love to experiment with old and new techniques and materials, that's how Studio Boot has become so well known in the Netherlands. Because we are also living together, we can never stop working and thinking about design."

»Studio Boot hat nichts mit Stiefeln (boots) zu tun – außer, dass Sie jederzeit bei uns hereinstiefeln können. Wir sind eine Agentur für Werbegrafik und Illustration, die starke Bilder mit illustrativer Typografie verbinden. Wir sind immer auf der Suche nach neuen Lösungen, und die Verschiedenheit unserer Auftraggeber hat zur Folge, dass wir wir immer wieder anders an Designprojekte herangehen. Wir experimentieren gerne mit alten und neuen Techniken und Materialien; dafür sind wir in den Niederlanden bekannt geworden. Weil wir auch zusammen leben, können wir nie aufhören zu arbeiten und über Gestaltungsfragen nachzudenken.«

« Studio Boot n'a rien à voir avec des bottes si ce n'est qu'on peut toujours y mettre un pied. Nous sommes une agence de graphisme et d'illustration qui crée des images fortes en ayant recours à la typographie de façon illustrative. Nous sommes toujours à la recherche de nouvelles solutions. La nature variée de notre clientèle reflète cette approche du graphisme. Nous aimons jouer avec des techniques et des matériaux anciens et nouveaux, et c'est comme ça que Studio Boot est devenu célèbre aux Pays-Bas. Parce que nous vivons aussi ensemble, nous n'arrêtons jamais je travailler et de penser design. »

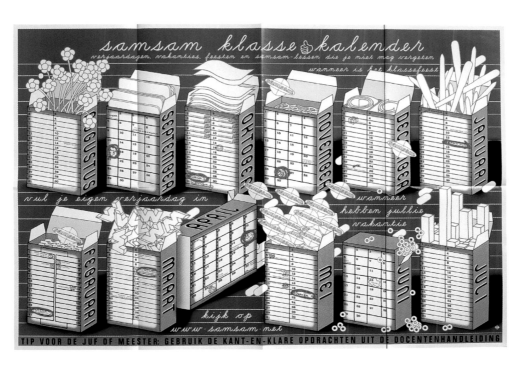

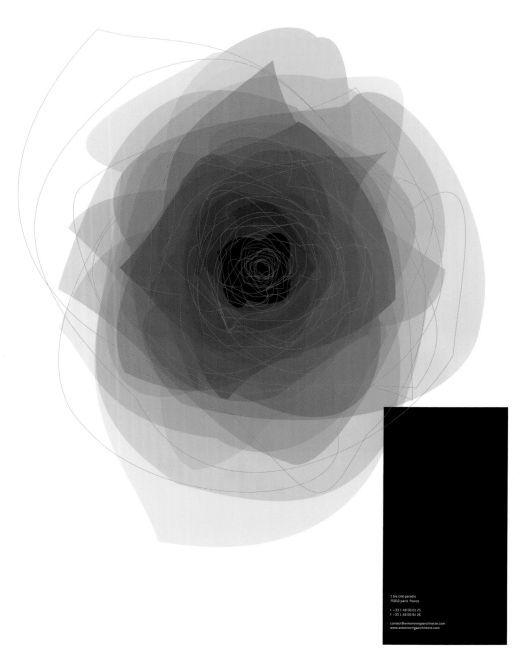

1 bis cité paradis
75010 paris france

t +33 1 48 00 01 25
f +33 1 48 00 81 26

contact@antoniovirgaarchitecte.com
www.antoniovirgaarchitecte.com

SUBURBIA

"Aesthetics/Ideas"

Suburbia
74 Rochester Place
London NW1 9JX
UK
T +44 207 424 068 0
info@suburbia-media.com
www.suburbia-media.com

Design group history
1998 Co-founded by Lee
Swillingham and Stuart
Spalding in London, England

Founders' biographies
Lee Swillingham
1969 Born in Manchester,
England
1988–1991 Studied graphic
design, Central Saint Martins
College of Art & Design,
London
1992–1998 Art Director,
The Face magazine,
London
1998+ Creative Director,
Suburbia, London
2001 Created and launched
Pop magazine for Emap
Publishing
Stuart Spalding
1969 Born in Hawick,
Scotland
1987 Foundation Level Art
& Design, Manchester
Polytechnic
1988–1991 Studied graphic

design, Newcastle upon Tyne
Polytechnic
1992–1998 Art Editor,
The Face magazine,
London
1998+ Creative Director,
Suburbia, London
1999+ Consultant to
Waddell Publishing–
publisher of Dazed and
Confused
2001 Created and launched
Pop magazine for Emap
Publishing

Recent awards
1999 Magazine of the Year,
Society of Publication
Designers, New York
2000 Merit Award, Art
Directors Club, New York
2001 Magazine of the Year,
Society of Publication
Designers, New York
2002 Cover of the Year, ECM
Awards, London
2003 The Annual Award,
London

Clients
Alexander McQueen; Bluma-
rine; BMG Music Group;
Bottega Venetta; Christian
Dior Beauty; Comme des
Garçons; Emap; Giles Deacon;
Gucci; Jigsaw UK; Katherine
Hamnett UK; Lancome; Levi's
Europe; Luella; Mercury
Records; Missoni; Nike
Europe; Universal Music
Group; Virgin Records

STUDIO
FM MILANO

"The shape of significance"

Studio FM Milano
Via Luigi Manfredini 6
20154 Milan
Italy
T +39 02 349 380 11
info@studiofmmilano.it
www.studiofmmilano.it

Founders' biographies
Barbara Forni
1966 Born in Milan, Italy
1985–1987 Studied graphic design at Scuola Politecnica di Design, Milan
1988–1992 Studied painting at the Accademia di Belle Arti di Brera, Milan
1992–1996 Graphic designer and illustrator, Sottsass Associati, Milan
2004 Taught a workshop in visual communication at the Politecnico di Milano, Milan
Sergio Menichello
1967 Born in Milan, Italy
1982–1986 Studied graphic

Design group history
1996 Founded by Barbara Forni and Sergio Menichello in Milan, Italy
2000 Cristiano Bottino joined the studio as a partner

design at Istituto statale d'arte, Monza
1986/87 Studied graphic design at ISIA, Urbino
1988–1996 Worked in several design studios in Milan, including Studio Lissoni, Sottsass Associati, Centro Ricerche Domus Academy, Studio De Lucchi
2001+ Teaches visual communication at the Politecnico di Milano
2004+ Teaches on master programme at the Scuola Politecnica di Design, Milan
2007+ Teaches art direction course at NABA's Art and Design Academy, Milan
Christiano Bottino
1970 Born in Milan, Italy
1990–1995 Studied fine art, architecture and environmental design at Parsons School of Design, New York
1994–1996 Studied photo-

graphy at the New School for Social Research, New York
Worked in an architectural studio in New York
1997–1999 Worked as a stage set designer with Franco Zeffirelli and Edoardo Sanchi at Verona's Arena and Rome's Opera Theatre
1999 Began working at Studio FM in Milan

Recent exhibitions
2001 "Swiss Inside ADV Contest", Victorinox Kunzi, Milan
2002 "Brno Graphic Design Biennial", Brno
2004 "Teach Me", IUAV (Istituto Universitario d'Architettura Venezia), Venice
2005 "Teach Me 3", IUAV (Istituto Universitario d'Architettura Venezia), Venice
2006 "Aiap Community", Perugia; "Give Peace Another

Chance", VI Salone dell'Editoria di Pace, Venice
2007 "The New Italian Design", Triennale di Milano, Milan

Recent awards
2003 Winner of the contest for the logo of the Museo di Fotografia Contemporanea, Cinisello Balsamo, Milan
2005 Best Cultural Event of the Year, BEA Prize, Milan (in collaboration with Connexine)
2006 EULDA The European Logo Design Award 2006, Milan

Clients
Altagamma; Abitare – Segesta; Arnoldo Mondadori; Autorità per l'Energia Elettrica e il Gas; B&B Italia; Boffi; Bticino; Central Groucho; Cesanamedia; Council of European Energy Regulators; Comune

di Milano; Editrice Compositore ENI; EPBM Paravia Bruno Mondadori; Fondazione Enrico Mattei; Fondazione Made in Italy; Gabrius; Gianfranco Ferré; Living Divani; Lupetti; Marni; Massimo De Carlo; Mescal Records; MUD Art Foundation; Museo di Fotografia Contemporanea di Cinisello Balsamo; Mutti & Architetti; Opera Private Equity; Orme Editori; Palazzo Reale Milano; Provincia di Milano; Regione Lombardia; Saipem; Sergio Rossi; Stream TV; Svizzera Turismo/Consorzio Svizzero; T Magazine (The New York Times Magazine); Tecno; Tema Celeste; Urmet Domus; Vallecchi; Versace

POP

+

Miss Moss in an amazing portfolio of London's beautiful and damned by Mert & Marcus Also starring Lily Allen, Peaches Geldof, Francesca Versace, Jonny Woo & more!!!

World Exclusive

Kate Fights Back

R45

9 771470 451005

1 0>

AUTUMN ISSUE   OCTOBER 2006
COVER 1 OF 2 No.13 £5.00

"Being involved in the world of fashion and magazines is proving more and more challenging for the art director and graphic designer. Often one is faced with conceptualizing and art directing a shoot for a person (whether they are a pop singer, actor or novelist), only to discover that the product the said person was promoting has already entered and departed the pop charts, their film has been released on DVD and consigned to the bargain bins, or their book has become a bad mini-series on cable TV. Surely Andy Warhol's prescient 'Fifteen Minute' adage should be changed to 'Fifteen Seconds' to keep in step with the twenty-first century? Consequently here at Suburbia we are, in conjunction with Professor Samuel Himperftoff at the University of Manchester Institute of Science and Technology, developing the Quantum Zeitgeist Predictor (QZP). This device will provide invaluable access to information relating to the coming trends in fashion/music/celebrity, thus allowing us to continue to create the trend-setting forward-thinking work we are so known for. As you can imagine, development of such technology is incredibly expensive and so we are accepting donations to the project through our website address."

»Die Tätigkeit in der Welt der Mode und Zeitschriften erweist sich für einen Art-Director und Grafiker als immer größere Herausforderung. Oft wird man vor die Aufgabe gestellt, ein Fotoshooting für einen Prominenten (sei er Popsänger, Schauspieler oder Autor) zu planen und durchzuführen, um dann zu entdecken, dass dessen zu bewerbendes Produkt bereits auf den Hitlisten stand und schon wieder daraus verschwunden ist, dass dessen Film bereits auf DVD verfügbar und schon in den Krabbelkisten gelandet ist, oder dass dessen Roman inzwischen schon als schlechte Miniserie im Kabelfernsehen läuft. Andy Warhols prophetische ›Fünfzehn Minuten‹ sollten auf jeden Fall in ›Fünfzehn Sekunden‹ abgeändert werden, um mit dem 21. Jahrhundert Schritt zu halten, oder? Deshalb arbeiten wir zusammen mit Professor Samuel Himperftoff vom Wissenschafts- und Technik-Institut der Universität Manchester an der Entwicklung des Quantum Zeitgeist Predictors (QZP), der uns wertvolle Informationen über kommende Trends in den Bereichen Mode, Musik und Prominenz liefern und uns ermöglichen wird, auch weiterhin die vorausschauende, trendige Grafik zu machen, für die wir bekannt sind. Wie Sie sich ja denken können, ist die Entwicklung einer derartigen Technologie wahnsinnig teuer, weshalb wir Spenden für das Projekt über unsere Website dankbar annehmen würden.«

«La collaboration avec le monde de la mode et de la presse magazine s'avère de plus en plus difficile pour les directeurs artistiques et les graphistes. Ils se retrouvent souvent à devoir conceptualiser ou diriger un projet pour quelqu'un d'autre (qu'il s'agisse d'un chanteur de rock, d'un acteur ou d'un romancier) pour finalement se rendre compte que le produit dont cette personne veut faire la promotion est déjà entré et sorti du Top 50, que son film est sorti en DVD et a été remisé sur l'étagère occasions ou que leur livre a été adapté en mini-série pour le câble. L'adage prémonitoire d'Andy Warhol sur les 'Quinze minutes' devrait être changé en 'Quinze secondes' pour suivre la cadence du 21e siècle. C'est pour cette raison qu'ici, chez Suburbia, nous développons en collaboration avec le Professeur Samuel Himperftoff de l'Institut de Sciences et de Technologie de l'Université de Manchester le Quantum Zeitgeist Predictor (QZP). Ce dispositif fournira des informations d'une valeur inestimable sur les tendances futures dans la mode, la musique et les autres domaines à célébrités. Ce projet nous permet aussi de continuer à mener à bien le travail innovateur et avant-gardiste pour lequel nous sommes si réputés. Comme vous pouvez l'imaginer, le développement d'une telle technologie est incroyablement coûteux et nous acceptons donc les dons pour financer nos recherches à travers notre site Web.»

Previous page:
Project: "Pop Issue 13 – Kate Boxing" magazine cover, 2007 (photo: Mert Alas & Marcus Piggott)
Client: Pop magazine/Emap Publishing

Above:
Project: "Pop Logo – Mirror Board Version" logo design, 2003
Client: Pop magazine/Emap Publishing

Following page top:
Project: "Pop Issue 1 – Trash White Fluro" magazine title spread, 2003 (photo: Mert Alas & Marcus Piggott)
Client: Pop magazine/Emap Publishing

Following page centre:
Project: "Pop Issue 1 – Push It!" magazine title spread, 2003 (photo: David Simms)
Client: Pop magazine/Emap Publishing

Following page bottom:
Project: "Shystie: Diamond In the Dirt" 12-inch vinyl gatefold record sleeve, 2005 (photo: Stephane Gallois)
Client: Polydor Records

TRASH WHITE... CLOTHING FLURO

photography by Mert Alas and Marcus Piggott fashion editor Katie Grand

PUSH IT!

Top:
Project: *"Moloko"*
12-inch vinyl record covers, 2004
Client: *Echo Records*

Above:
Project: *"Pop Issue 9 – Gothic"*
magazine spread, 2004
Client: *Pop magazine/Emap
Publishing*

Following page top:
Project: *"New York Fashion
week show invite"*
invitation card, 2004
Client: *Luella Bartley*

Following page bottom:
Project: *"Air collection" product
guide box and fold out, 2005
(photo: Mathew Donaldson)*
Client: *Nike*

Stella S/S 2004

ph: David Sims

Sunday 14th September 1:00 pm Bryant at Bryant Park

RSVP: 212.625.1000 x58

The Air Force One Insideout

20.22 HR

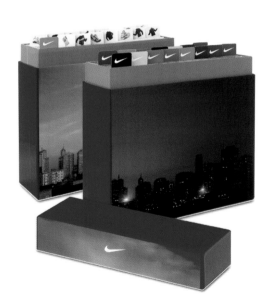

SWEDEN
GRAPHICS

*"In the land of the blind graphic designers,
the one-eyed graphic designer is king!"*

Sweden Graphics
Blekingegatan 46
11 662 Stockholm
Sweden
T +46 8 652 006 6
hello@swedengraphics.com
www.swedengraphics.com

Design group history
1997 Co-founded by Nille
Svensson and Magnus Åström
in Stockholm, Sweden

Founders' biographies
Nille Svensson
1970 Born in Stockholm,
Sweden
1993–1997 Studied graphic
design and illustration,
Konstfack University

College of Arts, Craft &
Design, Stockholm
Magnus Åström
1969 Born in Umeå, Sweden
1994–1997 Studied graphic
design and illustration,
Konstfack University

College of Arts, Craft &
Design, Stockholm

Clients
AIGA NY; Arena; Big Maga-
zine; BLM; Bonnier Amigo;
Don't Panic Media; MTV

Idents; Nando Costa; När Var
Hur; Neo21psum; onedotzero/
Channel 4; Smith and Jones;
Tokyo Style; Universal Music;
Victionary; Wilhelmssons
Arkitekter

"Professional life goes on and what more can we say than that we try to deliver something that is of high quality (thanks to experience), interesting (thanks to experiment), and bold (thanks to integrity). It is still important to be a free agent… To be able to move freely through a wide range of projects and to maintain a variation to the workflow."

»Das Berufsleben geht weiter. Was können wir also mehr sagen, als dass wir etwas zu liefern versuchen, das von hoher Qualität ist (dank unserer Erfahrung), interessant (dank unserer Experimente) und mutig (dank unserer Integrität). Es ist immer noch wichtig, als Freiberufler auch frei zu bleiben … sich frei durch eine Vielfalt unterschiedlicher Projekte hindurchzuarbeiten und die Arbeit abwechslungsreich zu gestalten.«

« La vie professionnelle suit son cours et que dire à part que nous essayons de transmettre un produit de qualité (grâce à l'expérience), intéressant (grâce à l'expérimentation) et hardi (grâce à l'intégrité). Il est toujours important d'être un électron libre… D'être capable de se mouvoir librement dans un large éventail de projets et de conserver une variété dans le flux de travail. »

Previous page:
Project: *"Territory"*
stills from animated short film
about borders, 2001
Client: *onedotzero/Channel 4*

Above:
Project: *"Kokomemedada"*
CD cover, 2003
Client: *Komeda/Universal*
Music

Following page top left:
Project: *"US-UN"*
poster, 2004
Client: *Don't Panic*

Following page top right:
Project: *"China 50 Years"*
editorial illustration, 2002
Client: *DN Förlaget*

Following page bottom:
Project: *"Put the Money Where*
the Mouths Are"
artwork project, 2002
Client: *NEO2 Magazine*

Top:
Project: *"OddJob: Koyo"*
CD cover, 2003
Client: *Bonnier Amigo*

Above:
Project: *"Döda" editorial*
illustration and design, 2003
Client: *BLM Magazine*

Following page top left:
Project: *"Drugs"*
editorial illustration, 2003
Client: *Arena Magazine*

Following page top right:
Project: *"M/M Paris vs. GTF"*
invitation poster, 2004
Client: *AIGA/New York Chapter*

Following page bottom left:
Project: *"Gooh Floor"*
ceramic floor tiles design, 2006
Client: *Wilhelmsson Arkitekter*

Following page bottom right:
Project: *"Where It's At"*
wallpaper design, 2003
Client: *Graphic Magazine*

312   **Sweden Graphics**

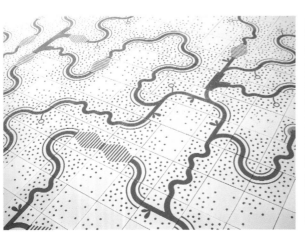

KAM
TANG

*"Drawing and thinking
go hand-in-hand
like a pen and paper."*

Kam Tang
18 Southwell Road
London SE5 9PG
UK
T +44 207 737 III 3
mail@kamtang.co.uk
www.kamtang.co.uk

Biography
1971 Born in London, England
1991–1994 Studied graphic design, Brighton University
1994–1996 Studied graphic design, Royal College of Art, London

Professional experience
1996+ Freelance designer
2004+ Represented by Big Active

Recent exhibitions
2002 "Picture This", worldwide touring exhibition; "Versus Exhibition", Japan
2005 "Who Let You In?", Tokyo
2006 "BWWT 2006" (Be@rbrick World Wide Tour), Medicom, New York/Florence/Milan

Recent awards
1998 Futures Award (for illustration), Creative Review

Clients
Adidas; Burberry; Coutts; Design Museum, London; Medicom; Nike; Royal Mail; Sony Music; Virgin; Warner

THE DESIGNERS REPUBLIC

"Brain Aided Design."

The Designers Republic
The Workstation
15 Paternoster Row
Sheffield S1 2BX
UK
T +44 114 275 498 2
disinfo@
thedesignersrepublic.com
www.
thedesignersrepublic.com

Design group history
1986 Founded by Ian Anderson in Sheffield, England

Recent exhibitions
2002 "Brain Aided Design", La Capella Gallery, Barcelona; "Latent Utopias" (with Sadar Vuga Arhitekti), Landesmuseum Joanneum, Graz

2003 "Brain Aided Design (222 Edit)", 222 Gallery, Philadelphia; "TDR/SCAA", Academy of Fine Arts, Sarajevo; "TDR en Ecuador", Museo de Arte Contemporaneo, Quito, Ecuador; "The Peoples Bureau For Consumer Information", Galerija Škuc, Ljubljana;

"TDR Unplugged", Shift Gallery, Tokyo
2004 "Brain Aided Design V.03", Umetnostna Galerija, Maribor; "MITDR: From SoYo With Love", Maxalot Gallery, Barcelona; "Communicate: British Graphic Design since the Sixties", Barbican Art Gallery, London

2005 "Selling Sound", Wakefield Art Gallery, Wakefield; "Brain Aided Design, SoYo", Millennium Galleries, Sheffield
2006 British Pavilion, Venice Architecture Biennale

Clients
Beatink; British Council; Coca-Cola; Deutsche Bank; EMAP; Hutchison 3G; MPC (Moving Picture Company); Nickelodeon; Nokia; Orange; Smirnoff; Sony; Telia Communications; University of Sheffield; Urban Splash; Warp Records

"Brain Aided Design. Brain Aided Design."

»Intelligentes Design. Intelligentes Design.«

«Design Assisté par Cerveau. »

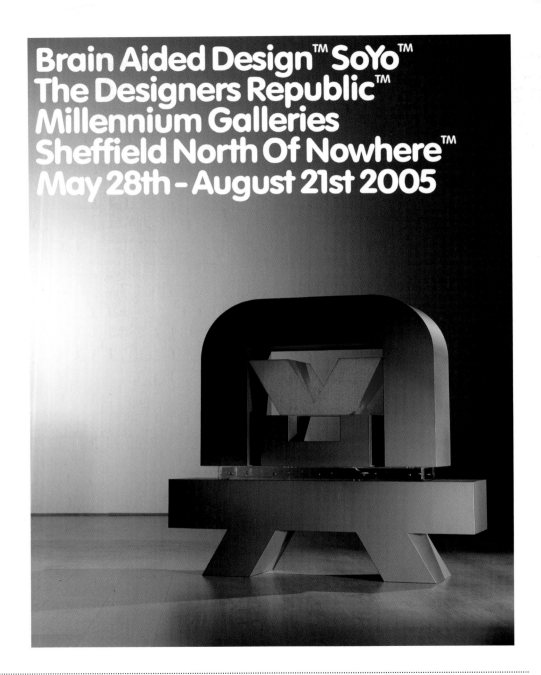

Brain Aided Design™ SoYo™
The Designers Republic™
Millennium Galleries
Sheffield North Of Nowhere™
May 28th – August 21st 2005

Page 319:
Project: *"Lovebeing – M5 project" design for soft-drinks bottle, 2005*
Client: *The Coca-Cola Company*

Previous page top:
Project: *"We are all prostitutes (The godlike genius of Mark Stuart) v. 2.0" graphic print, 2003*
Client: *Henry Peacock Gallery*

Previous page bottom left:
Project: *Food wall installation for Electroglide Festival, 2004*
Client: *Beatnik*

Previous page bottom right:
Project: *TPBFC website, 2002*
Client: *The Peoples Bureau for Consumer Information*

Above:
Project: *"Brain Aided Design SoYo" poster for "TDR" exhibition, 2005*
Client: *Millennium Galleries, Sheffield*

Previous page top:
Project: *"Call up, Tune in,
Chill out" advertisement for
Nokia 3300, 2003*
Client: *Bates Singapore*

Previous page bottom left:
Project: *"Warp Records"
website, 2000*
Client: *Warp Records*

Previous page bottom right:
Project: *"Bleep" website, 2004*
Client: *Warp Records*

Above:
Project: *"Squeezed out, Sucked
in, Spat out. Done in" poster for
Grafik "Felt-Tip" exhibition, 2006*
Client: *Grafik Magazine*

The Designers Republic 323

THIRST

"I'm devoted to design with real human presence."

Thirst
117 South Cook Street, USA
PMB 333
Barrington, IL 60010
USA
T +1 847 842 022 2
info@3st.com
www.3st.com

Design group history
1989 Founded by Rick Valicenti in Barrington, Illinois, USA

Founder's biography
Rick Valicenti
1951 Born in Pittsburgh, Pennsylvania, USA

1973 BFA, Bowling Green State University
1976 MA Photography, University of Iowa
1977 MFA Photography, University of Iowa

Professional experience
1981+ Contributed his time and energies to college and high school students in the form of workshops, personal critiques, and conversations about design and professional practice

Recent exhibitions
2000 "National Design Triennial", Cooper-Hewitt Nacional Design Museum, New York
2006 "National Design Triennial", Cooper-Hewitt Museum, New York

Recent awards
2005 Nomination, I. D. Fifty, representing Illinois; Nomination, 2004 AIGA Chicago Chapter Fellow
2006 AIGA Medal

Clients
Fireorb; Gilbert Paper; Herman Miller; The Lyric Opera of Chicago; Smithfield Properties; Wright Auctions

"If I knew all or any of the answers surrounding the practice of design, I would not wake up to pursue something different each and every day. I suppose I will stop my design practice when I get it right, but in the meantime, I will continue to delight in the joys my creative, elusive, and fragile gift affords me. I must add that as a generous person, I do delight in sharing the fruits of my curiosities."

»Wenn ich alle Antworten (oder auch nur eine) auf die Fragen hätte, die in der Praxis des Grafikdesigns auftauchen, würde ich nicht an jedem Tag etwas Neues ausprobieren. Ich vermute mal, ich werde mein Büro aufgeben, sobald ich einmal alles richtig hingekriegt habe, aber bis dahin werde ich weiterhin die Freuden genießen, die meine schöpferische, schwer zu fassende und labile Begabung mir bereitet. Ich muss hinzufügen, dass ich es als großzügiger Mensch liebe, die Früchte meiner Neugierde mit anderen zu teilen.«

« Si j'avais ne serait-ce qu'une réponse aux questions qui entourent la pratique du design, je ne me lèverais pas pour partir en quête de quelque chose de différent chaque matin. J'imagine que j'abandonnerai le design le jour où j'aurai tout compris, mais en attendant, je vais continuer à me régaler des plaisirs que m'octroie mon talent créatif, insaisissable et fragile. Je dois ajouter qu'étant une personne généreuse je prends aussi un grand plaisir à partager les fruits de mes investigations. »

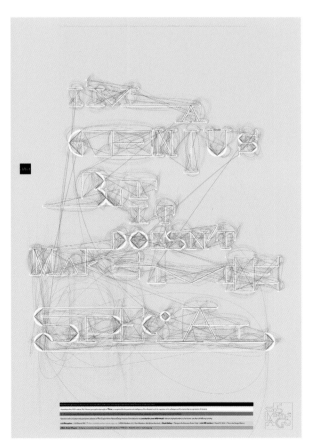

Previous page:
Project: "Emotion as Promotion – A Book of Thirst" book cover, 2005
Client: Monacelli Press

Above left:
Project: "I'm A Genius But It Doesn't Make Me Special" poster, 2007
Client: AIGA/Miami

Above right:
Project: "Happy Gone Lucky" poster, 2007
Client: AIGA/Miami

Following page top:
Project: "For Better or for Worth" book cover, 2006
Client: Real Eyes Communication

Following page bottom:
Project: "Intelligent Design: Creating an Evolved Red vs Blue State of Mind" book, 2006
Client: Self

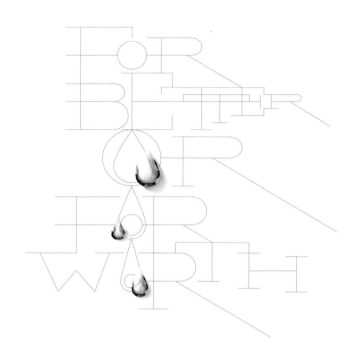

TOFFE

"My work is a production system for graphic action, a visual display process, somewhere between printed matter and screen work."

Toffe (Christophe Jacquet)
6, rue Thomas Francine
75014 Paris
France
T + 33 1 456 542 10
toffe@toffe.net
www.toffe.net

Biography
1955 Born in Paris, France
1975–1979 Studied at the École Nationale Supérieure des Beaux-Arts, Paris
1980+ Works as freelance graphic and industrial designer

Professional experience
1983 Began working with computers
2006 Lecturer, Esad, École Supérieure Art et Design, Amiens

1998–2006 Workshops, lectures, visiting professor in different schools of art and contemporary art centres: Paris, Pau, Chaumont, Limoges, Nancy, Rouen, Rennes, Valence, Lorient, Cergy, Nevers, Tel-Aviv, Rio, Warsaw, Palermo, Santiago, Buenos Aires, Mexico, Barcelona, etc.
2004–2006 Member of the Commission Nationale Allocation de Recherche, Centre National des Arts Plastiques, Ministère de la Culture et de la Communication, France

Recent awards
1997 Lauréat Villa Médicis Hors les murs, Association Française d'Action Artistique, Ministère des Affaires Etrangères, France
2002 Aide individuelle à la creation (grant), Ministère de la Culture et de la Communication, France

Recent exhibitions
2003 "Projection Générale: La Chaufferie", Galerie École Supérieure des Arts Décoratifs, Strasburg
2005 "Reproduction générale: XVIe Festival International des Arts graphiques", Chaumont; "Reproduction générale", Centre Culturel Français d'Alger, Algeria

Clients
Cut and Splice: Music Festival; Centre Culturel Français d'Alger; CNEAI, Centre National de l'Estampe et de l'Art Imprimé, Chatou; AFAA; Magazine Double; Musées de la Cour d'Or, Metz; Le Lit National; Fgr&Associés; Fing, Fondation Internet Nouvelle Génération; Direction Régionale des Affaires Culturelles Haute-Normandie; Woolmark; RATP

du 14 au 23 septembre 2004
* six journées * seize rendez-vous *
* *béni-saf* * *oran* * *alger* *
* *spectacles* * *expositions* * *films* *
* *rencontres littéraires* * *récitals poétiques* *

pour
jean sénac

centres culturels français en Algérie

AIR FRANCE

"My graphic production is political and utopian. Political in the primary sense of a conception that is an organization of codes and concepts. It is a minimum service done to my environment. As such, it refers to several principles inherited from the modernist thought in its aspiration for ergonomics of standards. But the comparison goes no further, since the graphic system I implement is not one that determines but rather generates apparitions, graphic matter and previously unthought-of and unlikely images. It is a utopian system where the tension between graphic and plastic elements is tangible. A space where graphic design and art live together within a terminology signifying the working process. Having been under digital influence for several years, I often wonder about its purpose: constructing a unique image, globalizing and open, in the heat of action. For me it is the energy put into the service of the creation, organization, installation or construction of the finished object that is often as important as the finished product itself."

»Meine Arbeit als Grafikdesigner ist zugleich politisch als auch utopisch. Politisch im ursprünglichen Sinn einer Gesamtkonzeption, die aus Codes und Unterkonzepten besteht. Es handelt sich um einen kleinen Beitrag für meine Umwelt. Es ist eine Arbeit, die Grundsätzen folgt, die – was ihr Streben nach ergonomischen Standards angeht – sich auf die Prinzipien der Moderne bezieht. Damit hört der Vergleich mit der Moderne aber auch schon auf, denn ich nutze kein Grafiksystem, das Bilder festlegt, sondern eher Erscheinungen, grafische Materie und zuvor noch unvorstellbare und unwahrscheinliche Bilder erzeugt. Es ist ein utopisches System, in dem die Spannung zwischen grafischen und plastischen Elementen greifbar wird. Ein Raum, in dem Grafikdesign und Kunst in einer Begriffswelt zusammenleben, die den Arbeitsprozess bezeichnet. Da ich seit mehreren Jahren mit Grafiksoftware arbeite (und davon beeinflusst bin), mache ich mir oft Gedanken über das Ziel, in der Hitze des Gefechts ein einzigartiges, globalisierendes und offenes Bild zu konstruieren. Für mich ist die Energie, die in die Gestaltung, Gliederung, Installation oder Konstruktion eines Objekts investiert wird, oft ebenso wichtig wie das fertige Endprodukt.«

«Ma production graphique est politique et utopiste. Politique au sens propre, c'est-à-dire une organisation de codes et de concepts. C'est un service minimal que je rends au monde qui m'entoure. Elle se réfère ainsi à quelques principes hérités de la pensée moderniste et de sa quête d'ergonomie des normes. Mais la comparaison s'arrête là, parce que le système graphique que je crée n'est pas de ceux qui déterminent mais plutôt génèrent des apparitions, un matériau graphique et des images jusqu'alors inimaginables et improbables. C'est aussi un système utopiste où la tension entre éléments graphiques et plastiques est tangible. Un espace où le graphisme et l'art cohabitent au sein d'une terminologie qui incarne la méthode de travail. J'ai été sous l'influence du numérique pendant plusieurs années et je me suis souvent demandé à quoi il sert : à construire une image unique, mondialisée et ouverte dans le feu de l'action. Pour moi, l'énergie mise au service de la création, de l'organisation, de l'installation et de la construction de l'objet fini est souvent aussi importante que le produit fini en lui-même. »

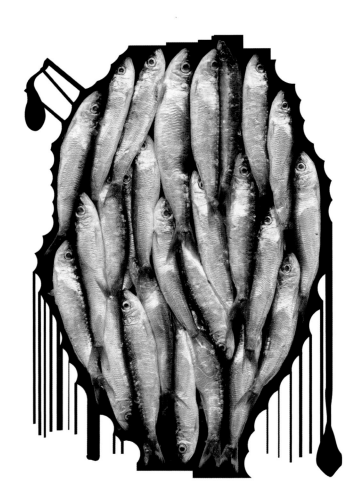

Page 329:
Project: *"Pour Jean Sénac"*
poster, 2004 (designed in collabo-
ration with Giancarlo Oprandi)
Client: *Centre Culturel Français*
d'Alger

Previous page:
Project: *"Reproduction*
générale" installation for the
Chaumont Festival, 2005
Client: *XVIᵉ Festival Inter-*
national des Arts graphiques,
Chaumont

Top:
Project: *"REFI25, fish figure"*
digital print, 2005
Client: *XVIᵉ Festival Inter-*
national des Arts graphiques,
Chaumont

Above:
Project: *"Reproduction*
générale"
digital heading, 2003–2005
Client: *XVIᵉ Festival Inter-*
national des Arts graphiques,
Chaumont

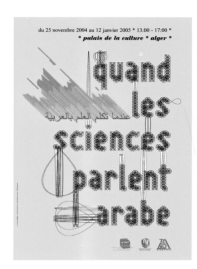

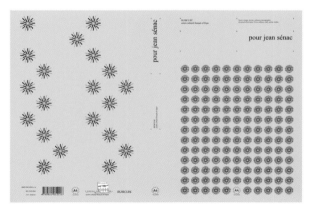

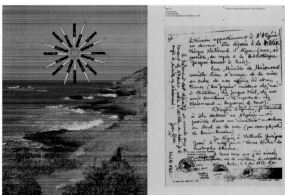

Top left and centre:
Project: *"Quand les sciences parlent arabe"* posters, 2004 *(designed in collaboration with*   Giancarlo Oprandi) Client: *Centre Culturel Français d'Alger*

Top right:
Project: *"Cut and Splice, Acousmonium"* music festival poster, 2006   Client: *Sonic Arts Network*

Above:
Project: *"Pour Jean Sénac"* book (cover/spreads), 2004 *(designed in collaboration*   with Giancarlo Oprandi) Client: *Centre Culturel Français d'Alger*

Top left and right:
Project: *"Jazzair" posters*, 2006
(designed in collaboration with
Giancarlo Oprandi)

Client: *Centre Culturel Français
d'Alger*

Above:
Project: *"Toffe.Edition générale"
graphic design book (cover)*, 2003
Client: *La Chaufferie Editions/*

Unvisible Editions/Toffe

CHRISTOPHER WILLIAMS

"Figure out what fascinates you and embrace it unabashedly, even if only for a moment."

Christopher Williams
677 Metropolitan Ave #6D
Brooklyn, NY 11211
USA
T +1 248 302 175 5
contact@thechriswilliams.com
www.thechriswilliams.com

Biography
1975 Born in Indianapolis, Indiana, USA
2004–2006 Studied 2D design, Cranbrook Academy of Art, Bloomfield Hills, Michigan

Professional experience
1996 Established his own record label, Witching Hour Records, in Indianapolis
2001 Worked as a designer for "would rather not say" and Indianapolis creative agency
2002 Co-founded Ghastly Cave, a collective multi-displinary studio with Mike Little in Indianapolis
2006 Moved to New York

Recent exhibitions
2000 Digital art group exhibition, Pittsburgh Museum of Art

2001 Group exhibition, J. Martin Gallery, Indianapolis
2004 "Werewolves and Rainbows", Bodner Studios, Indianapolis; "Graphic Noise", Museum of Design, Atlanta
2006 "From Here On Out", Cranbrook Academy of Art, Bloomfield Hills; "Can I Borrow A Spaceship", Contemporary Art Institute of Detroit

Recent awards
2004 Regional Design Annual Award
2005 Nuvo 30 Under 30 Award
2006 Fistful of Rock Art Award; Finalist, Daimler Chrysler Emerging Artist

Clients
31G Records; Beautiful/Decay Magazine; Clear Channel Entertainment; Coca-Cola; Cranbrook Academy of Art; Walt Disney; FedEx Kinkos; Hydra-Head; Indiana University; Level-Plane Records; New York Arts Magazine; The New Yorker Magazine; Secretly Canadian Records; Swindle Magazine

"This work loves and breathes on/from the complexity in which we live. It makes relationships, compares, and re-contextualizes images by borrowing from different aesthetics, tenets and social classes. It reuses anything from everywhere to create a melting pot of truth, fantasy and the everyday. This body of work resides as a marker of the moment in time in which it was created."

»Diese Entwürfe lieben und leben durch die Komplexität des heutigen Lebens. Sie stellen Beziehungen her, vergleichen Bilder und stellen sie in neue Zusammenhänge. Dabei bedienen sie sich verschiedener Stile, Grundsätze und Gesellschaftsschichten. Sie recyceln alles von überall her, um daraus einen Schmelztiegel aus Wahrheit, Fantasie und Alltäglichem zu schaffen. Das resultierende Werk steht stellvertretend für den Augenblick seiner Erschaffung.«

«Ce travail aime et respire la complexité dans laquelle nous vivons. Il crée des liens, compare et replace les images dans un contexte en empruntant à différentes esthétiques, doctrines et classes sociales. Il réutilise toutes sortes d'éléments venus de partout pour créer un *melting-pot* de vérité, de fantasme et de quotidien. Cet œuvre se veut une borne marquant le moment où il a été créé.»

Previous page:
Project: *"Know Thy Kingdom"*
poster, 2005
Client: *Self*

Above left:
Project: *"The Gross Grill"*
artwork featured in "The People Say Publication", 2006
Client: *Cranbrook 2D Design*

Above right:
Project: *"Meltomas"*
poster, 2004
Client: *The Vogue*

Following page top:
Project: *"Now That's Time Travel" poster,* 2006
Client: *Self*

Following page bottom:
Project: *"Storyboards for Lifelongfriendshipsociety"*
artwork, 2007
Client: *MTVU*

Above:
Project: "Untitled"
poster, 2004
Client: Birdy's

Following page top:
Project: "Enoch Ardon"
album cover, 2007
Client: Existencia

Following page centre:
Project: "The People Say Publi-
cation" magazine cover, 2006
Client: Cranbrook 2D Design

Following page bottom:
Project: "Not Much More Than
Music Fest" poster, 2005
Client: Viva La Vinyl

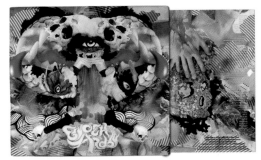

MARTIN WOODTLI

"Meticulous Resistance"

Martin Woodtli
Schöneggstr. 5
8004 Zurich
Switzerland
T +41 1 291 241 9
martin@woodt.li
www.woodt.li

Biography
1971 Born in Bern, Switzerland
1990–1995 Studied graphic design, School of Design, Bern
1996–1998 Studied visual communication, Academy of Art and Design, Zurich

Professional experience
1998/99 Worked in New York with David Carson and Stefan Sagmeister
1999 Founded own studio in Zurich

2000 Became youngest member of Alliance Graphique Internationale (AGI)
2001 First book about work published
2002 Taught at the School of Design, Biel
2002+ Taught at the Academy of Art and Design, Lucerne
2002/03 Professor at the Staatliche Akademie der Bildenden Künste, Stuttgart

Recent exhibitions
2004 "Young Swiss Graphic Design", 8th Tehran International Poster Biennial
2006 "The 4th Ningbo International Poster Biennial", Ningbo Museum of Art

Recent awards
1999 Swiss Federal Design Prize
2000 40 under 30 Award, I. D. Magazine
2001 "IDEA 285", Japan;

"The Most Beautiful Swiss Books" and "Book of the Jury", Swiss Federal Office of Culture
2005 1st Prize, International Poster and Graphic Arts Festival of Chaumont; 2nd Prize, Competition for the artistic design of the new Swiss banknote series
2006 Bronze Award, Poster Triennial, Toyama

Clients
Die Gestalten Verlag; Freitag AG; GDI; Kunstraum Walcheturm, Zurich; Migros Kulturprozent; Museum für Gestaltung, Zurich; Schaffhauser Jazzfestival; soDa Magazine; Stadtgalerie Bern; Swiss National Bank; Wired Magazine

AUSSTELLUNGSSTRASSE 60, 8005 ZÜRICH

TAKE AWAY

MUSEUM FÜR GESTALTUNG ZÜRICH
14.12.05–19.3.06

DI – DO 10 – 20 UHR, FR – SO 10 – 17 UHR

24.12., 31.12. 10 – 16 UHR, 26.12., 2.1. 10 – 17 UHR   MONTAGS SOWIE 25.12. UND 1.1. GESCHLOSSEN

"Design as such is a broad concept and has many aspects. Some are more free, others more applied. Perhaps the question behind this is: what motivates someone to go in for this occupation? I think it's impossible if you don't enjoy it. I'm not the least interested in being trendy. I have my own obsessions. Whatever I experience goes into my work in one way or another, that is almost inevitable anyway. When you're on the ball, you see certain developments, and reach an interpretation of what something should look like at the moment. Design should explain itself and have a certain 'entertainment' in it. In contrast to postmodern iconoclasm and eclectic self-indulgence, I try time and again to find a new, 'self-contained' idea and its visual expression, which focus on their own implementation. That is strenuous, but that's what ultimately makes it interesting, otherwise it would be boring."

»Gestalten an und für sich ist ein weiter Begriff und hat viele Aspekte. Gewisse sind freier, andere angewandter. Vielleicht steht dahinter die Frage, was die Motivation ist, diesen Beruf auszuüben? Ich glaube, ohne Lust an der Sache geht es nicht. Trendy zu sein interessiert mich nicht im Geringsten. Ich habe meine eigenen Obsessionen, was immer ich erlebe, fließt auf gewisse Art und Weise in die Arbeit mit ein, das lässt sich auch schwer vermeiden. Wenn man ein bisschen wach ist, sieht man bestimmte Entwicklungen und kommt zu einer Interpretation dessen, wie etwas im Moment aussehen muss. Gestaltung sollte sich selbst erklären einen gewissen ›Unterhaltungswert‹ haben. Im Gegensatz zum postmodernen Ikonoklasmus und zum eklektizistischen Vergnügen, versuche ich immer wieder aufs Neue, auf eine ›eigenständige‹ Idee und deren Bildschöpfung zu kommen und die ihr eigene Umsetzung zum Thema machen. Das ist anstrengend, dafür letztlich interessanter, sonst wird es einem langweilig.«

« Le graphisme est un vaste champ et recouvre de nombreux aspects, dont certains sont plus libres, d'autres plus profanes. La question la plus importante est probablement celle de la motivation qui vous pousse à exercer ce métier. Je pense qu'il n'est pas possible de travailler dans ce métier si l'on n'y prend pas plaisir. Personnellement, être à la mode ne m'intéresse pas le moins du monde. J'ai mes propres obsessions, et tout ce qui m'arrive informe d'une manière ou d'une autre mon travail ; de toute façon, c'est presque inévitable. Lorsqu'on est un tant soit peu attentif, on observe certains développements qui permettent de tirer des conclusions quant à l'aspect qu'un objet donné doit avoir à un certain moment. Le graphisme devrait s'expliquer de lui-même et receler un certain degré de 'divertissement'. Contrairement à l'iconoclasme postmoderne et au plaisir éclectique, je cherche toujours à dégager une idée 'autonome' et sa correspondance iconographique et, par ailleurs, à faire de sa réalisation le sujet même du travail. C'est fatigant, mais en fin de compte plus intéressant ; à défaut de quoi, on risque de s'ennuyer. »

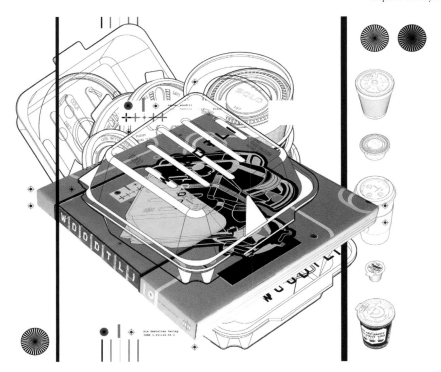

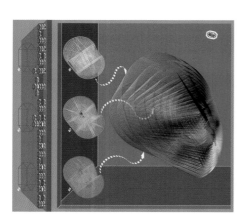

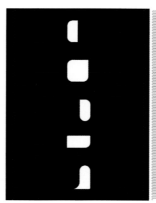

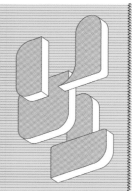

MUSEUM FÜR GESTALTUNG ZÜRICH

SPORT DESIGN

13. NOVEMBER 2004–13. MÄRZ 2005

DI–DO 10–20h / FR–SO 11–18h / 24.12., 31.12., 11–16h / MONTAGS SOWIE 25.12., 1.1. GESCHLOSSEN / AUSSTELLUNGSSTRASSE 60, 8005 ZÜRICH

Previous page:
Project: *"Play"*
poster for design exhibition, 2005
Client: *Museum für Gestaltung, Zurich*

Above:
Project: *"Sport Design"*
poster for design exhibition, 2004
Client: *Museum für Gestaltung, Zurich*

YACHT ASSOCIATES

"Measure twice. Cut once."

Yacht Associates
Unit 7, Stephendale Yard
Stephendale Road
London SW6 2LR
UK
T +44 207 371 878 8
info@yachtassociates.com
www.yachtassociates.com

Design group history
1996 Co-founded by Richard Bull and Christopher Steven Thomson in Kensington, London
2004 Christopher Steven Thomson left Yacht Associates

Founder's biography
Richard Bull
1968 Born in London, England
1987–1989 Studied art and design, Chelsea School of Art, London
1989–1992 Studied graphic design, Chelsea School of Art, London

Recent exhibitions
1998 Opening Installation, Urban Outfitters, London
1999 Furniture Design Exhibition, sponsored by Sony, Haus, London
2001 "Yacht Associates: Five Year Retrospective", Waterstones Piccadilly, London

Recent awards
2000 Best Album Design, Music Week Awards
2001 Best Photography, Music Week Awards; Editorial & Book Design Award, D&AD; Record Packaging Award, D&AD
2002 Best Album Design, Music Week Awards
2005 Bronze Award, The Consort Royal Graphic Design & Print Awards

Clients
19 Management; A&M Records; Blag Magazine; Columbia Records; Def Soul UK; Eagle Rock; EMI Chrysalis; GettyStone; Independiente; Jam; London Records; Mercury Records; Myla; Next Level Magazine; Parlophone; Penguin Books; Polydor; Sketch; Sony/BMG; Talk-in'Loud; Toshiba EMI; Universal; Virgin Records; Warner Music; WEA; WOWBOW

EMBRACE
GRAVITY
30/08/04

"Brief.
Conceive.
Create.
Pitch.
Win.
Pre-Produce.
Commission.
Recce.
Pre-Produce some more.
Direct.

Edit.
Visualize.
Edit some more.
Present.
Post Produce.
Re-Create.
Re-Present.
Approve.
Print."

»Briefing.
Konzipieren.
Entwerfen.
Fein einstellen.
Gewinnen.
Ausarbeiten.
Beauftragen.
Lage peilen.
Weiter ausarbeiten.
Anleiten.

Bearbeiten.
Visualisieren.
Erneut bearbeiten.
Präsentieren.
Nachbearbeiten.
Neu entwerfen.
Erneut präsentieren.
Bestätigen.
Drucken.«

«Consignes.
Concevoir.
Créer.
Bonimenter.
Gagner.
Préproduire.
Commander.
Reconnaître.
Re-Préproduire.
Diriger.

Mettre au point.
Visualiser.
Remettre au point.
Présenter.
Post-Produire.
Re-Créer.
Re-Présenter.
Approuver.
Imprimer. »

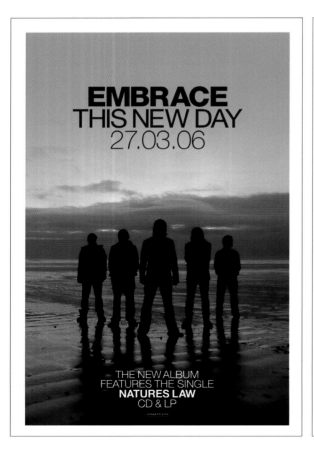

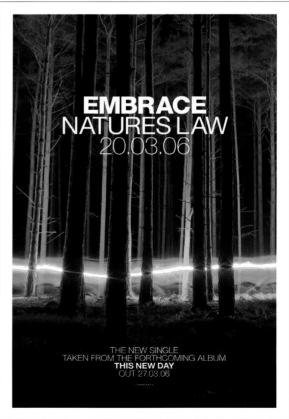

Acknowledgements

Firstly, a big thank you to all the graphic designers who agreed to participate in this project – if it wasn't for your kind cooperation there wouldn't be a book. We would also like to acknowledge the excellent inputs of our research assistant, Quintin Colville, and our editor, Thomas Berg. Thanks must also go to Anthony Oliver for the new photography he generated for the project, and to Ute Wachendorf in TASCHEN's production department who, as ever, has done a wonderful job collating and organizing the images. A special mention must also go to Annette Wiethüchter and Alice Petillot for their translations. Lastly, we are immensely grateful to Andy Disl for his superb graphic design of the book. For us it has been a real pleasure working with such talented and dedicated people.

Danksagung

Zunächst ein großes Dankeschön an alle Grafikdesigner, die sich bereit gefunden haben, an diesem Buchprojekt mitzuwirken. Ohne Ihre freundliche Zusammenarbeit wäre dieses Buch nicht zustande gekommen. Außerdem möchten wir den hervorragenden Einsatz unseres Assistenten Quintin Colville und unseres Lektors Thomas Berg dankend erwähnen. Dank schulden wir auch Anthony Oliver für die neuen Fotoaufnahmen, die er für das Buch angefertigt hat, und Ute Wachendorf in der Herstellungsabteilung von TASCHEN, die – wie immer – bei der Beschaffung, Auswahl und Bearbeitung der Bildvorlagen ausgezeichnete Arbeit geleistet hat. Annette Wiethüchter und Alice Petillot möchten wir für ihre Übersetzungen danken. Andy Disl gilt unserer besonderer Dank für seine ausgezeichnete Buchgestaltung. Es war für uns ein großes Vergnügen, mit so talentierten und engagierten Menschen zusammenzuarbeiten.

Remerciements

Tout d'abord un grand merci à tous les graphistes qui ont accepté de participer à ce projet – sans votre aimable coopération, ce livre n'existerait pas. Nous aimerions aussi saluer les excellentes contributions de notre assistant de recherches, Quintin Colville, et de notre éditeur, Thomas Berg. Nos remerciements vont aussi à Anthony Oliver pour la nouvelle photo qu'il a crée pour le projet, ainsi qu'à Ute Wachendorf, du département fabrication de TASCHEN, qui, comme toujours, a admirablement rassemblé et assemblé les images. Mention spéciale également à Annette Wiethüchter et Alice Pétillot pour leurs traductions. Enfin, nous sommes immensément reconnaissants à Andy Disl pour sa sublime maquette. Ce fut un réel plaisir pour nous de travailler avec des personnes si talentueuses et dévouées.

CONTEMPORARY GRAPHIC DESIGN

Grafikdesign der Gegenwart
Le graphisme contemporain

CONTEMPORARY GRAPHIC DESIGN: COMPLEX AND EVER CHANGING IN FORM, IT SYNTHESIZES AND TRANSMITS INFORMATION TO THE PUBLIC WHILE, AT THE SAME TIME, REFLECTING SOCIETY'S CULTURAL ASPIRATIONS AND MORAL VALUES.